The World's Story
A History of the World in Story, Song and Art

Volume 5
U.S. History – American Revolution, France

Edited by Eva March Tappan

Libraries of Hope

The World's Story
A History of the World
In Story, Song and Art

Volume 5
U.S. History – American Revolution,
France

The World's Story, A History of the World in Story, Song and Art, edited by Eva March Tappan. (Original copyright 1914)

Cover Image: Arrest of Louis XVI and His Family, by Thomas Falcon Marshall (1854). In public domain, source Wikimedia Commons.

Libraries of Hope, Inc.

Appomattox, Virginia 24522

Website www.librariesofhope.com

Email: librariesofhope@gmail.com

Printed in the United States of America

CONTENTS

THE UNITED STATES

I. WAR IN THE WEST AND ON THE OCEAN

How Daniel Boone saved Boonesborough
Charles C. B. Seymour 3
From "Self-made Men."

A Campaign through the Water . *George Rogers Clark* 13
How the Women brought Water to Bryan's Station
Cyrus Townsend Brady 24
From "Border Fights and Fighters."

The First Salute to the Flag *Sarah Orne Jewett* 32
From "The Tory Lover."

John Paul Jones in the Revolution *Joel Tyler Headley* 36
From "Washington and his Generals."

II. THE COLONIES WIN THEIR FREEDOM

Congress and Valley Forge . . *John Fiske* 36
From "The American Revolution."

The Message of Lydia Darrah . *Elizabeth F. Ellet* 68
From "The Women of the American Revolution."

Mollie Pitcher . . *Kate Brownlee Sherwood* 74

The Capture of Major André *Jared Sparks* 76
From "Benedict Arnold."

A Visit to General Marion *Charles Carleton Coffin* 81
From "The Boys of '76."

When Cornwallis surrendered *Burton Egbert Stevenson* 85
From "The Heritage."

George III. acknowledges the Independence of the
Colonies *Elkanah Watson* 90
From "Men and Times of the Revolution."

When Washington resigned his Commission *R. M. Devens* 94
From "Our First Century."

III. LIFE IN REVOLUTIONARY DAYS

The Meschianza at Philadelphia *John F. Watson* 101
From "Annals of Philadelphia and Pennsylvania."

A New England Thanksgiving Dinner in 1779
Juliana Smith 107
From "Colonial Holidays," compiled by Walter Tittle

CONTENTS

A CALL ON LADY WASHINGTON IN 1780   .*Charles D. Platt*   112
    From "Ballads of New Jersey in the Revolution."
HOW PEOPLE TRAVELED IN REVOLUTIONARY TIMES
                              John Bach McMaster   114
    From "A History of the People of the United States."
ABRAHAM DAVENPORT   . *John G. Whittier*   123

FRANCE

I. IN THE DARK AGES

THE CHRISTMAS OF 496 .   *J. C. Bateman*   131
    From "Ierne of Armorica."
THE FAMOUS VICTORY OF CHARLES MARTEL .   *A. W. Grube*   143
    From "Heroes of History and Legend."
THE LAMENT OF CHARLEMAGNE FOR ROLAND.   *Unknown*   146
    From "The Song of Roland."
CHARLEMAGNE, EMPEROR OF THE WEST   *A. W. Grube*   150
    From "Heroes of History and Legend."
ROLLO THE VIKING .   *Eva March Tappan*   157
    From "European Hero Stories."

II. STORIES OF THE HUNDRED YEARS' WAR

THE BATTLE OF CRÉCY   *Sir John Froissart*   165
HOW QUEEN PHILIPPA SAVED THE BURGHERS   *Sir John Froissart*   171
    From "Froissart's Chronicles."
THE COMING OF THE MAID OF ORLÉANS
                Johann Christoph Friedrich von Schiller   176
    From "The Maid of Orléans."
THE DEATH OF JEANNE D'ARC   *Mary Rogers Bangs*   185
    From "Jeanne d'Arc."

III. FRANCE UNDER THE VALOIS KINGS

WHERE LOUIS XI SAID HIS PRAYERS   . *Victor Hugo*   193
    From "The Hunchback of Notre Dame."
ANNE OF BRITTANY AND HER COURT   *Catherine Charlotte*   209
    From "The Court of France in the Sixteenth Century."
THE DEATH OF THE CHEVALIER BAYARD
                      From the Old Chronicles   215
KING FRANCIS I AND THE GOLDSMITH   *Benvenuto Cellini*   221
    From "Memoirs of Benvenuto Cellini."

CONTENTS

IV. THE HOUSE OF BOURBON

THE BATTLE OF IVRY . . . . *Thomas Babington Macaulay* 231
CARDINAL RICHELIEU AND HIS ENEMY .*Edward Bulwer-Lytton* 237
  From "Richelieu."
IN THE DAYS OF THE FRONDE *Alexandre Dumas* 250
  From "Twenty Years After."
THE DEATH OF LOUIS XIV *Julia Pardoe* 268
  From "Louis XIV and the Court of France."

V. ON THE EVE OF THE FRENCH REVOLUTION

WHEN MARIE ANTOINETTE ENTERED PARIS *Marie Antoinette* 277
HOW THE QUEEN WAS SERVED . . . . . *Madame Campan* 279
THE WARDROBE OF MARIE ANTOINETTE . *Madame Campan* 281
  From "Memoirs of the Private Life of Marie Antoinette."
THE FALL OF THE BASTILLE • *Alexandre Dumas* 284
  From "Ange Pitou."
THE FLIGHT OF LOUIS XVI *Charles Duke Yonge* 292
  From "Life of Marie Antoinette."
THE MARSEILLAISE • • • . . *Claude Joseph Rouget de Lisle* 302

VI. THE REIGN OF TERROR

THE EXECUTION OF LOUIS XVI • • • • • *Edmond Biré* 307
  From "The Diary of a Citizen of Paris during 'The Terror.'"
IN THE REVOLT OF THE VENDÉE • • • • • . *Victor Hugo* 317
  From "Ninety-three."
AT THE GUILLOTINE • *Charles Dickens* 329
  From "A Tale of Two Cities."
THE FALL OF ROBESPIERRE • *Thomas Carlyle* 336
  From "The French Revolution."

VII. NAPOLEON BONAPARTE

THE BATTLE OF EYLAU • • • . . *Isaac McLellan* 351
THE RETREAT FROM MOSCOW • • • • . *Victor Hugo* 354
THE COMING OF LOUIS XVIII *"Louisa Mühlbach"*
  From "Queen Hortense." *(Clara Mundt)* 359
THE RETURN OF NAPOLEON FROM ELBA *Anonymous* 364
  From "Memoirs of Napoleon Bonaparte," by Bourrienne.
WHEN NAPOLEON RETURNED FROM ELBA *Napoleon Bonaparte* 370

CONTENTS

WATERLOO . . . . *Victor Hugo* 372
    From "Les Miserables."
THE DEATH OF NAPOLEON .   *Isaac McLellan* 394

VIII. THE FRANCO–PRUSSIAN WAR

THE WHITE FLAG OF SEDAN   *Émile Zola* 399
    From "The Downfall."
ONE DAY UNDER THE COMMUNE .   *John Leighton* 416
    From "Paris under the Commune."

UNITED STATES

I

WAR IN THE WEST AND ON THE OCEAN

HISTORICAL NOTE

DURING the Revolution the border warfare in the West was constant and pitiless, and from Kentucky to the Great Lakes the outlying settlements were devastated by the Tories and their Indian allies. In 1778 the border villages of New York and Pennsylvania were so cruelly harried by Chief Brant and Colonel Butler that in the following year General Sullivan led an army into the country of the Six Nations, the most powerful of the Indian tribes, and avenged the massacres so sternly that this great tribe never recovered its former position.

In 1778 the British planned to unite the Indian tribes and destroy the little settlements in what was then the "Far West," or what is now Indiana and Illinois. This might well have come to pass if, through the efforts of a young Virginian surveyor named George Rogers Clark, they had not been driven back and Vincennes and other places captured. This one man saved the vast expanse of country between the Ohio and the Great Lakes, and as far west as the Mississippi.

At the time of the Revolution the colonies had, of course, no navy of their own, and in consequence the coast was practically at the mercy of the English. Congress felt this handicap early in the war, but little was done except the equipment of privateers and cruisers for the destruction of British commerce. During the first half of the war more than six hundred British vessels were taken by these privateers, but during the same period nine hundred American vessels were captured by British cruisers, and the fisheries and coasting trade of New England were almost destroyed.

There was one captain who, more than all others, terrorized British shipping and spread the fame of American seamen throughout Europe — John Paul Jones, a Scotch sailor who had settled in Virginia shortly before the outbreak of hostilities. As commander of the Ranger in 1778 and the Bon Homme Richard in 1779, he wrought havoc along the British coast, burned the shipping in British ports, and finally captured the man-of-war Serapis after one of the most desperate sea-fights in history.

HOW DANIEL BOONE SAVED
BOONESBOROUGH

[1775]

BY CHARLES C. B. SEYMOUR

In the spring of the year 1775, Boone was employed by a company of land speculators (who imagined they had secured a valid title to the land in Kentucky by virtue of a deed of purchase from the Cherokees) to survey and lay out roads in Kentucky. He was placed at the head of a body of well-armed men, and proceeded to his work with great willingness. The party had arrived within fifteen miles of Boonesborough, when they were fired on by Indians, and suffered a loss of two killed and two wounded. Three days later they were again attacked, and had two killed and three wounded. Boone was not the sort of man to be deterred by a calamity even of this severe kind. He pressed forward, and on a favorable site erected a fort (called Boonesborough), sufficiently strong and large to afford protection against any further attack. He was so well satisfied with its security, that, shortly afterward, he returned to Clinch River for his wife and family. They arrived safely, his "wife and daughters being the first white women that ever stood on the banks of the Kentucky River." A number of families followed their example, and the little place soon became cheerful and populated.

The Indians did not venture to attack the settlers so long as they remained within sight of the fort, but it was

3

very well known that they hovered about the outskirts, ready for a descent on any unhappy wight who might expose himself unguardedly to their vengeance. The men were suspicious and careful and never went out without their rifles. In spite of these precautions, a most thrilling and tragic incident occurred. On the 14th of July, 1776, three young girls belonging to the fort (one of them was Boone's daughter) heedlessly crossed the river in a canoe late in the afternoon. When they got to the other side they commenced playing and splashing with the paddles, as gay young girls, unconscious of danger, might naturally do, until the canoe, floating with the current, drifted close to the shore, which at this part was thickly covered with trees and shrubs. Concealed in this natural ambuscade lay three savage Indians. They had been watching every motion of the girls, and were prepared now to seize their opportunity. One of the coppery rascals dropped stealthily into the stream, caught hold of the rope that hung from the bow of the canoe, and drew it out of view of the fort. The girls, aroused to a sense of their danger, screamed as loud as they could, and were heard at the fort; but, before assistance could come, their captors hurried them on shore and bore them to the interior.

"Next morning by daylight," says Colonel Floyd, who was one of the actors in what he describes, "we were on the track, but found they had totally prevented our following them by walking some distance apart through the thickest canes they could find. We observed their course, and on which side they had left their sign, and traveled upward of thirty miles. We then imagined that they would be less cautious in traveling, and made a turn in order to cross their trace, and had gone but a few miles before we found their tracks in a buffalo path; pursued and overtook them on going about ten miles, just as they were kindling a fire to cook. Our study had been more to get the prisoners, without giving the Indians time to murder them, after they discovered us, than to kill them.

"We discovered each other nearly at the same time. Four of us fired, and all rushed on them, which prevented them from carrying away anything except one shotgun without ammunition. Mr. Boone and myself had a pretty fair shot just as they began to move off. I am well convinced I shot one through, and the one he shot dropped his gun; mine had none. The place was very thick with canes, and being so much elated on recovering the three little broken-hearted girls prevented our making further search. We sent them off without their moccasins, and not one of them with so much as a knife or a tomahawk."

The simplicity of this narrative exceeds its clearness, but, with all its involutions, is it not graphic, and does it not convey an excellent idea of the rough indifference to danger so characteristic of true pioneer life?

After this it was necessary to be doubly watchful, for the Indians became more aggressive, and apprehensions were felt that a general attack would be made on the fortified stations. These fears appeared to be so well founded, that it was only the oldest and bravest of the pioneers who could withstand their influence. The land speculators and other adventurers, to the number of nearly three hundred, left the country, and newcomers, although prepared for danger, were with difficulty pre-

vailed upon to remain. The year 1777 passed in this
gloomy way, marked only by frequent attacks on the
various stations by the Indians. Two attempts were
made on the fort, but each time the besiegers were
beaten off. The brave little garrison lost two men killed
and five wounded. With all means of transit cut off by
their wary foes, great privations were necessarily suffered by the little band. The immediate necessaries of
life they could of course procure, but some articles
which were essential to the preservation of health they
were without. This was especially the case with regard
to salt. Boone, while in the wilderness, could do without
this article of luxury, but the families in the fort sorely
felt its need, and all kinds of efforts were made to
obtain a supply. At length it was determined to fit out
an expedition, consisting of thirty men, with Boone at
its head, to effect this desirable object. It was necessary
to proceed to the Lower Blue Licks, on Licking River,
and there manufacture the article, which, in due course,
was to be forwarded by pack-horses to the fort.

The enterprise, which seemed at first to promise success, cost Boone and his companions their liberty. One
day, while hunting a short distance from his comrades,
he was surprised by a party of Indians, one hundred and
two in number. He attempted to escape, but their
swiftest runners were put on his trail, and he soon
abandoned all idea of doing so. The sagacity and presence of mind of the old hunter had now to be exercised.
He parleyed with the Indians, professed all sorts of
friendship for them, succeeded in gaining their confidence, and finally made honorable terms for the surrender of his men, who became prisoners of war. Boone

has been blamed for not offering resistance, but a moment's reflection will demonstrate that the course he pursued was the wisest and safest. Had he offered resistance, his little band would have been overpowered, and the next point of attack would have been the fort, which, from the absence of the garrison, would have been entirely at the mercy of the savages. To avert a certain massacre, he surrendered his men, after having made excellent conditions for the safety of their lives. "The generous usage the Indians had promised before, in my capitulation," says Boone, "was afterward fully complied with, and we proceeded with them as prisoners to Old Chillicothe, the principal Indian town on Little Miami, where we arrived, after an uncomfortable journey in very severe weather, on the 18th of February, and received as good treatment as prisoners could expect from savages. On the 10th day of March following, I and ten of my men were conducted by forty Indians to Detroit, where we arrived on the 30th day, and were treated by Governor Hamilton, the British commander at that post, with great humanity." The governor endeavored to obtain Boone's liberation by purchase, but his captors were not willing to part with him. He had so ingratiated himself in their good graces that they were determined to have him for a chief, and insisted on carrying him back to their town for the purpose of adoption. He bade farewell to his friends in Detroit, and under the friendly escort of his pertinacious admirers, returned to Chillicothe, where he was adopted by an illustrious individual of the name of Blackfish, to supply the place of a deceased son and warrior. He was treated with great kindness, and in a short time became universally popular. He was careful to avoid all cause for suspicion, and to appear constantly happy, although, of course, he was forever dreaming of his wife and family, and praying for the happy day that should enable him to escape to them.

Early in the following June he was taken to the Salt Springs, on the Scioto, to assist in making salt. On his return, he was alarmed to see a fearful array of four hundred and fifty warriors, and still more so when he discovered that they were bound on an expedition against Boonesborough. He determined to effect his escape, and, on the following morning, the 16th of June, 1778, he arose and went forth as usual without exciting suspicion. He never returned, and Blackfish had to adopt another son. Boone succeeded in reaching the fort in safety. His sudden appearance greatly astonished the people there, for they had given him up, and his wife, with some of the children, had actually departed for North Carolina. Not a moment was to be lost in making the necessary preparations for the defense of the settlement. The fort, which had fallen into a very rickety condition, was put in thorough repair, and the garrison mustered and drilled so as to be in perfect readiness. The Indians, however, changed their minds. Alarmed, probably, at the escape of Boone, they postponed their expedition for three weeks, but, in the mean time, they made some additions to their strength in the shape of French and Canadian officers.

On the 7th of September, the Indian army, numbering four hundred and forty-four, with Captain Duquesne and eleven other Canadians, appeared before Boonesborough. The Indians were commanded by Boone's would-be adopted father, Mr. Blackfish, and the Canadians by Captain Duquesne. When this alarming foe had assembled before the unhappy little fort, a summons was issued to "surrender, in the name of His Britannic Majesty." The garrison consisted of between sixty and seventy men, and a large number of women and children. If they *had* surrendered, it would have been nothing remarkable, but they did not even think of doing such a thing. Boone expected reinforcements from Holston, and it became necessary, therefore, to procure as much delay as possible. For this purpose, he desired that he might have two days to consider the proposition of His Britannic Majesty. Strange as it may appear, this proposition was acceded to. About five minutes were sufficient for the garrison to arrive at a determination, and this was that they would fight it out to the last. All the cows and horses were collected within the fort, and every vessel filled with water from the spring, the latter task being performed by the ladies. When the hour arrived for giving an answer to bold Captain Duquesne, it was done in this wise by Boone: "We laugh at your formidable preparations, but thank you for giving notice and time to prepare for defense." Captain Duquesne was not incensed at this reply, but still insisted on a capitulation. He declared his orders from Colonel Hamilton were to take the garrison captives, to treat them as prisoners of war, and not to injure, much less to murder them; and that they had horses to take the women and children, and all others who could not bear the fatigue of traveling on foot. He then proposed that, if the garrison would depute nine persons to come out of the fort and hold a treaty, the terms should be liberal. It is impossible at this time, after the demise of every person concerned in the affair, to account for the singular course of Captain Duquesne and his Indian allies.

Although Duquesne's affectionate course savored of treachery, Boone thought it desirable to accede to his proposition, as it would at least secure a little more delay. Nine commissioners were selected for the purpose of discussing the treaty, Boone being one of the number. A plot of ground in front of the fort was selected for the conference, all parties to go unarmed. Before leaving for this hazardous interview, Boone took the precaution to place a number of experienced riflemen in advantageous positions, so that, if the commissioners retreated hastily, they might be protected. The parties met, and the treaty proposed was of the most liberal kind. It simply demanded that the residents and garrison of the fort should acknowledge the British authorities, and take the oath of allegiance to the king; in return for which they were to remain unmolested. After these points had been settled, the Indians proposed that, as a commemoration of the joyous occasion, they should revive an ancient custom of their tribe, which consisted of two Indians shaking hands with one white man at the same moment. Boone and his companions knew exactly what this meant, but they did not betray any uneasiness. Eighteen stalwart, muscular Indians now advanced, and, in the way prescribed by the very ancient custom before mentioned, endeavored to drag off the white men. But the iron frames of the pioneers were braced for a struggle. Being without weapons, they appealed to their Anglo-Saxon knowledge of fisticuffs, and in a very little while had tumbled the red villains in the dust. In the excitement which followed they made good their retreat to the fort, and the riflemen immediately opened a murderous fire to keep off the pursuers. Hostilities now commenced on both sides. The Indians kept up a brisk fire at the fort, but owing to its favorable situation, could not effect much mischief. The garrison, on the contrary, never fired a charge without an especial object. A regular siege, conducted in the usual Indian style, was kept up for nine days, but with no result. The Kentuckians never flinched for a moment. Even the women assisted in the defense, for they loaded the rifles, moulded bullets, and supplied refreshments. On one occasion the fort was fired by the enemy, but a heroic young man extinguished the flames, in spite of a shower of bullets which greeted his appearance with the buckets on the roof. Foiled in this, the Indians, under the direction of the Canadians, commenced digging a mine; but Boone was equal to this emergency. He began a counter-mine, and threw all the dirt into their works, so that they had the pleasure of shoveling it away before they could make the slightest progress. On the 20th of September they raised the siege and took their departure, after having suffered a loss of thirty-seven killed and many more wounded. The loss on the pioneer side was two killed and four wounded: it would not have been so great but for the desertion of a vagabond negro who went over to the enemy, carrying with him an excellent rifle. During the siege, this rascal placed himself in a tree on the other side of the river, and was able, owing to the excellence of his weapon, to fire into the fort. He had killed one and wounded another, when

Boone caught a glimpse of his woolly head. It was suffi-cient; the next moment Sambo rolled from the tree. After the retreat his body was found, and in the center of the forehead an explanatory hole told the story of his death. The old hunter brought him down at a distance of one hundred and seventy-five yards.

A CAMPAIGN THROUGH THE WATER

[1778]

BY GEORGE ROGERS CLARK

[BY means of the two bold campaigns of George Rogers Clark, the United States was, at the close of the Revolution, in possession of the land west of the Ohio, and so was able to secure the Mississippi instead of the Ohio as a western boundary.

The Editor.]

EVERYTHING being ready, on the 5th of February, after receiving a lecture and absolution from the priest, we crossed the Kaskaskia River with one hundred and seventy men, marched about three miles and encamped, where we lay until the 7th, and set out. The weather wet (but fortunately not cold for the season) and a great part of the plains under water several inches deep. It was difficult and very fatiguing marching. My object was now to keep the men in spirits. I suffered them to shoot game on all occasions, and feast on it like Indian war-dancers, each company by turns inviting the others to their feasts, which was the case every night, as the company that was to give the feast was always supplied with horses to lay up a sufficient store of wild meat in the course of the day, myself and principal officers putting on the woodsmen, shouting now and then, and running as much through the mud and water as any of them. Thus, insensibly, without a murmur, were those men led on to the banks of the Little Wabash, which we

13

reached on the 13th, through incredible difficulties, far surpassing anything that any of us had ever experienced. Frequently the diversions of the night wore off the thoughts of the preceding day. We formed a camp on a height which we found on the bank of the river, and suffered our troops to amuse themselves. I viewed this sheet of water for some time with distrust; but, accusing myself of doubting, I immediately set to work, without holding any consultation about it, or suffering anybody else to do so in my presence; ordered a pirogue to be built immediately, and acted as though crossing the water would be only a piece of diversion. As but few could work at the pirogue at a time, pains were taken to find diversion for the rest to keep them in high spirits. . . . In the evening of the 14th, our vessel was finished, manned, and sent to explore the drowned lands on the opposite side of the Little Wabash, with private instructions what report to make, and, if possible, to find some spot of dry land. They found about half an acre, and marked the trees from thence back to the camp, and made a very favorable report.

Fortunately, the 15th happened to be a warm, moist day for the season. The channel of the river where we lay was about thirty yards wide. A scaffold was built on the opposite shore (which was about three feet under water), and our baggage ferried across, and put on it. Our horses swam across, and received their loads at the scaffold, by which time the troops were also brought across, and we began our march through the water. . . .

By evening we found ourselves encamped on a pretty height, in high spirits, each party laughing at the other, in consequence of something that had happened in the course of this ferrying business, as they called it. A little antic drummer afforded them great diversion by floating on his drum, etc. All this was greatly encouraged; and they really began to think themselves superior to other men, and that neither the rivers nor the seasons could stop their progress. Their whole conversation now was concerning what they would do when they got about the enemy. They now began to view the main Wabash as a creek, and made no doubt but such men as they were could find a way to cross it. They wound themselves up to such a pitch that they soon took Post Vincennes, divided the spoil, and before bedtime were far advanced on their route to Detroit. All this was, no doubt, pleasing to those of us who had more serious thoughts. . . . We were now convinced that the whole of the low country on the Wabash was drowned, and that the enemy could easily get to us, if they discovered us, and wished to risk an action; if they did not, we made no doubt of crossing the river by some means or other. Even if Captain Rogers, with our galley, did not get to his station agreeable to his appointment, we flattered ourselves that all would be well, and marched on in high spirits. . . .

The last day's march through the water was far superior to anything the Frenchmen had an idea of. They were backward in speaking; said that the nearest land to us was a small league called the Sugar Camp on the bank of the river. A canoe was sent off, and returned without finding that we could pass. I went in her myself, and sounded the water; found it deep as to my neck. I returned with a design to have the men transported on board the canoes to the Sugar Camp, which I knew

15

would spend the whole day and ensuing night, as the vessels would pass slowly through the bushes. The loss of so much time, to men half-starved, was a matter of consequence. I would have given now a great deal for a day's provision or for one of our horses. I returned but slowly to the troops, giving myself time to think. On our arrival, all ran to hear what was the report. Every eye was fixed on me. I unfortunately spoke in a serious manner to one of the officers. The whole were alarmed without knowing what I said. I viewed their confusion for about one minute, whispered to those near me to do as I did: immediately put some water in my hand, poured on powder, blackened my face, gave the war whoop, and marched into the water without saying a word. The party gazed, and fell in, one after another, without saying a word, like a flock of sheep. I ordered those near me to begin a favorite song of theirs. It soon passed through the line, and the whole went on cheerfully. I now intended to have them transported across the deepest part of the water; but, when about waist deep, one of the men informed me that he thought he felt a path. We examined and found it so, and concluded that it kept on the highest ground, which it did; and, by taking pains to follow it, we got to the Sugar Camp without the least difficulty, where there was about half an acre of dry ground, at least not under water, where we took up our lodging. The Frenchmen that we had taken on the river appeared to be uneasy at our situation. They begged that they might be permitted to go in the two canoes to town in the night. They said that they would bring from their own houses provisions, without a possibility of any persons knowing it; that some of our men should go with them as a surety of their good conduct; that it was impossible we could march from that place till the water fell, for the plain was too deep to march. Some of the officers believed that it might be done. I would not suffer it. I never could well account for this piece of obstinacy, and give satisfactory reasons to myself or anybody else why I denied a proposition apparently so easy to execute and of so much advantage; but something seemed to tell me that it should not be done, and it was not done.

The most of the weather that we had on this march was moist and warm for the season. This was the coldest night we had. The ice, in the morning, was from one half to three quarters of an inch thick near the shores and in still water. The morning was the finest we had on our march. A little after sunrise I lectured the whole. What I said to them I forget, but it may easily be imagined by a person that could possess my affections for them at that time. I concluded by informing them that passing the plain that was then in full view and reaching the opposite woods would put an end to their fatigue, that in a few hours they would have a sight of their long-wished-for object, and immediately stepped into the water without waiting for any reply. A huzza took place. As we generally marched through the water in a line, before the third entered I halted, and called to Major Bowman, ordering him to fall to the rear with twenty-five men, and put to death any man who refused to march, as we wished to have no such person among us. The whole gave a cry of approbation, and on we went. This was the most trying of all the difficulties we had experienced. I generally kept fifteen or twenty of the strongest men

17

next myself, and judged from my own feelings what must be that of others. Getting about the middle of the plain, the water about mid-deep, I found myself sensibly failing; and, as there were no trees nor bushes for the men to support themselves by, I feared that many of the most weak would be drowned. I ordered the canoes to make the land, discharge their loading, and play backward and forward with all diligence, and pick up the men; and, to encourage the party, sent some of the strongest men forward, with orders, when they got to a certain distance, to pass the word back that the water was getting shallow, and when getting near the woods to cry out, "Land!" This stratagem had its desired effect. The men, encouraged by it, exerted themselves almost beyond their abilities; the weak holding by the stronger. . . . The water never got shallower, but continued deepening. Getting to the woods, where the men expected land, the water was up to my shoulders; but gaining the woods was of great consequence. All the low men and the weakly hung to the trees, and floated on the old logs until they were taken off by the canoes. The strong and tall got ashore and built fires. Many would reach the shore, and fall with their bodies half in the water, not being able to support themselves without it.

This was a delightful dry spot of ground of about ten acres. We soon found that the fires answered no purpose, but that two strong men taking a weaker one by the arms was the only way to recover him; and, being a delightful day, it soon did. But, fortunately, as if designed by Providence, a canoe of Indian squaws and children was coming up to town, and took through part of this plain as a nigh way. It was discovered by our canoes as they were out after the men. They gave chase, and took the Indian canoe, on board of which was near half a quarter of a buffalo, some corn, tallow, kettles, etc. This was a grand prize, and was invaluable. Broth was immediately made, and served out to the most weakly with great care. Most of the whole got a little; but a great many gave their part to the weakly, jocosely saying something cheering to their comrades. This little refreshment and fine weather by the afternoon gave new life to the whole. Crossing a narrow deep lake in the canoes, and marching some distance, we came to a copse of timber called the Warrior's Island. We were now in full view of the fort and town, not a shrub between us, at about two miles' distance. Every man now feasted his eyes, and forgot that he had suffered anything, saying, that all that had passed was owing to good policy and nothing but what a man could bear; and that a soldier had no right to think, etc., — passing from one extreme to another, which is common in such cases. It was now we had to display our abilities. The plain between us and the town was not a perfect level. The sunken grounds were covered with water full of ducks. We observed several men out on horseback, shooting them, within a half mile of us, and sent out as many of our active young Frenchmen to decoy and take one of these men prisoner in such a manner as not to alarm the others, which they did. The information we got from this person was similar to that which we got from those we took on the river, except that of the British having that evening completed the wall of the fort, and that there were a good many Indians in town.

Our situation was now truly critical, — no possibility

19

of retreating in case of defeat, and in full view of a town that had, at this time, upward of six hundred men in it. — troops, inhabitants, and Indians. The crew of the galley, though not fifty men, would have been now a reenforcement of immense magnitude to our little army (if I may so call it), but we would not think of them. We were now in the situation that I had labored to get ourselves in. The idea of being made prisoner was foreign to almost every man, as they expected nothing but torture from the savages, if they fell into their hands. Our fate was now to be determined, probably in a few hours. We knew that nothing but the most daring conduct would insure success. I knew that a number of the inhabitants wished us well, that many were lukewarm to the interest of either, and I also learned that the grand chief, the Tobacco's son, had but a few days before openly declared, in council with the British, that he was a brother and friend to the Big Knives. These were favorable circumstances; and, as there was but little probability of our remaining until dark undiscovered, I determined to begin the career immediately, and wrote the following placard to the inhabitants: —

To the Inhabitants of Fort Vincennes:

Gentlemen, — Being now within two miles of your village, with my army, determined to take your fort this night, and not being willing to surprise you, I take this method to request such of you as are true citizens and willing to enjoy the liberty I bring you to remain still in your houses; and those, if any there be, that are friends to the king will instantly repair to the fort, and join the hair-buyer general,[1] and fight like men. And if any such

---

[1] Hamilton offered rewards for American scalps.

as do not go to the fort shall be discovered afterward, they may depend on severe punishment. On the contrary, those who are true friends to liberty may depend on being well treated; and I once more request them to keep out of the streets. For every one I find in arms on my arrival I shall treat him as an enemy.

(Signed)

G. R. CLARK.

I had various ideas on the supposed result of this letter. I knew that it would do us no damage, but that it would cause the lukewarm to be decided, encourage our friends, and astonish our enemies. . . . We anxiously viewed this messenger until he entered the town, and in a few minutes could discover by our glasses some stir in every street that we could penetrate into, and great numbers running or riding out into the commons, we supposed, to view us, which was the case. But what surprised us was that nothing had yet happened that had the appearance of the garrison being alarmed, — no drum nor gun. We began to suppose that the information we got from our prisoners was false, and that the enemy already knew of us, and were prepared. . . . A little before sunset we moved, and displayed ourselves in full view of the town, crowds gazing at us. We were plunging ourselves into certain destruction or success. There was no midway thought of. We had but little to say to our men, except inculcating an idea of the necessity of obedience, etc. We knew they did not want encouraging, and that anything might be attempted with them that was possible for such a number, — perfectly cool, under proper subordination, pleased with the prospect before them, and much attached to their officers. They all declared that they were convinced that an implicit obedience to orders was the only thing that would insure success, and hoped that no mercy would be shown the person that should violate them. Such language as this from soldiers to persons in our station must have been exceedingly agreeable. We moved on slowly in full view of the town; but, as it was a point of some consequence to us to make ourselves appear as formidable, we in leaving the covert that we were in, marched and countermarched in such a manner that we appeared numerous. In raising volunteers in the Illinois, every person that set about the business had a set of colors given him, which they brought with them to the amount of ten or twelve pairs. These were displayed to the best advantage; and, as the low plain we marched through was not a perfect level, but had frequent risings in it seven or eight feet higher than the common level (which was covered with water), and as these risings generally ran in an oblique direction to the town, we took the advantage of one of them, marching through the water under it, which completely prevented our being numbered. But our colors showed considerably above the heights, as they were fixed on long poles procured for the purpose, and at a distance made no despicable appearance; and, as our young Frenchmen had, while we lay on the Warrior's Island, decoyed and taken several fowlers with their horses, officers were mounted on these horses, and rode about, more completely to deceive the enemy. In this manner we moved, and directed our march in such a way as to suffer it to be dark before we had advanced more than half-way to the town. We then suddenly altered our direction, and crossed ponds where they could not have suspected us, and about eight o'clock gained the heights back of the town. As there was yet no hostile appearance, we were impatient to have the cause unriddled. Lieutenant Bayley was ordered, with fourteen men, to march and fire on the fort. The main body moved in a different direction, and took possession of the strongest part of the town.

[The attack upon the town continued for some thirty-six hours. Then the audacious young leader sent a demand for surrender. It was promptly refused; nevertheless, the surrender took place before the close of the day.]

HOW THE WOMEN BROUGHT WATER TO BRYAN'S STATION

[1782]

BY CYRUS TOWNSEND BRADY

THERE had been terrible doings on the frontier during the spring and summer of 1782. The British and Indians had made raid after raid through the land. Two years before a certain Colonel William Byrd of Westover, Virginia, a Tory, who seems to have been a gentleman and a soldier, led some eight hundred Indians with a detachment of soldiers and some artillery into Kentucky. None of the forts was proof against artillery, nor was there any in the territory except that in the possession of George Rogers Clark, which was not available. Two stations, Martin's and Ruddle's, were attacked in succession and easily captured. Their garrisons and inhabitants were murdered and tortured with shocking barbarity. It is to the eternal credit of Colonel Byrd, that, finding himself unable to control the Indians, he abandoned his expedition and withdrew, otherwise the whole land would have been desolated. The bulk of the invading Indians were Wyandots, who were easily first among the savages of the northwest for ferocious valor and military skill. The opposing forces being exactly equal, a detachment of them defeated a certain Captain Estill by a series of brilliant military maneuvers which would have done credit to a great captain, being indeed upon a

24

small scale Napoleonic in their conception and execution.

Two years after Byrd had withdrawn, William Campbell and Alexander McKee, notorious renegades, with the infamous Simon Girty, whose name has been a hissing and a byword ever since he lived, led a formidable war party consisting of a few Canadians and four hundred Indians into Kentucky. The first place they attacked was Bryan's Station. Another place called Hoy's Station was menaced by a different party of Indians, and express messengers had ridden to Bryan's Station to seek aid, which the settlers were ready to grant.

The American party was being made up to go to Hoy's Station early in the morning of the 16th of August, 1782, when as they approached the gate to ride out of it, a party of Indians was discovered on the edge of the woods in full view. The party was small in number, comparatively speaking, yet its members exposed themselves, out of rifle range, of course, with such careless indifference to consequences or to a possible attack, as inevitably to suggest to the mind of Captain John Craig, who commanded the fort at the time, that they were desirous of attracting the attention of the garrison in the hope that their small numbers might induce the men of the station to leave the fort and pursue them.

Craig was an old Indian fighter who had been trained in Daniel Boone's own school. He was suspicious of any maneuver of that kind. Checking the departure of the relief party, he called his brother and the principal men of the station into a council and they concluded at once that the demonstration in the front of the fort was a mere feint, that the Indians were anxious to be pursued and that the main attack would come from the other direction.

The surmise was correct. With cunning adroitness Campbell had massed the main body of his forces in the woods back of the fort with strict instructions for them to remain concealed and not show themselves on any account until they heard the fire coming from the front of the station, which would convince them that their ruse had succeeded. Then they were to break from cover and rush for the back wall of the fort, which they supposed would be undefended, scale it, and have the little garrison at their mercy. It so happened that the spring, from which the fort got its water supply, lay within a short distance of the main body concealed in the thick woods which surrounded the clearing with the fort in the center. The situation was perfectly plain to Craig and his men. They determined to meet ruse with ruse and if possible to defeat the Indians at their own game.

Before they could do anything, however, they must have a supply of water. On that hot August day life in that stockade, especially when engaged in furious battle, would become unsupportable without water. Only the ordinary amount sufficient for the night had been brought in the day before. The receptacles were now empty. After swift deliberations the commandant turned to the women and children crowded around the officers, and explained the situation plainly to them. He proposed that the women, and children who were large enough to carry water, should go down to the spring with every vessel they could carry and bring back the water upon which their lives depended. He also explained to them that the spring was probably covered by concealed masses of the enemy who were waiting for the success of the demonstration in front of the fort to begin the attack.

He said further that it was the opinion of those in command, that if the women would go to the spring as they did under ordinary circumstances, as was their custom every morning that is, the Indians would not molest them, not being desirous of breaking up the plan by which they hoped to take the fort and have everything at their mercy. The men in the fort would cover the women with their rifles so far as they could. It would be impossible for them to go and get water; as it was not the habit of the men to do that, the unusual proceeding would awaken the suspicions of the Indians, and the men would be shot down, and the fort and all its inmates would be at the mercy of the savages.

Every woman there was able to see the situation. The theory upon which they were proceeding might be all wrong. The Indians might be satisfied with the certainty of capturing the women thus presented, and the women and children might be taken away under the very eyes of the helpless men. On the other hand, it was probable, though by no means certain, that Craig's reasoning was correct and that the Indians would not discover themselves, and the women and children would be allowed to return unmolested. Still nobody could tell what the Indians would do and the situation was a terrible one. Capture at the very best meant death by torture. The women in the fort had not lived on the frontier in vain. They realized the dilemma instantly. A shudder of terror and apprehension went through the crowd. What would they do? They must have the water; the men could not get it, the women did!

Mrs. Jemima Suggett Johnson, the wife of an intrepid pioneer and the daughter and sister of others, instantly volunteered for the task. She was the mother of five little children and her husband happened to be away in Virginia at the time. Leaving her two little boys and her daughter Sally to look after the baby in his dug-out cradle, she offered to go for the water. This baby was that Richard Mentor Johnson, who afterward became so celebrated at the battle of the Thames where Tecumseh was killed, and who was subsequently Vice-President of the United States.

Taking her little daughter Betsy, aged ten, her eldest child, by the hand, the fearless woman headed a little band of twelve women and sixteen children, who had agreed to follow where she led; among them were the wives and children of the Craig brothers. The little ones carried wooden piggins, and the women noggins and buckets. The piggin was a small bucket with one upright stave for a handle — a large wooden dipper as it were — while the larger noggin had two upright staves for handles.

Carefully avoiding any suspicious demonstration of force on the part of his men, Captain Craig opened the gate and the women marched out. Chatting and laughing in spite of the fact that they were nearly perishing from apprehension and terror, they tramped down the hill to the spring near the creek some sixty yards away, with as much coolness and indifference as they could muster. It was indeed a fearful moment for the women, and no wonder that some of the younger ones and the older children found it difficult to control their agitation; but the composed manner of those valiant and heroic matrons like Mrs. Johnson somewhat reassured the others and completely deluded the Indians. Probably the younger children did not realize their frightful danger, and their unconsciousness helped to deceive the foes in ambush.

It took some time to fill the various receptacles from the small spring, but, by the direction of Mrs. Johnson, no one left the vicinity until all were ready to return. This little party then marched deliberately back to the fort as they had come. Not a shot was fired. The Indians concealed within a stone's throw in the underbrush had looked at them with covetous eyes, but such was the unwonted discipline in which they were held that they refrained from betraying themselves, in the hope of afterward carrying out their stratagem. As they neared the gate some of the younger ones broke into a run crowding into the door of the stockade which never looked so hospitable as on that sunny summer morning, and some of the precious water was spilled, but most of it was carried safe into the inclosure.

With what feelings of relief the fifty-odd men in the station saw their wives and children come back again can scarcely be imagined. Dispatching two daring men on horseback to break through the besiegers and rouse the country, Craig immediately laid a trap for the Indians. Selecting a small body he sent them out to the front of the fort to engage the Indians there, instructing them to make as much noise and confusion as possible. Then he posted the main body of his men at the loopholes back of the fort, instructing them not to make a move, nor fire a gun, until he gave the order.

The ruse was completely successful. Deceived by the hullabaloo in front, the Indians in the rear, imagining that their plan had succeeded, broke from cover and instantly dashed up to the stockade, shouting their war cries, and expecting an easy victory. What was their surprise to find it suddenly bristling with rifles as Craig and his men poured a steady withering fire into the mass crowded before them, fairly decimating them. They ran back instantly, and concealment being at an end, returned the fire ineffectually. Immediately thereafter from every side a furious fire from four hundred rifles burst upon the defenders. All day long the siege was maintained. Once in a while a bullet ploughing through a crevice in the stockade struck down one of the brave garrison, but the casualties in the station were very few.

On the other hand, when an Indian exposed himself he was sure to be killed by a shot from some unerring rifle. One or two Indians climbed a tree seeking to command the fort therefrom, but they were quickly detected and shot before they had time to descend. At last they attempted to burn the fort by shooting flaming arrows up in the air to fall perpendicularly upon the buildings. The children, the little boys, that is, and some of the older girls, were lifted up on the inclined roofs, where they were safe from direct rifle fire, though in imminent danger of being pierced by the dropping arrows, with instructions to put out the fires as fast as the arrows kindled them, which they succeeded in doing. Meanwhile, the women were busy moulding bullets and load-

ing rifles for the men, and many of them took their
places on the walls and aided in the defense.

> "The mothers of our forest land,
>   Their bosoms pillowed men;
> And proud were they by such to stand
>   In hammock, fort, or glen;
> To load the sure old rifle,
>   To run the leaden ball,
> To watch a battling husband's place,
>   And fill it should he fall."

Finding their efforts unavailing, the Indians ravaged
the surrounding country. They killed all the cattle
belonging to the pioneers, burned and destroyed the
fields of grain, and turned the environment into a bloody
desert. In the afternoon a succoring party from Boone's
Station appeared, but without Boone, for he was absent
at the time, and succeeded in entering the fort.

THE FIRST SALUTE TO THE FLAG

[1778]

BY SARAH ORNE JEWETT

IN midwinter something happened that lifted every true heart on board. There had been dull and dreary weeks on board the Ranger, with plots for desertion among the crew, and a general look of surliness and reproach on all faces. The captain was eagerly impatient in sending his messengers to Nantes when the Paris post might be expected, and was ever disappointed at their return. The discipline of the ship became more strict than before, now that there was little else to command or insist upon. The officers grew tired of one another's company, and kept to their own quarters, or passed each other without speaking. It was easy, indeed, to be displeased with such a situation, and to fret at such an apparently needless loss of time, even if there were nothing else to fret about.

At last there was some comfort in leaving Nantes, and making even so short a voyage as to the neighboring port of L'Orient, where the Ranger was overhauled and refitted for sea; yet even here the men grumbled at their temporary discomforts, and above all regretted Nantes, where they could amuse themselves better ashore. It was a hard, stormy winter, but there were plenty of rich English ships almost within hand's reach. Nobody could well understand why they had done nothing, while such easy prey came and went in those waters, from

Bordeaux and the coast of Spain, even from Nantes itself.

On a certain Friday orders were given to set sail, and the Ranger made her way along the coast to Quiberon, and anchored there at sunset, before the bay's entrance, facing the great curve of the shores. She had much shipping for company: farther in there lay a fine show of French frigates with a convoy, and four ships of the line. The captain scanned these through his glass, and welcomed a great opportunity: he had come upon a division of the French navy, and one of the frigates flew the flag of a rear admiral, La Motte Piqué.

The wind had not fallen at sundown. All night the Ranger tossed about and tugged at her anchor chains, as if she were impatient to continue her adventures, like the men between her sides. All the next day she rode uneasily, and clapped her sailcloth and thrummed her rigging in the squally winter blast, until the sea grew quieter toward sundown. Then Captain Paul Jones sent a boat to the king's fleet to carry a letter.

The boat was long gone. The distance was little, but difficult in such a sea, yet some of the boats of the country came out in hope of trading with the Ranger's men. The poor peasants would venture anything, and a strange-looking, swarthy little man who got aboard nobody knew how, suddenly approached the captain where he stood, ablaze with impatience, on the quarter. At his first word Paul Jones burst with startling readiness into Spanish invective, and then, with a look of pity at the man's poverty of dress in that icy weather, took a bit of gold from his pocket. "Barcelona?" said he. "I have had good days in Barcelona, myself," and bade the Spaniard begone. Then he called him back and asked a few questions, and, summoning a quartermaster, gave orders that he should take the sailor's poor gear, and give him a warm coat and cap from the slop chests.

"He has lost his ship, and got stranded here," said the captain, with compassion, and then turned again to watch for the boat. "You may roll the coat and cap into a bundle; they are quaint-fashioned things," he added carelessly, as the quartermaster went away.

The bay was now alive with small Breton traders, and at a short distance away there was a droll little potato fleet making hopefully for the Ranger. The headmost boat, however, was the Ranger's own, with an answer to the captain's letter. He gave an anxious sigh and laid down his glass. He had sent to say frankly to the rear admiral that he flew the new American flag, and that no foreign power had yet saluted it, and to ask if his own salute to the Royal Navy of France would be properly returned. It was already in the last fluster of the February wind, and the sea was going down; there was no time to be lost. He broke the great seal of his answer with a trembling hand, and at the first glance pressed the letter to his breast.

The French frigates were a little apart from their convoy, and rolled sullenly in a solemn company, their tall masts swaying like time-keepers against the pale winter sky. The low land lay behind them, its line broken here and there by strange mounds, and by ancient altars of the druids, like clumsy, heavy-legged beasts standing against the winter sunset. The captain gave orders to hoist the anchor, nobody knew why, and to spread the sails, when it was no time to put to sea.

He stood like a king until all was done, and then passed the word for his gunners to be ready, and steered straight in toward the French fleet.

They all understood now. The little Ranger ran slowly between the frowning ships, looking as warlike as they; her men swarmed like bees into the rigging; her colors ran up to salute the flag of his most Christian Majesty of France, and she fired one by one her salute of thirteen guns.

There was a moment of suspense. The wind was very light now; the powder smoke drifted away, and the flapping sails sounded loud overhead. Would the admiral answer, or would he treat this bold challenge like a handkerchief waved at him from a pleasure boat? Some of the officers on the Ranger looked incredulous, but Paul Jones still held his letter in his hand. There was a puff of white smoke, and the great guns of the French flagship began to shake the air, — one, two, three, four, five, six, seven, eight, *nine;* and then were still, save for their echoes from the low hills about Carnac and the great druid mount of St. Michael.

"Gardner, you may tell the men that this was the salute of the King of France to our Republic, and the first high honor to our colors," said the captain proudly to his steersman. But they were all huzzaing now along the Ranger's decks, — that little ship whose name shall never be forgotten while her country lives.

"We hardly know what this day means, gentlemen," he said soberly to his officers, who came about him. "I believe that we are at the christening of the greatest nation that was ever born into the world."

He lifted his hat, and stood looking up at the flag.

JOHN PAUL JONES IN THE REVOLUTION

[1775–1781]

BY JOEL TYLER HEADLEY

IN 1775, when the American Revolution broke out, the young Scotchman commenced his brilliant career. His offer to Congress, to serve in the navy, was accepted, and he was appointed first lieutenant in the Alfred. As the commander-in-chief of the squadron came on board, Jones unfurled the national flag — the first time its folds were ever given to the breeze. What that flag was, strange as it may seem, no record or tradition can certainly tell. It was not the stars and the stripes, for they were not generally adopted till two years after. The generally received opinion is that it was a pine tree, with a rattlesnake coiled at the roots, as if about to spring, and underneath, the motto, "Don't tread on me." At all events, it unrolled to the breeze, and waved over as gallant a young officer as ever trod a quarter-deck. If the flag bore such a symbol, it was most appropriate to Jones, for no serpent was ever more ready to strike than he. Fairly afloat — twenty-nine years of age — healthy — well knit, though of light and slender frame, — a commissioned officer in the American navy — the young gardener saw, with joy, the shores receding as the fleet steered for the Bahama Isles. A skillful seaman — at home on the deck, and a bold and daring man — he could not but distinguish himself, in whatever circumstances he might be placed. The result of this expedition was the capture of New Providence, with a hundred cannon, and an abundance of military stores. It came near failing, through the bungling management of the commander-in-chief, and would have done so but for the perseverance and daring of Paul Jones.

As the fleet was returning home, he had an opportunity to try himself in battle. The Glasgow, an English ship, was chased by the whole squadron, yet escaped. During the running fight, Jones commanded the lower battery of the Alfred, and exhibited that coolness and daring which afterwards so characterized him.

Soon after, he was transferred to the sloop Providence, and ordered to put to sea on a six weeks' cruise. It required no ordinary skill or boldness to keep this little sloop hovering amid the enemy's cruisers, and yet avoid capture. Indeed, his short career seemed about to end, for he found himself one day chased by the English frigate Solebay; and despite of every exertion overhauled, so that at the end of four hours his vessel was brought within musket-shot of the enemy, whose heavy cannon kept thundering against him. Gallantly returning the fire with his light guns, Jones, though there seemed no chance of escape, still kept his flag flying, and saved himself by his extraordinary seamanship. Finding himself lost in the course he was pursuing, he gradually worked his little vessel off till he got the Solebay on his weather quarter, when he suddenly exclaimed, "Up helm," to the steersman, and setting every sail that would draw, stood dead before the wind, bearing straight down on the English frigate, and passing within pistol-shot of her. Before the enemy could recover his surprise at this bold and unexpected maneuver, or bring his ship into the same position, Jones was showing him a clean pair of heels. His little sloop could outsail the frigate before the wind, and he bore proudly away.

He soon after had another encounter with the English frigate Milford. He was lying to near the Isle of Sable, fishing, when the Milford hove in sight. Immediately putting his ship in trim, he tried the relative speed of the two vessels, and finding that he could outsail his antagonist, let him approach. The Englishman kept rounding to as he advanced, and pouring his broadsides on the sloop, but at such a distance that not a shot told. Thus Jones kept irritating his more powerful enemy, keeping him at just such a distance as to make his firing ridiculous. Still it was a hazardous experiment, for a single chance shot, crashing through his rigging, might have reduced his speed so much as to prevent his escape. But to provoke the Englishman still more, Jones, as he walked quietly away, ordered one of his men to return each of the enemy's broadsides with a single musket-shot. This insulting treatment made a perfect farce of the whole chase, and must have enraged the commander of the Milford beyond measure.

He continued cruising about, and at the end of forty-seven days sailed into Newport with sixteen prizes. He next planned an expedition against Cape Breton, to break up the fisheries; and, though he did not wholly succeed, he returned to Boston in about a month, with four prizes and a hundred and fifty prisoners. The clothing on its way to the Canada troops, which he captured, came very opportunely for the destitute soldiers of the American army. During this expedition, Jones had command of the Alfred, but was superseded on his return, and put on board his old sloop, the Providence. This was the commencement of a series of unjust acts on the part of our Government towards him, which as yet could not break away from English example, and make brave deeds the only road to rank. It insisted, according to the old Continental rule, with which Bonaparte made such wild work, on giving the places of trust to the sons of distinguished gentlemen. Jones remonstrated against this injustice, and pressed the Government so closely with his importunities and complaints, that, to get rid of him, it sent him to Boston to select and fit out a ship for himself. In the mean time, he recommended measures to the Government, respecting the organizing and strengthening of the navy, which show him to have been the most enlightened naval officer in our service, and that his sound and comprehensive views were equal to his bravery. Most of his suggestions were adopted, and the foundation of the American navy laid.

Soon after (June, 1777), he was given command of the Ranger, and informed in his commission that the flag of the United States was to be thirteen stripes, and the union thirteen stars on a blue field, representing a new constellation in the heavens. With joy he hoisted this new flag and put to sea in his badly equipped vessel — steering for France, where he was, by order of his Government, to take charge of a large vessel, there to be purchased for him by the American Commissioners. Failing in this enterprise, he again set sail in the Ranger, and steered for Quiberon Bay. Here, passing through the French fleet with his brig, he obtained a national salute, the first ever given our colors. Having had the honor first to hoist our flag on the water, and the first to hear the guns of a powerful nation thunder forth their recognition of it, he again put to sea, and boldly entered the Irish Channel, capturing several prizes.

Steering for the Isle of Man, he planned an expedition which illustrates the boldness and daring that characterized him. He determined to burn the shipping in Whitehaven, in retaliation for the injuries inflicted on our coast by English ships. More than three hundred vessels lay in this port, protected by two batteries, composed of thirty pieces of artillery, while eighty rods distant was a strong fort. To enter a port so protected and filled with shipping, with a single brig, and apply the torch, under the very muzzles of the cannon, was an act unrivaled in daring. But Jones seemed to delight in these reckless deeds — there appeared to be a sort of witchery about danger to him, and the greater it was, the more enticing it became. Once, when Government was making arrangements to furnish him with a ship, he urged the necessity of giving him a good one, "for," said he, "*I intend to go in harm's way.*" This was true, and he generally managed to carry out his intentions.

It was about midnight, on the 22d of April, 1778, when Jones stood boldly in to the port of Whitehaven. Having got sufficiently near, he took two boats and thirty-one men, and rowed noiselessly away from his gallant little ship. He commanded one boat in person, and took upon himself the task of securing the batteries. With a mere handful of men he scaled the breastwork, seized the sentinel on duty before he could give the alarm, and rushing forward took the astonished soldiers prisoners and spiked the cannon. Then leaving Lieutenant Wallingsford to fire the shipping, he hastened forward with *only one man* to take the fort. All was silent as he approached, and boldly entering, he spiked every cannon, and then hurried back to his little band. He was surprised, as he approached, not to see the shipping in a blaze; and demanded of his lieutenant why he had not fulfilled his orders. The latter replied that his light had gone out; but he evidently did not like his mission, and purposely neglected to obey orders. Everything had been managed badly, and to his mortification he saw the day beginning to dawn, and his whole plan, at the moment when it promised complete success, overturned. The people, rousing from their slumbers, saw with alarm a band of men with half-burnt candles in their hands standing on the pier — and assembled in crowds. Jones, however, refused to depart, and indignant at the failure of the expedition, entered alone a large ship, and coolly sat down and kindled a fire in the steerage. He then hunted about for a barrel of tar, which having found, he poured it over the flames. The blaze shot up around the lofty spars, and wreathed the rigging in their spiral folds, casting a baleful light over the town. The terrified inhabitants, seeing the flames shoot heavenward, rushed toward the wharves; but Jones posted himself by the entrance to the ship, with a cocked pistol in his hand, threatening to shoot the first who should approach. They hesitated a moment and then turned and fled. Gazing a moment on the burning ship and the panic-struck multitude, he entered his boat, and leisurely rowed back to the Ranger, that sat like a sea gull on the water. The bright sun had now risen, and was bathing the land and sea in its light, revealing to the inhabitants the little craft that had so boldly entered their waters; and they hastened to their fort to open their cannon upon it. To their astonishment they found them spiked. They, however, got possession of two guns, which they began to fire; but the shot fell so wide of the mark, that the sailors, in contempt, fired back their pistols.

The expedition had failed through the inefficiency of his men, and especially one deserter, who remained behind to be called the "savior of Whitehaven"; but it showed to England that her own coast was not safe from the hands of the spoiler; and that the torch she carried into our ports might be hurled into hers also. In carrying it out, Jones exhibited a daring and coolness never surpassed by any man. The only drawback to it was, that it occurred in the neighborhood of his birthplace, and amid the hallowed associations of his childhood. One would think that the familiar hilltops and mountain ranges, and the thronging memories they would bring back on the bold rover, would have sent him to other portions of the coast to inflict distress. It speaks badly for the man's sensibilities, though so well for his courage.

He next entered Kirkcudbright Bay in a single boat, for the purpose of taking Lord Selkirk prisoner. The absence of the nobleman alone prevented his success.

The next day, as he was off Carrickfergus, he saw the Drake, an English ship of war, working slowly out of harbor to go in pursuit of his vessel, that was sending such consternation along the Scottish coast. Five small vessels, filled with citizens, accompanied her part of the way. A heavy tide was setting landward, and the vessel made feeble headway; but at length she made her last tack, and stretched boldly out into the channel. The Ranger, when she first saw the Drake coming out of the harbor, ran down to meet her, and then lay to till the latter had cleared the port. She then filled away, and stood out into the center of the channel. The Drake had, in volunteers and all, a crew of a hundred and sixty men, besides carrying two guns more than the Ranger. She also belonged to the regular British navy, while Jones had a crew imperfectly organized, and but partially used to the discipline of a vessel of war. He, however, saw with delight his formidable enemy approach, and when the latter hailed him, asking what ship it was, he replied: "The American Continental ship Ranger! We are waiting for you — come on!"

Alarm fires were burning along both shores, and the hilltops were covered with spectators, witnessing the meeting of these two ships. The sun was only an hour high, and as the blazing fire-ball stooped to the western wave, Jones commenced the attack. Steering directly across the enemy's bow, he poured in a deadly broadside, which was promptly returned; the two ships moved gallantly away, side by side, while broadside after broadside thundered over the deep. Within close musket-shot they continued to sweep slowly and sternly onward for an hour, wreathed in smoke, while the incessant crash of timbers on board the Drake told how terrible was the American's fire. First, her fore- and main-topsails were carried away — then the yards began to tumble, one after another; until at length her ensign, fallen also, draggled in the water. Jones kept pouring in his destructive broadsides, which the Drake answered, but with less effect; while the topmen of the Ranger made fearful havoc amid the dense crew of the enemy. As the last sunlight was leaving its farewell on the distant mountain-tops, the commander of the Drake fell, shot through the head with a musket-ball, and the British flag was lowered to the Stripes and Stars — a ceremony which, in after years, became quite common.

Jones returned with his prizes to Paris, and offered his services to France. In hopes of getting command of a larger vessel he gave up the Ranger, but soon had cause to regret it, for he was left for a long time without employment. He had been promised the Indian; and the Prince of Nassau, pleased by the daring of Jones, had promised to accompany him as a volunteer. But this fell through, together with many other projects, and but for the firm friendship of Franklin, he would have fared but poorly in the French capital. After a long series of annoyances and disappointments, he at length obtained command of a vessel, which, out of respect to Franklin, he named the Bon Homme Richard, the "Poor Richard." With seven ships in all — a snug little squadron for Jones, had the different commanders been subordinate — he set sail from France, and steered for the coast of Ireland. The want of proper subordination was soon made manifest, for in a week's time the vessels, one after another, parted company, to cruise by themselves, till Jones had with him but the Alliance, Pallas, and Vengeance. In a tremendous storm he bore away, and after several days of gales and heavy seas, approached the shore of Scotland. Taking several prizes near the Firth of Forth, he ascertained that a twenty-four-gun ship, and two cutters were in the roads. These he determined to cut out, and, landing at Leith, lay the town under contribution. The inhabitants supposed his little fleet to be English vessels in pursuit of Paul Jones; and a member of Parliament, a wealthy man in the place, sent off a boat, requesting powder and balls to defend himself, as he said, against the "pirate Paul Jones." Jones very politely sent back the bearer with a barrel of powder, expressing his regrets that he had no shot to spare. Soon after, in his pompous, inflated manner, he summoned the town to surrender; but the wind blowing steadily off the land, he could not approach with his vessel.

At length, however, the wind changed, and the Richard stood boldly in for the shore. The inhabitants, as they saw her bearing steadily up towards the place, were filled with terror, and ran hither and thither in affright; but the good minister, Rev. Mr. Shirra, assembled his flock on the beach, to pray the Lord to deliver them from their enemies. He was an eccentric man, one of the quaintest of the quaint Scotch divines, so that his prayers, even in those days, were often quoted for their oddity and even roughness.

Whether the following prayer is literally true or not, it is difficult to tell, but there is little doubt that the invocation of the excited, eccentric old man was sufficiently odd. It is said that, having gathered his congregation on the beach in full sight of the vessel, which, under a press of canvas, was making a long tack that brought her close to the town, he knelt down on the sand, and thus began: "Now, dear Lord, dinna ye think it a shame for ye to send this vile pirate to rob our folk o' Kirkaldy; for ye ken they're puir enow already, and hae naething to spare. The way the wind blaws he'll be here in a jiffy, and wha kens what he may do; he's nae too good for onything. Mickle's the mischief he has done already. He'll burn their houses, tak their very claes, and tirl them to the sark. And waes me! wha kens but the bluidy villain might take their lives! The puir weemen are maist frightened out o' their wits, and the bairns skirling after them. I canna think of it! I canna think of it! I hae been long a faithful servant to ye, Lord; but gin ye dinna turn the wind about, and blaw the scoundrel out of our gate, I'll nae stir a foot: but will just sit here till the tide comes. Sae tak ye'r will o't." To the no little astonishment of the good people, a fierce gale at that moment began to blow, which sent one of Jones's prizes ashore, and forced him to stand out to sea. This fixed forever the reputation of good Mr. Shirra; and he did not himself wholly deny that he believed his intercessions brought on the gale, for whenever his parishioners spoke of it to him, he always replied, "I prayed, but the Lord sent the wind."

Stretching from thence along the English coast, Jones cruised about for a while, and at length fell in with the Alliance, which had parted company with him a short time previous. With this vessel, the Pallas and Vengeance, — making, with the Richard, four ships, — he stood to the north; when, on the afternoon of September 23d, 1779, he saw a fleet of forty-one sail hugging the coast. This was the Baltic fleet, under the convoy of the Serapis, of forty-one guns, and the Countess of Scarborough, of twenty guns. Jones immediately issued his orders to form line of battle, while with his ship he gave chase. The convoy scattered like wild pigeons, and ran for the shore, to place themselves under the protection of a fort, but the two warships advanced to the conflict.

It was a beautiful day, the wind was light, so that not a wave broke the smooth surface of the sea — and all was smiling and tranquil on land, as the hostile forces slowly approached each other. The piers of Scarborough were crowded with spectators, and the old promontory of Flamborough, over three miles distant, was black with the multitude assembled to witness the engagement. The breeze was so light that the vessels approached each other slowly, as if reluctant to come to the mortal struggle, and mar that placid scene and that beautiful evening with the sound of battle. It was a thrilling spectacle, those bold ships with their sails all set, moving sternly up to each other. At length the cloudless sun sank behind the hills, and twilight deepened over the waters. The next moment the full round moon pushed its broad disk over the tranquil waters, bathing in her soft beams the white sails that now seemed like gentle moving clouds on the deep.

The Pallas stood for the Countess of Scarborough, while the Alliance, after having also come within range, withdrew and took up a position where she could safely contemplate the fight. Paul Jones, now in his element, paced the deck to and fro, impatient for the contest; and at length approached within pistol-shot of the Serapis. The latter was a new ship, with an excellent crew, and throwing, with every broadside, seventy-five pounds more than the Richard. Jones, however, rated this lightly, and with his old, half-worn-out merchantman, closed fearlessly with his powerful antagonist. As he approached the latter, Captain Pearson hailed

47

him with "What ship is that?" "I can't hear what you
say," was the reply. "What ship is that?" rang back.
"Answer immediately, or I shall fire into you." A shot
from the Richard was the significant answer, and immediately both vessels opened their broadsides. Two of the
three old eighteen-pounders of the Richard burst at the
first fire, and Jones was compelled to close the lower
deck ports, which were not opened again during the
action. This was an ominous beginning, for it reduced
the force of the Richard to one third below that of the
Serapis. The broadsides now became more rapid, presenting a strange spectacle to the people on shore, the
flashes of the guns amid the cloud of smoke, followed by
the roar that shook the coast, the dim moonlight, serving to but half-reveal the struggling vessels, conspired
to render it one of terror and of dread. The two vessels
kept moving alongside, constantly crossing each other's
track; now passing each other's bow, and now the stern;
pouring in such terrific broadsides as made both friend
and foe stagger. Thus fighting and maneuvering, they
swept onward, until at length the Richard got foul of
the Serapis, and Jones gave the orders to board. His
men were repulsed, and Captain Pearson hailed him to
know if he had struck. "I have not yet begun to fight,"
was the short and stern reply of Jones; and backing his
topsails, while the Serapis kept full, the vessels parted,
and again came alongside, and broadside answered broadside with fearful effect. But Jones soon saw that this
mode of fighting would not answer. The superiority in
weight of metal gave them great advantage in this heavy
cannonading; especially as his vessel was old and rotten,
while every timber in that of his antagonist was new

and stanch; and so he determined to throw himself aboard of the enemy. In doing this, he fell farther than he intended, and his vessel catching a moment by the jib boom of the Serapis, carried it away, and the two ships swung close alongside of each other, head and stern, the muzzles of the guns touching. Jones immediately ordered them to be lashed together; and in his eagerness to secure them, helped with his own hands to tie the lashings. Captain Pearson did not like this close fighting, for it destroyed all the advantage his superior sailing and heavier guns gave him, and so let drop an anchor to swing his ship apart. But the two vessels were firmly clenched in the embrace of death; for, added to all the lashings, a spare anchor of the Serapis had hooked the quarter of the Richard, so that when the former obeyed her cable, and swung round to the tide, the latter swung also. Finding that he could not unlock the desperate embrace in which his foe had clasped him, the Englishman again opened his broadsides. The action then became terrific; the guns touched muzzles, and the gunners, in ramming home their cartridges, were compelled frequently to thrust their ramrods into the enemy's ports. Never before had an English commander met such a foeman nor fought such a battle. The timbers rent at every explosion; and huge gaps opened in the sides of each vessel, while they trembled at each discharge as if in the mouth of a volcano. With his heaviest guns burst, and part of his deck blown up, Jones still kept up this unequal fight, with a bravery unparalleled in naval warfare. He, with his own hands, helped to work the guns; and blackened with powder and smoke, moved about among his men with the stern expression never to yield, written on his delicate features in lines not to be mistaken. To compensate for the superiority of the enemy's guns, he had to discharge his own with greater rapidity, so that after a short time they became so hot that they bounded like mad creatures in their fastenings; and at every discharge the gallant ship trembled like a smitten ox, from kelson to crosstrees, and heeled over till her yardarms almost swept the water. In the mean time his topmen did terrible execution. Hanging amid the rigging, they dropped hand grenades on the enemy's decks with fatal precision. One daring fellow walked out on the end of the yard with a bucket full of these missiles in his hand, and hurling them below, finally set fire to a heap of cartridges. The blaze and explosion which followed were terrific — arms and legs went heavenward together, and nearly sixty men were killed or wounded by this sudden blow. They succeeded at length in driving most of the enemy below decks. The battle then presented a singular aspect — Jones made the upper deck of the Serapis too hot for her crew, while the latter tore his lower decks so dreadfully with her broadsides that his men could not remain there a moment. Thus they fought, one above and the other beneath, the blood in the mean time flowing in rills over the decks of both. Ten times was the Serapis on fire, and as often were the flames extinguished. Never did a man struggle braver than the English commander, but a still braver heart opposed him. At this juncture the Alliance came up, and instead of pouring her broadsides into the Serapis, hurled them against the Poor Richard! — now poor, indeed! Jones was in a transport of rage, but he could not help himself.

JOHN PAUL JONES IN THE REVOLUTION

In this awful crisis, fighting by the light of the guns, for the smoke had shut out that of the moon, the gunner and carpenter both rushed up, declaring the ship was sinking. The shot-holes which had pierced the hull of the Richard between wind and water had already sunk below the surface, and the water was pouring in like a torrent. The carpenter ran to pull down the colors, which were still flying amid the smoke of battle, while the gunner cried, "Quarter, for God's sake, quarter!" Still keeping up this cry, Jones hurled a pistol, which he had just fired at the enemy, at his head, which fractured his skull, and sent him headlong down the hatchway. Captain Pearson hailed to know if he had struck, and was answered by Jones with a "No," accompanied by an oath, that told that, if he could do no better, he would go down, with his colors flying. The master-at-arms, hearing the gunner's cry, and thinking the ship was going to the bottom, released a hundred English prisoners into the midst of the confusion. One of these, passing through the fire to his own ship, told Captain Pearson that the Richard was sinking, and if he would hold out a few moments longer, she must go down. Imagine the condition of Jones at this moment — with every battery silenced, except the one at which he still stood unshaken, his ship gradually settling beneath him, a hundred prisoners swarming his deck, and his own consort raking him with her broadsides, his last hope seemed about to expire. Still he would not yield. His officers urged him to surrender, while cries of quarter arose on every side. Undismayed and resolute to the last, he ordered the prisoners to the pumps, declaring if they refused to work he would take them to the bottom with him. Thus making panic fight panic, he continued the conflict. The spectacle at this moment was awful — both vessels looked like wrecks, and both were on fire. The flames shot heavenward around the mast of the Serapis, and at length, at half-past ten, she struck. For a time, the inferior officers did not know which had yielded, such a perfect tumult had the fight become. For three hours and a half had this incessant cannonade, within yard-arm and yardarm of each other, continued, piling three hundred dead and wounded men on those shattered decks. Nothing but the courage and stern resolution of Jones never to surrender saved him from defeat.

When the morning dawned, the Bon Homme Richard presented a most deplorable appearance — she lay a complete wreck on the sea, riddled through, and liter-ally stove to pieces. There were six feet of water in the hold, while above she was on fire in two places. Jones had put forth every effort to save the vessel in which he had won such renown, but in vain. He kept her afloat all the following day and night, but next morning she was found to be going. The waves rolled through her — she swayed from side to side, like a dying man — then gave a lurch forward, and went down head foremost. Jones stood on the deck of the English ship, and watched her as he would a dying friend, and finally, with a swell-ing heart, saw her last mast disappear, and the eddy-ing waves close, with a rushing sound, over her as she sank with the dead, who had so nobly fallen on her decks. They could have wished no better coffin or burial.

Captain Pearson was made a knight, for the bravery with which he had defended his ship. When it was told to Jones, he wittily remarked that if he ever caught him at sea again, he would make a lord of him.

Landais, of the Alliance, who had evidently designed to destroy Jones, then take the English vessel and claim the honor of the victory, was disgraced for his conduct. Franklin could not conceal his joy at the result of the action, and received the heroic Jones with transport.

The remainder of this year was one of annoyance to Jones. Landais continued to give him trouble, and the French Government constantly put him off in his requests to be furnished with a ship. But at length the Alliance, which had borne such a disgraceful part in the engagement with the Serapis, was placed under his command, and he determined to return to America. But he lay wind-bound for some time in the Texel, while an English squadron guarded the entrance of the port. During this delay he was subject to constant annoyances from the Dutch admiral of the port. The latter inquired whether his vessel was French or American; and demanded, if it was French, that he should hoist the national colors, and if American, that he should leave immediately. Jones would bear no flag but that of his adopted country, and promised to depart, notwithstanding the presence of the English squadron watching for him, the moment the wind would permit. At length, losing all patience with the conduct of the Dutch admiral, he coolly sent word to him that, although he commanded a sixty-four, if the two vessels were out to sea, his insolence would not be tolerated a moment.

The wind finally shifting, he hoisted sail, and with the Stripes floating in the breeze, stood fearlessly out of the harbor. With his usual good luck, he escaped the vigilance of the English squadron, cleared the Channel, and with all his sails set, and under a "staggering breeze," stretched away toward the Spanish coast. Nothing of consequence occurred during this cruise, and the next year we find him again in Paris, and in hot water respecting the infamous Landais, whom Arthur Lee, one of the American Commissioners at Paris, presumed to favor. At length, however, he was appointed to the Ariel, and ordered to leave for America with military stores. In the mean time, however, the French king had presented him with a magnificent sword, and bestowed on him the cross of military merit.

On the 7th of September he finally put to sea, but had hardly left the coast when the wind changed, and began to blow a hurricane. Jones attempted to stretch northward and clear the land, but in vain. He found himself close on a reef of rocks, and unable to carry a rag of canvas. So fierce was the wind, that, although blowing simply on the naked spars and deck, it buried the ship waist-deep in the sea, and she rolled so heavily that her yards would frequently be under water. Added to all the horrors of his position, she began to leak badly, while the pumps would not work. Jones heaved the lead with his own hand, and found that he was rapidly shoaling water. There seemed now no way of escape; yet as a last feeble hope he let go an anchor; but so fierce and wild were the wind and sea, that it did not even bring the ship's head to, and she kept driving broadside toward the rocks. Cable after cable was spliced on, yet still she surged heavily landward. He then cut away the foremast, when the anchor, probably catching in a rock, brought the ship round. That good anchor held like the hand of Fate, and though the vessel jerked at every blow of the billows, as if she would wrench everything apart, yet still she lay chained amid the chaos of waters. At length the mainmast fell with a crash against the mizzenmast, carrying that away also, and the poor Ariel, swept to her decks, lay a complete wreck on the waves. In this position she acted like a mad creature chained by the head to a ring that no power can sunder. She leaped, and plunged, and rolled from side to side, as if striving with all her untamed energy to rend the link that bound her, and madly rush on the rocks, over which the foam rose like the spray from the foot of a cataract. For two days and three nights did Jones thus meet the full terror of the tempest. At last it abated, and he was enabled to return to port. The coast was strewed with wrecks, and the escape of the Ariel seemed almost a miracle. But Jones was one of those fortunate beings, who, though ever seeking the storm and the tumult, are destined finally to die in their beds.

Early the next year he reached Philadelphia, and received a vote of thanks from Congress. After vexatious delays in his attempts to get the command of a large vessel he at length joined the French fleet in its expedition to the West Indies. Peace soon after being proclaimed, he returned to France, and failing in a projected expedition to the Northwest coast, sailed again for the United States. Congress voted him a gold medal, and he was treated with distinction wherever he went. Failing again in his efforts to get command of a large vessel, he returned to France. Years had now passed away, and Jones was forty years of age. He had won an imperishable name, and the renown of his deeds been spread throughout the world. The title of chevalier had been given him by the French king, and he was at an age when it might be supposed he would repose on his laurels.

But Russia, then at war with Turkey, sought his services, and made brilliant offers, which he at last accepted, and prepared to depart for St. Petersburg. On reaching Stockholm he found the Gulf of Bothnia so blocked with ice that it was impossible to cross it; but impatient to be on his way, he determined to sail round the ice, to the southward, in the open Baltic. Hiring an open boat, about thirty feet long, he started on his perilous expedition. Knowing that the boatmen would refuse to accompany him, if made acquainted with his desperate plan, he kept them in ignorance until he got fairly out to sea, then drew his pistol, and told them to stretch away into the Baltic. The poor fellows, placed between Scylla and Charybdis, obeyed, and the frail craft was soon tossing in the darkness. Escaping every danger, he at length on the fourth day reached Revel, and set off for St. Petersburg, amid the astonishment of the people, who looked upon his escape as almost miraculous. He was received with honor by the Empress, who immediately conferred on him the rank of rear admiral. A brilliant career now seemed before him. Nobles and foreign ambassadors thronged his residence, and there appeared no end to the wonder his adventurous life had created. He soon after departed for the Black Sea, and took command of a squadron under the direction of Prince Potemkin, the former lover of the Empress, and the real Czar of Russia. Jones fought gallantly under this haughty prince, but at length, disgusted with the annoyances to which he was subjected, he came to an open quarrel, and finally returned to St. Petersburg. Here he for a while fell into disgrace, on account of some unjust accusations against his moral character; but finally, through Count Ségur, the French ambassador, was restored to favor.

In 1792 he was taken sick at Paris, and gradually declined. He had been making strenuous efforts in behalf of the American prisoners in Algiers, but never lived to see his benevolent plans carried out. On the 18th of July, 1792, he made his will, and his friends, after witnessing it, bade him good-evening and departed. His physician coming soon after, perceived his chair vacant; and, going to his bed, found him stretched upon it dead. A few days after, a dispatch was received from the United States, appointing him commissioner to treat with Algiers for the ransom of the American prisoners in captivity there. The National Assembly of France decreed that twelve of its members should assist at the funeral ceremonies of "Admiral Paul Jones," and a eulogium was pronounced over his tomb.

Thus died Paul Jones, at the age of forty-five — leav-ing a name that shall live as long as the American navy rides the sea.

THE FIGHT BETWEEN THE SERAPIS AND THE BON HOMME RICHARD

FROM AN OLD ENGRAVING

"TEN o'clock at night, and the full moon shining, and the
     leaks on the gain, and five feet of water reported,
The master-at-arms loosing the prisoners confined in the
     after-hold, to give them a chance for themselves.

"The transit to and from the magazine was now stopped by
     the sentinels,
They saw so many strange faces, they did not know whom to
     trust.

"Our frigate was afire,
The other asked if we demanded quarter?
If our colors were struck, and the fighting done?

"I laughed content when I heard the voice of my little
     captain,
'*We have not struck*,' he composedly cried. '*We have just
     begun our part of the fighting.*'

"Only three guns were in use,
One was directed by the captain himself against the ene-
     my's mainmast,
Two, well-served with grape and canister, silenced his
     musketry and cleared his decks.

"The tops alone seconded the fire of this little battery,
     especially the main-top,
They all held out bravely during the whole of the action.

"Not a moment's cease,
The leaks gained fast on the pumps — the fire eat toward
     the powder-magazine,
One of the pumps was shot away — it was generally thought
     we were sinking.

"Serene stood the little captain,
He was not hurried — his voice was neither high nor low,
His eyes gave more light to us than our battle-lanterns.

"Toward twelve at night, there in the beams of the moon,
     they surrendered to us."

Walt Whitman.

II
THE COLONIES WIN THEIR FREEDOM

HISTORICAL NOTE

In the Middle States affairs were going badly for the Continentals. In September, 1777, the British won the battle of Brandywine and captured Philadelphia. After an unsuccessful attack on the British lines at Germantown, Washington went into winter quarters at Valley Forge, where the army suffered cruelly from cold and hunger. But meanwhile the capture of Burgoyne's army had shown Europe that the colonies were a worthy foe for the mother country, and in February, 1778, France struck a blow at her ancient enemy by recognizing the United States and sending a fleet and army to aid them in their struggle for independence.

After the evacuation of Philadelphia by the British, in the summer of 1778, the scene of warfare shifted to the Southern colonies. Here the British at first met with complete success. In 1779 and 1780, Georgia and South Carolina were overrun by their forces, and in June, 1780, the American army under Gates was so badly defeated at the battle of Camden that for some time after the only resistance in the South was by partisan bands under such leaders as General Marion. In the same year Benedict Arnold's plot to surrender West Point to the British was discovered. This period was perhaps the darkest of the whole war.

But with the destruction of a British force at King's Mountain by the backwoodsmen of Carolina, the tide of victory turned against the British. Gates was replaced by Greene, and after a brilliant campaign the new commander succeeded in driving the British from Carolina. When the summer of 1781 arrived, Cornwallis, commander of the British forces in Virginia, was at Yorktown, expecting the English ships. The only force opposing him was under Lafayette, whom Cornwallis called "the boy." Suddenly Washington made one of his unexpected moves and appeared before Yorktown with a large army. At the same time a strong French fleet cut off all hope of succor from the sea. On the 19th of October, 1781, Cornwallis surrendered and the colonies were free, although it was not until September 3, 1783, that the formal treaty of peace was signed.

CONGRESS AND VALLEY FORGE

[1777–1778]

BY JOHN FISKE

THE army suffered under . . . drawbacks, which were immediately traceable to the incapacity of Congress; just as afterwards, in the War of Secession, the soldiers had often to pay the penalty for the sins of the politicians. A single specimen of the ill-timed meddling of Congress may serve as an example. At one of the most critical moments of the year 1777, Congress made a complete change in the commissariat, which had hitherto been efficiently managed by a single officer, Colonel Joseph Trumbull. Two commissary-generals were now appointed, one of whom was to superintend the purchase and the other the issue of supplies; and the subordinate officers of the department were to be accountable, not to their superiors, but directly to Congress; this was done in spite of the earnest opposition of Washington, and the immediate result was just what he expected. Colonel Trumbull, who had been retained as commissary-general for purchases, being unable to do his work properly without controlling his subordinate officers, soon resigned his place. The department was filled up with men selected without reference to fitness, and straightway fell into hopeless confusion, whereby the movements of the armies were grievously crippled for the rest of the season. On the 22d of December, Washington was actually prevented from executing a most promising movement against General Howe, because two brigades had become mutinous for want of food. For three days they had gone without bread, and for two days without meat. The quartermaster's department was in no better condition. The dreadful sufferings of Washington's army at Valley Forge have called forth the pity and the admiration of historians; but the point of the story is lost unless we realize that this misery resulted from gross mismanagement rather than from the poverty of the country. As the poor soldiers marched on the 17th of December to their winter-quarters, their route could be traced on the snow by the blood that oozed from bare, frost-bitten feet; yet at the same moment, says Gordon, "hogsheads of shoes, stockings, and clothing were lying at different places on the roads and in the woods, perishing for want of teams, or of money to pay the teamsters." On the 23d, Washington informed Congress that he had in camp 2898 men "unfit for duty, because they are barefoot, and otherwise naked." For want of blankets, many were fain "to sit up all night by fires, instead of taking comfortable rest in a natural and common way." Cold and hunger daily added many to the sick-list; and in the crowded hospitals, which were for the most part mere log huts or frail wigwams woven of twisted boughs, men sometimes died for want of straw to put between themselves and the frozen ground on which they lay. In the deficiency of oxen and draft-horses, gallant men volunteered to serve as beasts of burden, and, yoking themselves to wagons, dragged into camp such meager supplies as they could obtain for their sick and exhausted comrades. So great was the distress that there were times when, in case of an attack by the enemy, scarcely two thousand men could have been got under arms. When one thinks of these sad consequences wrought by a negligent quartermaster and a deranged commissariat, one is strongly reminded of the remark once made by the eccentric Charles Lee, when with caustic alliteration he described Congress as "a stable of stupid cattle that stumbled at every step."

BARON STEUBEN DRILLING THE COLONIAL TROOPS AT VALLEY FORGE

BY EDWIN A. ABBEY

(*American artist*, 1852)

"IN 1777, the French Government was seriously contemplating giving aid to the American colonies in their struggle for independence. It was clear that, brave as were the colonial troops, they had little organization or training, and the French sent over Baron von Steuben, one of the most experienced soldiers of Germany, to remedy this lack. Washington's little army was in winter quarters at Valley Forge, cold, hungry, and in need of everything. Drilling troops was the work of a sergeant, the English had always thought, but this honored officer took a musket in his own hands and taught them."

"Generals, colonels, and captains were fired by the contagion of his example, and his tremendous enthusiasm," says John Fiske, "and for several months the camp was converted into a training-school, in which masters and pupils worked with incessant and furious energy. Steuben was struck with the quickness with which the common soldiers learned their lessons. He had a harmlessly choleric temper, which was part of his overflowing vigor, and sometimes, when drilling an awkward squad, he would exhaust his stock of French and German oaths, and shout for his aide to come and curse the blockheads in English. 'Viens, mon ami Walker,' he would cry, — 'viens, mon bon ami. Sacre-bleu! Gott vertamn de gaucherie of dese badauts. Je ne puis plus; I can curse dem no more!' Yet in an incredibly short time, as he afterward wrote, these awkward fellows had acquired a military air, had learned how to carry their arms, and knew how to form into columns, deploy, and execute maneuvers with precision."

THE MESSAGE OF LYDIA DARRAH

[1777]

BY ELIZABETH F. ELLET

On the 2d day of December, 1777, late in the afternoon, an officer in the British uniform ascended the steps of a house in Second Street, Philadelphia, immediately opposite the quarters occupied by General Howe, who at that time had full possession of the city. The house was plain and neat in its exterior, and well known to be tenanted by William and Lydia Darrah, members of the Society of Friends. It was the place chosen by the superior officers of the army for private conference, whenever it was necessary to hold consultations on subjects of importance; and selected, perhaps, on account of the unobtrusive character of its inmates, whose religion inculcated meekness and forbearance, and forbade them to practice the arts of war.

The officer, who seemed familiar with the mansion, knocked at the door. It was opened; and in the neatly furnished parlor he met the mistress, who spoke to him, calling him by name. It was the adjutant general; and he appeared in haste to give an order. This was to desire that the back room abovestairs might be prepared for the reception that evening of himself and his friends, who were to meet there and remain late. "And be sure, Lydia," he concluded, "that your family are all in bed at an early hour. I shall expect you to attend to this request. When our guests are ready to leave the house, I will myself give you notice, that you may let us out and extinguish the fire and candles."

Having delivered this order with an emphatic manner which showed that he relied much on the prudence and discretion of the person he addressed, the adjutant-general departed. Lydia betook herself to getting all things in readiness. But the words she had heard, especially the injunction to retire early, rang in her ears; and she could not divest herself of the indefinable feeling that something of importance was in agitation. While her hands were busy in the duties that devolved upon her, her mind was no less actively at work. The evening closed in, and the officers came to the place of meeting. Lydia had ordered all her family to bed, and herself admitted the guests, after which she retired to her own apartment, and threw herself, without undressing, upon the bed.

But sleep refused to visit her eyelids. Her vague apprehensions gradually assumed more definite shape. She became more and more uneasy, till her nervous restlessness amounted to absolute terror. Unable longer to resist the impulse — not of curiosity, but surely of a far higher feeling — she slid from her bed, and taking off her shoes, passed noiselessly from her chamber and along the entry. Approaching cautiously the apartment in which the officers were assembled, she applied her ear to the keyhole. For a few moments she could distinguish but a word or two, amid the murmur of voices; yet what she did hear but stimulated her eager desire to learn the important secret of the conclave.

At length there was profound silence, and a voice was heard reading a paper aloud. It was an order for the troops to quit the city on the night of the 4th, and march out to a secret attack upon the American army, then encamped at White Marsh.

Lydia had heard enough. She retreated softly to her own room, and laid herself quietly on the bed. In the deep stillness that reigned through the house, she could hear the beating of her own heart — the heart now throbbing with emotions to which no speech could give utterance. It seemed to her that but a few moments had elapsed when there was a knocking at her door. She knew well what the signal meant, but took no heed. It was repeated, and more loudly; still she gave no answer. Again, and yet more loudly, the knocks were repeated; and then she rose quickly, and opened the door.

It was the adjutant-general, who came to inform her they were ready to depart. Lydia let them out, fastened the house, and extinguished the lights and fire. Again she returned to her chamber, and to bed; but repose was a stranger for the rest of the night. Her mind was more disquieted than ever. She thought of the danger that threatened the lives of thousands of her countrymen, and of the ruin that impended over the whole land. Something must be done, and that immediately, to avert this widespread destruction. Should she awaken her husband and inform him? That would be to place him in special jeopardy, by rendering him a partaker of her secret; and he might, too, be less wary and prudent than herself. No; come what might, she would encounter the risk alone. After a petition for heavenly guidance, her resolution was formed; and she waited with composure, though sleep was impossible, till the dawn of day. Then she waked her husband, and informed

70

him flour was wanted for the use of the household, and that it was necessary she should go to Frankford to procure it. This was no uncommon occurrence; and her declining the attendance of the maidservant excited little surprise. Taking the bag with her, she walked through the snow; having stopped first at headquarters, obtained access to General Howe, and secured his written permission to pass the British lines.

The feelings of a wife and mother — one whose religion was that of love, and whose life was but a quiet round of domestic duties — bound on an enterprise so hazardous, and uncertain whether her life might not be the forfeit, may be better imagined than described. Lydia reached Frankford, distant four or five miles, and deposited her bag at the mill. Now commenced the dangers of her undertaking; for she pressed forward with all haste towards the outposts of the American army. Her determination was to apprise General Washington of the danger.

She was met on her way by an American officer, who had been selected by General Washington to gain information respecting the movements of the enemy. According to some authorities, this was Lieutenant-Colonel Craig, of the light horse. He immediately recognized her, and inquired whither she was going. In reply, she prayed him to alight and walk with her; which he did, ordering his men to keep in sight. To him she disclosed the secret, after having obtained from him a solemn promise not to betray her individuality, since the British might take vengeance on her and her family.

The officer thanked her for her timely warning, and

directed her to go to a house near at hand, where she might get something to eat. But Lydia preferred returning at once; and did so, while the officer made all haste to the commander-in-chief. Preparations were immediately made to give the enemy a fitting reception.

With a heart lightened and filled with thankfulness, the intrepid woman pursued her way homeward, carrying the bag of flour which had served as the ostensible object of her journey. None suspected the grave, demure Quakeress of having snatched from the English their anticipated victory. Her demeanor was as usual, quiet, orderly, and subdued, and she attended to the duties of her family with her wonted composure. But her heart beat, as late on the appointed night, she watched from her window the departure of the army — on what secret expedition bound, she knew too well! She listened breathlessly to the sound of their footsteps and the trampling of horses, till it died away in the distance, and silence reigned through the city.

Time never appeared to pass so slowly as during the interval which elapsed between the marching out and the return of the British troops. When at last the distant roll of the drum proclaimed their approach, when the sounds came nearer and nearer, and Lydia, who was watching at the window, saw the troops pass in martial order, the agony of anxiety she felt was too much for her strength, and she retreated from her post, not daring to ask a question, or manifest the least curiosity as to the event.

A sudden and loud knocking at her door was not calculated to lessen her apprehensions. She felt that the safety of her family depended on her self-possession at this critical moment. The visitor was the adjutant-general, who summoned her to his apartment. With a pale cheek, but composed, for she placed her trust in a higher power, Lydia obeyed the summons.

The officer's face was clouded, and his expression stern. He locked the door with an air of mystery when Lydia entered, and motioned her to a seat. After a moment of silence, he said —

"Were any of your family up, Lydia, on the night when I received company in this house?"

"No," was the unhesitating reply. "They all retired at eight o'clock."

"It is very strange" — said the officer, and mused a few minutes. "You, I know, Lydia, were asleep; for I knocked at your door three times before you heard me — yet it is certain that we were betrayed. I am altogether at a loss to conceive who could have given the information of our intended attack to General Washington! On arriving near his encampment we found his cannon mounted, his troops under arms, and so prepared at every point to receive us, that we have been compelled to march back without injuring our enemy, like a parcel of fools."

It is not known whether the officer ever discovered to whom he was indebted for the disappointment.

But the pious Quakeress blessed God for her preservation, and rejoiced that it was not necessary for her to utter an untruth in her own defense. And all who admire examples of courage and patriotism, especially those who enjoy the fruit of them, must honor the name of Lydia Darrah.

MOLLIE PITCHER

[1787]

BY KATE BROWNLEE SHERWOOD

'T was hurry and scurry at Monmouth Town,
    For Lee was beating a wild retreat;
The British were riding the Yankees down,
    And panic was pressing on flying feet.

Galloping down like a hurricane
    Washington rode with his sword swung high,
Mighty as he of the Trojan plain,
    Fired by a courage from the sky.

"Halt, and stand by the guns!" he cried,
    And a bombardier made swift reply.
Wheeling his comrades into the tide;
    He fell 'neath the shot of a foeman nigh.

Mollie Pitcher sprang to his side,
    Fired as she saw her husband do.
Telling the king in his stubborn pride
    Women like men to their homes are true.

Washington rode from the bloody fray
    Up to the gun that a woman manned.
"Mollie Pitcher, you save the day,"
    He said, as he gave her a hero's hand.

MOLLIE PITCHER

He named her sergeant with manly praise,
  While her war-brown face was wet with tears —
(A woman has ever a woman's ways,)
  And the army was wild with cheers.

THE CAPTURE OF MAJOR ANDRÉ

[1780]

BY JARED SPARKS

[BENEDICT ARNOLD, a trusted officer in the Continental army, offered, for a large sum of money, and a commission in the British army, to betray to the British West Point, the strongest fort on the Hudson River. Major André, a young British officer, was sent by the English to meet an agent of Arnold and make the final arrangements. The following extract tells the story of his capture. He was hanged as a spy; but every one wished that the traitor Arnold could have been in his place.

The Editor.]

WHEN he [André] and Smith [his guide, a Loyalist] separated, it seems to have been understood that André would pursue the route through White Plains, and thence to New York; but after crossing Pine's Bridge he changed his mind, and took what was called the Tarrytown Road. He was probably induced to this step by the remarks he had heard the evening before from Captain Boyd, who said the Lower Party had been far up the Tarrytown Road, and it was dangerous to proceed that way. As the Lower Party belonged to the British, and André would of course be safe in their hands, it was natural for him to infer that he should be among friends sooner in that direction than in the other.

A law of the State of New York authorized any person to seize and convert to his own use all cattle or beef that should be driven or removed from the country in

the direction of the city beyond a certain line in West-
chester County. By military custom, also, the personal
effects of prisoners taken by small parties were assigned
to the captors as a prize.

It happened that, the same morning on which André
crossed Pine's Bridge, seven persons, who resided near
Hudson River, on the neutral ground, agreed volun-
tarily to go out in company armed, watch the road, and
intercept any suspicious stragglers, or droves of cattle,
that might be seen passing toward New York. Four of
this party were stationed on a hill, where they had a
view of the road for a considerable distance. The three
others, named John Paulding, David Williams, and
Isaac Van Wart, were concealed in the bushes at
another place and very near the road.

About half a mile north of the village of Tarrytown,
and a few hundred yards from the bank of Hudson
River, the road crosses a small brook, from each side of
which the ground rises into a hill, and it was at that
time covered over with trees and underbrush. Eight or
ten rods south of this brook, and on the west side of the
road, these men were hidden; and at that point André
was stopped, after having traveled from Pine's Bridge
without interruption.

The particulars of this event I shall here introduce,
as they are narrated in the testimony given by Paulding
and Williams at Smith's trial, written down at the time
by the judge-advocate, and preserved in manuscript
among other papers. This testimony having been taken
only eleven days after the capture of André, when every
circumstance must have been fresh in the recollection
of his captors, it may be regarded as exhibiting a greater

exactness in its details than any account hitherto published. In answer to the question of the court, Paulding said:—

"Myself, Isaac Van Wart, and David Williams were lying by the side of the road about half a mile above Tarrytown, and about fifteen miles above Kingsbridge, on Saturday morning, between nine and ten o'clock, the 23d of September. We had lain there about an hour and a half, as near as I can recollect, and saw several persons we were acquainted with, whom we let pass. Presently one of the young men, who were with me, said, 'There comes a gentlemanlike-looking man, who appears to be well dressed, and has boots on, and whom you had better step out and stop, if you don't know him.' On that I got up, and presented my firelock at the breast of the person, and told him to stand; and then I asked him which way he was going. 'Gentlemen,' said he, 'I hope you belong to our party.' I asked him what party. He said, 'The Lower Party.' Upon that I told him I did. Then he said, 'I am a British officer out of the country on particular business, and I hope you will not detain me a minute'; and to show that he was a British officer he pulled out his watch. Upon which I told him to dismount. He then said, 'My God, I must do anything to get along,' and seemed to make a kind of laugh of it, and pulled out General Arnold's pass, which was to John Anderson, to pass all guards to White Plains and below. Upon that he dismounted. Said he, 'Gentlemen, you had best let me go, or you will bring yourselves into trouble, for your stopping me will detain the general's business'; and said he was going to Dobb's Ferry to meet a person there and get intelligence for

General Arnold. Upon that I told him I hoped he would not be offended, that we did not mean to take anything from him; and I told him there were many bad people, who were going along the road, and I did not know but perhaps he might be one."

When further questioned, Paulding replied that he asked the person his name, who told him it was John Anderson; and that, when Anderson produced General Arnold's pass, he should have let him go, if he had not before called himself a British officer. Paulding also said that when the person pulled out his watch, he understood it as a signal that he was a British officer, and that he meant to offer it to him as a present.

All these particulars were substantially confirmed by David Williams, whose testimony in regard to the searching of André, being more unique than Paulding's, is here inserted.

"We took him into the bushes," said Williams, "and ordered him to pull off his clothes, which he did; but on searching him narrowly, we could not find any sort of writings. We told him to pull off his boots, which he seemed to be indifferent about; but we got one boot off, and searched in that boot, and could find nothing. But we found there were some papers in the bottom of the stocking next to his foot; on which we made him pull his stocking off, and found three papers wrapped up. Mr. Paulding looked at the contents, and said he was a spy. We then made him pull off his other boot, and there we found three more papers at the bottom of his foot within his stocking.

"Upon this we made him dress himself, and I asked him what he would give us to let him go. He said he would give us any sum of money. I asked him whether he would give us his horse, saddle, bridle, watch, and one hundred guineas. He said 'Yes,' and told us he would direct them to any place, even if it was that very spot, so that we could get them. I asked him whether he would not give us more. He said he would give us any quantity of dry goods, or any sum of money, and bring it to any place that we might pitch upon, so that we might get it. Mr. Paulding answered, 'No, if you would give us one thousand guineas, you should not stir one step.' I then asked the person, who had called himself John Anderson, if he would not get away if it lay in his power. He answered, 'Yes, I would.' I told him I did not intend he should. While taking him along we asked him a few questions, and we stopped under a shade. He begged us not to ask him questions, and said when he came to any commander he would reveal all.

"He was dressed in a blue overcoat, and a tight body-coat, that was of a kind of claret color, though a rather deeper red than claret. The buttonholes were laced with gold tinsel, and the buttons drawn over with the same kind of lace. He had on a round hat, and nankeen waistcoat and breeches, with a flannel waistcoat and drawers, boots, and thread stockings."

The nearest military post was at North Castle, where Lieutenant-Colonel Jameson was stationed with a part of Sheldon's regiment of dragoons. To that place it was resolved to take the prisoner; and within a few hours he was delivered up to Jameson, with all the papers that had been taken from his boots.

A VISIT TO GENERAL MARION

[1781]

BY CHARLES CARLETON COFFIN

GENERAL MARION was north of Charleston, not far from the Santee River, when a British officer came with a flag of truce to see him about exchanging prisoners, and was taken into the camp blindfolded. The officer had heard much about Marion; and instead of finding, as he had expected, a man of noble presence in an elegant uniform, he saw a small, thin man, in homespun clothes. Around were Marion's soldiers, some of them almost naked, some in British uniforms, which they had captured — a motley set, with all kinds of weapons, large muskets, rifles, shotguns, swords made by country blacksmiths from mill-saws. The business upon which the officer had come was soon settled.

"Shall I have the honor of your company to dinner?" said Marion.

The officer saw no preparation for dinner. A fire was burning, but there were no camp-kettles, no Dutch ovens, no cooking utensils.

"Give us our dinner, Tom!" said Marion to one of his men.

Tom was the cook. He dug open the fire with a stick, and poked out a fine mess of sweet potatoes. He pricked the large ones to see if they were done, blew the ashes from them, wiped them on his shirt-sleeve, placed the best ones on a piece of bark, and laid them on the log between Marion and the officer.

"I fear our dinner will not prove so palatable to you as I could wish, but it is the best we have," said Marion.

The British officer was a gentleman, and ate of the potatoes, but soon began to laugh. "I was thinking," he said, "what some of my brother officers would say if our Government were to give such a bill of fare as this. I suppose this is only an accidental dinner."

"Not so, for often we don't get even this."

"Though stinted in provisions, you, of course, draw double pay?"

"Not a cent, sir. We don't have any pay. We are fighting for our liberty."

The officer was astonished. They had a long and friendly talk, and the officer, bidding Marion good-bye, went back to Georgetown.

Colonel Watson was in command of the British there. "What makes you look so serious?" Colonel Watson asked.

"I have cause to look serious," the officer replied.

"Has Marion refused to treat?"

"No, sir; but I have seen an American general and his officers, without pay, almost without clothes, living on roots and drinking water, and all for liberty! What chance have we against such men?"

The officer was so impressed by what he had seen that he could fight no more, but disposed of his commission and returned to England.

General Greene sent Marion and Lee south to get between the British and Charleston, and cut off their supplies. They marched to Fort Watson, a strong fortification on the east bank of the Santee River, about fifty miles north of Charleston. It was built of logs, stood on a hill, and was garrisoned by one hundred and twenty men, commanded by Lieutenant M'Kay. They sent him a message to surrender; but he was a brave officer, and informed them that he intended to defend the fort. He knew that Lord Rawdon would soon be there to aid him with several hundred men. Marion and Lee knew that Lord Rawdon was on the march, and they resolved to capture the fort before he arrived.

They saw that there was no well in the fort, and that the garrison had to come out and creep down to the river to obtain water. The riflemen soon stopped that. Then M'Kay set his men at work digging a well, and carried it down to the level of the lake, and had a good supply of water.

Lee and Marion knew that there was a large amount of supplies in the fort, for, besides what was inside, there were boxes and barrels outside. Some of the militia tried to creep up and get a barrel; but the garrison killed one and wounded another. A brave negro, named Billy, with Marion, looked at the supplies, saw that one of the hogsheads was only a few feet from the edge of the bluff, and resolved to try what he could do. He crept very near without being seen, then, before the British could fire upon him, he was crouched behind the hogshead. The ground was a declivity, and soon the British soldiers saw that the hogshead was in motion. They fired at it, but they could only see some black fingers clasping the chimbs, and in a few minutes the hogshead disappeared down the hill.

. Billy obtained an axe, broke open the hogshead, and found that he had captured one hundred and fifty shirts, one hundred knapsacks, fifty blankets, and six cloaks.

He distributed them to the soldiers, many of whom had no shirts. Marion named the negro "Captain Billy," and every one treated the brave fellow with great respect.

Rawdon was close at hand. Marion and Lee could see the light of his camp fires on the hills in the west. Whatever was done must be done quickly. But what could they do? They had no cannon; and even if they had, they could not batter down the fort; but a bright thought came to Colonel Mahan — to build a tower which would overlook the fortification. As soon as night came, all the axes in the camp were in use. The British could hear the choppers, and wondered what was going on; but they were astonished in the morning when they saw a tower higher than the fort, and a swarm of men on the top firing through loopholes, and picking off with their rifles every man who showed his head above the parapet. Lord Rawdon had not come, and Lieutenant M'Kay saw that he would soon lose all his men, and that he must surrender. Before noon the Americans were in possession of the fort and all its supplies.

WHEN CORNWALLIS SURRENDERED

[1781]

BY BURTON EGBERT STEVENSON

SPRING and summer sped by quietly enough, with much visiting back and forth; but one crisp morning in early October our neighbor of Berkeley rode up to our door and plunged at once into the heart of the business which had brought him.

"You know, I suppose, Mrs. Randolph," he began, "that that old fox, Cornwallis, is caught at last at York-town, and must soon surrender?"

"Yes, thank God," said my mother.

"'T will be such a sight as may never again be witnessed in America. I am going to take my boy to see it, and I should be glad to have yours, too, if you'll let him go."

"Oh, mother!" I cried.

She looked at us a moment with frightened eyes.

"Take my boy into the midst of the fighting!" she protested.

"Oh, not so bad as that, madam," laughed Mr. Harrison. "We will view it all from a perfectly safe distance — I will answer for that. May he go?" I think his good humor and courtesy, as much as the passionate pleading in my eyes, won her over.

"Would you like to go, Stewart?" she asked, and I knew from her look that she consented.

"Right, madam!" cried our visitor heartily, as I

threw my arms about her. "You are right not to deny the boy."

My cup of happiness was full to overflowing, and as we rolled away that afternoon in the great Harrison coach, I fear it was only my mother who wept at parting. That was an enchanted journey down the peninsula, and I was almost sorry that it had come to an end when, toward evening of the second day, we rumbled up to Oldham, Mr. Samuel Harrison's place, some few miles above Yorktown on the river.

Such a sight as awaited us the next morning when we were led forth to view the contending armies. From the top of a little hill near the bank of the York, which the French had evacuated the day before in their advance, we could see a great part of their position quite clearly. On the right were our troops, with the artillery in the center, near the commander's quarters. There the French lines began, artillery first, and then the infantry, stretching to the very bank of the river below us. Away in the distance we could dimly see the British works closely girdling the little town, and still beyond this a half dozen British men-of-war lay anchored in the stream. Far out on the bay we could just discern the white sails of the blockading squadron of French ships.

Mr. Harrison pointed out to us how our troops were ever creeping nearer and nearer to the British works; but he had more important things to do, so he left us presently, confiding us to the care of old Shad, and warning us not to leave the hillock where we were stationed. We had small wish to do so, and we sat for hours looking at the scene, until suddenly, away on the right, the artillery began to thunder. The fire ran along the line until every battery, American and French alike, was pouring shot and shell into the British works, as fast as the sweating men could serve the guns. The enemy replied but feebly, and after a time fell silent altogether. A dense cloud of smoke settled over the ramparts, and was carried slowly out to sea, where it lay banked against the horizon like a great thundercloud.

We ate the lunch that Shad had brought for us, and spent the afternoon watching the cannonading. Mr. Harrison came back to us as evening fell, but we tarried where we were with no thought of dinner, for the French battery near the river had opened upon the British ships with red-hot ball, and presently we saw one of them wrapped in a torrent of flame. The fire spread with amazing speed, running along the rigging and to the very tops of the masts, while all around was thunder and lightning from the cannon. Even as we gazed there came a blinding flash of flame that rent the ship asunder, and ten seconds later a mighty roar, which told us the fire had reached the magazine. The blazing fragments fell back one by one into the river and disappeared.

"Come, boys, we must be going," said Mr. Harrison at last, and we followed him, awed and silent.

Another British ship was set in flames next day, and in the three days that followed we could see our soldiers working like beavers in the trenches, which advanced every hour nearer the enemy. Meanwhile, all Virginia had come to see the spectacle, and on the morning of the seventeenth was gathered in a great throng exultantly watching the work of our batteries, when of a sudden the firing ceased.

A murmur of anxiety ran through the crowd.

"What is it? What has happened?" asked every one, looking fearfully into his neighbor's face. Could it be that, after all, the prize was to escape? Some thought that the munitions had run out; some that the French ships had been driven away and a great force under Clinton landed; but presently came word that Cornwallis had had enough, and asked a parley. What joy there was that night at every board within reach of the good news, and in what mighty bumpers did loyal Virginia drink the health of the First of Virginians and his men!

How shall I describe the stirring spectacle which took place next afternoon? To the right of the Hampton road the Patriot army was drawn up, veterans of six years' service, with torn and faded regimentals; while to the left, facing them, were the French, brilliant as toy soldiers. Down the road for more than a mile stretched this living avenue. Presently there broke forth a great storm of cheering, and I saw the tears rolling unchecked down Mr. Harrison's face as he gazed at a man sitting a white charger, riding slowly along the line.

"'T is the general," he whispered. "This is his hour of triumph and reward — God knows how he has earned it!"

Near him, on a great bay horse, rode General Rochambeau, gorgeous in white and gold. He was no doubt a gallant soldier, and great general, but there was something in the quiet dignity of the other which caught and held the eye, which fired the imagination, which needed no ornament to set it forth. Men and women sobbed aloud as they saw him there that day, and cheered between their sobs like mad things, and thanked the God that had given him to America.

Then a great silence fell upon the crowd, there came the beat of a drum from the British line, and the conquered troops marched slowly out of their intrenchments, — seven thousand of them and more, — their colors cased, their arms reversed. Colors and arms alike were surrendered to the victors, while the regimental bands played a quaint old air, forgot these many years, "The World Turned Upside Down."

GEORGE III ACKNOWLEDGES THE INDEPENDENCE OF THE COLONIES

[1782]

BY ELKANAH WATSON

SOON after my arrival in England, having won at the insurance office one hundred guineas, on the event of Lord Howe's relieving Gibraltar, and dining the same day with Copley, the distinguished painter, who was a Bostonian by birth, I determined to devote the sum to a splendid portrait of myself. The painting was finished in most admirable style, except the background, which Copley and I designed to represent a ship, bearing to America the intelligence of the acknowledgment of Independence, with a sun just rising upon the Stripes of the Union, streaming from her gaff. All was complete save the flag, which Copley did not deem prudent to hoist under present circumstances, as his gallery is a constant resort of the royal family and the nobility. I dined with the artist, on the glorious 5th of December, 1782, after listening with him to the speech of the king, formally recognizing the United States of America as in the rank of nations. Previous to dining, and immediately after our return from the House of Lords, he invited me into his studio, and there with a bold hand, a master's touch, and I believe an American heart, attached to the ship the Stars and Stripes. This was, I imagine, the first American flag hoisted in Old England.

At an early hour on the 5th of December, 1782, in

conformity with previous arrangements, I was conducted by the Earl of Ferrers to the very entrance of the House of Lords. At the door he whispered, "Get as near the throne as you can; fear nothing." I did so, and found myself exactly in front of it, elbow to elbow with the celebrated Admiral Lord Howe. The Lords were promiscuously standing, as I entered. It was a dark and foggy day; and the windows being elevated, and constructed in the antiquated style, with leaden bars to contain the diamond-cut panes of glass, increased the gloom. The walls were hung with dark tapestry, representing the defeat of the Spanish Armada. I had the pleasure of recognizing, in the crowd of spectators, Copley, and West the painter, with some American ladies. I saw also some dejected American royalists in the group.

After waiting nearly two hours, the approach of the king was announced by a tremendous roar of artillery. He entered by a small door on the left of the throne, and immediately seated himself upon the Chair of State, in a graceful attitude, with his right foot resting upon a stool. He was clothed in royal robes. Apparently agitated, he drew from his pocket the scroll containing his speech. The Commons were summoned; and, after the bustle of their entrance had subsided, he proceeded to read his speech. I was near the king, and watched, with intense interest, every tone of his voice and expression of his countenance. After some general and usual remarks, he continued: —

"I lost no time in giving the necessary orders to prohibit the further prosecution of offensive war upon the continent of North America. Adopting, as my inclination will always lead me to do, with decision and effect, whatever I collect to be the sense of my Parliament and my people, I have pointed all my views and measures, in Europe, as in North America, to an entire and cordial reconciliation with the colonies. Finding it indispensable to the attainment of this object, I did not hesitate to go to the full length of the powers vested in me, and offer to declare them " — here he paused and was in evident agitation; either embarrassed in reading his speech, by the darkness of the room, or affected by a very natural emotion. In a moment he resumed: — " and offer to declare them free and independent States. In thus admitting their separation from the crown of these kingdoms, I have sacrificed every consideration of my own to the wishes and opinions of my people. I make it my humble and ardent prayer to Almighty God, that Great Britain may not feel the evils which might result from so great a dismemberment of the Empire, and that America may be free from the calamities which have formerly proved, in the mother country, how essential monarchy is to the enjoyment of constitutional liberty. Religion, language, interests, and affection may, and I hope will, yet prove a bond of permanent union between the two countries."

It is remarked that George III is celebrated for reading his speeches in a distinct, free, and impressive manner. On this occasion, he was evidently embarrassed; he hesitated, choked, and executed the painful duties of the occasion with an ill grace that does not belong to him. I cannot adequately portray my sensations in the progress of this address; every artery beat high, and swelled with my proud American blood. It was impossible not to revert to the opposite shores of the Atlantic, and to review, in my mind's eye, the misery and woe I had myself witnessed, in several stages of the contest, and the wide-spread desolation, resulting from the stubbornness of this very king, now so prostrate, but who had turned a deaf ear to our humble and importunate petitions for relief. Yet, I believe that George III acted under what he felt to be the high and solemn claims of constitutional duty.

The great drama was now closed. The battle of Lexington exhibited its first scene. The Declaration of Independence was a lofty and glorious event in its progress; and the ratification of our Independence by the king, consummated the spectacle in triumph and exultation. This successful issue of the American Revolution will, in all probability, influence eventually the destinies of the whole human race.

WHEN WASHINGTON RESIGNED HIS COMMISSION

[1783]

BY R. M. DEVENS

FOR the last time, he assembled them [his soldiers] at Newburgh, when he rode out on the field, and gave them one of those paternal addresses which so eminently characterized his relationship with his army. To the tune of "Roslin Castle," — the soldier's dirge, — his brave comrades passed slowly by their great leader, and filed away to their respective homes. It was a thrilling scene. There were gray-headed soldiers, who had grown old by hardships and exposures, and too old to begin life anew; tears coursed freely the furrowed cheeks of these veterans. Among the thousands passing in review before him were those, also, who had done valorous service when the destiny of the country hung tremblingly in the balance. As Washington looked upon them for the last time, he said, "I am growing old in my country's service and losing my sight; but I never doubted its justice or gratitude." Even on the rudest and roughest of the soldiery, the effect of his parting language was irresistible.

On the 4th of December, 1783, by Washington's request, his officers, in full uniform, assembled in Fraunces's tavern, New York, to take a final leave of their commander-in-chief. On entering the room, and finding himself surrounded by his old companions-in-arms, who had shared with him so many scenes of hardship, difficulty, and danger, his agitated feelings overcame his usual self-command. Every man arose with eyes turned towards him. Filling a glass of wine, and lifting it to his lips, he rested his benignant but saddened countenance upon them, and said: —

"With a heart full of love and gratitude, I now take leave of you. I most devoutly wish that your latter days may be as prosperous as your former ones have been honorable and glorious." Having drunk, he added, "I cannot come to each of you to take my leave, but shall be obliged to you, if each of you will come and take me by the hand."

A profound silence followed, as each officer gazed on the countenance of their leader, while the eyes of all were wet with tears. He then expressed again his desire that each of them should come and take him by the hand. The first, being nearest to him, was General Knox, who grasped his hand in silence, and both embraced each other without uttering a word. One after another followed, receiving and returning the affectionate adieu of their commander, after which he left the room in silence, followed by his officers in procession, to embark in the barge that was to convey him to Paulus Hook, now Jersey City. As he was passing through the light infantry drawn up on either side to receive him, an old soldier, who was by his side on the terrible night of his march to Trenton, stepped out from the ranks, and reaching out his arms, exclaimed, "Farewell, my dear General, farewell!" Washington seized his hand most heartily, when the soldiers forgot all discipline, rushed toward their chief, and bathed him with their tears.

The scene was like that of a good patriarch taking leave of his children, and going on a long journey, from whence he might return no more.

Having entered the barge, he turned to the weeping company upon the wharf, and waving his hat, bade them a silent adieu. They stood with heads uncovered, until the barge was hidden from their view, when, in silent and solemn procession, they returned to the place where they had assembled. Congress was at this time in session at Annapolis, Maryland, to which place Washington now proceeded, greeted along his whole route with enthusiastic homage, for the purpose of formally resigning his commission. He arrived on the 19th of December, 1783, and the next day he informed Congress of the purpose for which he had come, and requested to know whether it would be their pleasure that he should offer his resignation in writing, or at an audience. A committee was appointed by Congress, and it was decided that on Tuesday, December 23, the ceremonial should take place.

When the hour arrived, the president, General Mifflin, informed him that that body was prepared to receive his communications. With a native dignity, heightened by the solemnity of the occasion, the general rose. In a brief and appropriate speech he offered his congratulations on the termination of the war, and having alluded to his object in appearing thus in that presence, — that he might resign into the hands of Congress the trust committed to him, and claim the indulgence of retiring from the public service, — he concluded with those affecting words, which drew tears from the eyes of all in that vast assembly: —

"I consider it an indispensable duty to close this last

act of my official life by commending the interests of our dearest country to the protection of Almighty God, and those who have the superintendence of them, to his holy keeping. Having now finished the work assigned me, I retire from the theater of action, and, bidding an affectionate farewell to this august body, under whose orders I have so long acted, I here offer my commission, and take my leave of all the employments of public life."

After advancing to the chair, and delivering his commission to the president, he returned to his place, and remained standing, while General Mifflin replied, reviewing the great career thus brought to a close, and saying in conclusion: —

"The glory of your virtues will not terminate with your military command; it will continue to animate the remotest ages. We join with you in commending the interest of our country to Almighty God, beseeching Him to dispose the hearts and minds of its citizens to improve the opportunity afforded them of becoming a happy and respectful nation. And for you, we address to Him our warmest prayers, that a life so beloved may be fostered with all His care, that your days may be as happy as they have been illustrious, and that He will finally give you that reward which this world cannot bestow."

III
LIFE IN REVOLUTIONARY DAYS

HISTORICAL NOTE

"AT the commencement of the Revolution the colonists of America were husbandmen, merchants, mechanics, and fishermen, who were occupied in the ordinary duties of their respective callings, and were sober, honest, and industrious. But when the struggle for independence began, new fields for exertion were opened, and a great change was suddenly wrought in the American people. Many who were before only known in the humble sphere of peaceful occupations, soon shone forth in the cabinet or in the field. The war, too, did much to wear away local peculiarities and prejudices. But the Revolution introduced, at the same time, greater looseness of manners and morals. An army always carries deep vices in its train, and communicates its corruption to society around it. Besides this, the failure of public credit so far put it out of the power of individuals to perform private engagements, that the breach of them became common, and at length was scarcely disgraceful. Education suffered, in common with other kindred interests. In several colleges the course of instruction was suspended; the hall was exchanged for the camp, and the gown for the sword and epaulet. After the war, interest in education revived, and before the end of the period several colleges and other institutions of learning were established in different sections of the country.

"During the war, the commerce of the United States was suppressed, but it revived on the return of peace. Arts and manufactures made considerable progress in the United States during this period. Cut off by the war from foreign sources of supply, the people of the United States had been obliged to look to their own industry and ingenuity to furnish articles needed in the struggle and for the usual occupations of life. On the return of peace, many branches of manufacture had become so firmly established that they held their ground, even against the excessive importations that immediately followed. Agriculture was greatly interrupted, during the war, by the withdrawing of laborers to the camp, and by the distractions which disturbed all the occupations of society. But within a few years after peace was established the exports of products raised in the United States were again considerable." — *Charles A. Goodrich.*

THE MESCHIANZA AT PHILADELPHIA

[1778]

BY JOHN F. WATSON

[THE British spent the winter of 1777–78 in Philadelphia. To pass the time, they gave balls and other entertainments. The most noted of these was the "Meschianza."

The Editor.]

THIS is the appellation of the most splendid pageant ever exhibited in our country,[1] if we except the great "Federal Procession" of all trades and professions, through the streets of Philadelphia in 1788. The Meschianza was chiefly a tilt and tournament with other entertainments, as the term implies, and was given on Monday the 18th of May, 1778, at Wharton's country-seat in Southwark, by the officers of General Sir William Howe's army, to that officer, on his quitting the command to return to England. A considerable number of our city belles were present; which gave considerable offense afterwards to the whigs; and did not fail to mark the fair as the "Tory ladies." The ill-nature and the reproach have long since been forgotten.

The company began to assemble at three to four o'clock, at Knight's Wharf, at the water edge of Green Street in the Northern Liberties, and by half-past four o'clock in the afternoon the whole were embarked, in the pleasant month of May, in a "grand regatta" of three divisions. In the front of the whole were three flatboats,

---

[1] This was written in 1843.

101

with a band of music in each of them, "rowed regular to harmony." As this assemblage of vessels progressed, barges rowed on the flanks, "light skimming, stretch'd their oary wings," to keep off the multitude of boats that crowded from the city as beholders; and the houses, balconies, and wharves were filled with spectators all along the riversides.

When arrived at the fort below the Swedes' church, they formed a line through an avenue of grenadiers, and light horse in the rear. The company were thus conducted to a square lawn of one hundred and fifty yards on each side, and which was also lined with troops. This area formed the ground for a tilt or tournament. On the front seat of each pavilion were placed seven of the principal young ladies of the country, dressed in Turkish habits, and wearing in their turbans the articles which they intended to bestow on their several gallant knights. Soon the trumpets at a distance announced the approach of the seven white knights, habited in white and red silk, and mounted on gray chargers, richly caparisoned in similar colors. These were followed by their several esquires on foot; besides these there was a herald in his robe. These all made the circuit of the square, saluting the ladies as they passed, and then they ranged in line with their ladies; then their herald, Mr. Beaumont, after a flourish of trumpets, proclaimed their challenge, in the name of "the knights of the blended rose," declaring that the ladies of their order excelled in wit, beauty, and accomplishments those of the whole world, and they are ready to enter the lists against any knights who will deny the same, according to the laws of ancient chivalry; at the third repetition of the challenge, a sound of trumpets announced the entrance of another herald, with four trumpeters dressed in black and orange. The two heralds held a parley, when the black knight proceeded to proclaim his defiance in the name of "the knights of the burning mountain." Then retiring, there soon after entered "the black knights," with their esquires, preceded by the herald, on whose tunic was represented a mountain sending forth flames, and the motto, "I burn forever."

These seven knights, like the former ones, rode round the lists, and made their obeisance to the ladies, and then drew up fronting the white knights, and the chief of these having thrown down his gauntlet, the chief of the black knights directed his esquire to take it up. Then the knights received their lances from their esquires, fixed their shields on their left arms, and making a general salute to each other by a movement of their lances, turned round to take their career, and encountering in full gallop, shivered their spears! In the second and third encounter they discharged their pistols. In the fourth they fought with their swords.

From the garden they ascended a flight of steps, covered with carpets, which led into a spacious hall, the panels of which were painted in imitation of Siena marble, inclosing festoons of white marble. In this hall and the adjoining apartments, were prepared tea, lemonade, etc., to which the company seated themselves. At this time the knights came in, and on their knee received their favors from their respective ladies. From these apartments they went up to a ballroom, decorated in a light, elegant style of painting, and showing many festoons of flowers. The brilliancy of the whole was heightened by eighty-five mirrors, decked with ribbons and flowers, and in the intermediate spaces were thirty-four branches. On the same floor were four drawing-rooms, with sideboards of refreshments, decorated and lighted in the style of the ballroom. The ball was opened by the knights and their ladies; and the dances continued till ten o'clock, when the windows were thrown open, and a magnificent bouquet of rockets began the fireworks. These were planned by Captain Montressor, the chief engineer, and consisted of twenty different displays in great variety and beauty, and changing General Howe's arch into a variety of shapes and devices. At twelve o'clock (midnight) supper was announced, and large folding doors, before concealed, sprung open, and discovered a magnificent saloon of two hundred and ten feet by forty feet, and twenty-two feet in height, with three alcoves on each side, which served for sideboards. The sides were painted with vine leaves and festoon flowers, and fifty-six large pier-glasses ornamented with green silk artificial flowers and ribbons. There were also one hundred branches trimmed, and eighteen lusters of twenty-four lights hung from the ceiling. There were three hundred wax tapers on the supper tables, four hundred and thirty covers, and twelve hundred dishes. There were twenty-four black slaves in oriental dresses, with silver collars and bracelets.

Towards the close of the banquet, the herald with his trumpeters entered and announced the king and royal family's health, with other toasts. Each toast was followed by a flourish of music. After the supper, the company returned to the ballroom, and continued to dance until four o'clock in the morning.

THE MESCHIANZA AT PHILADELPHIA

I omit to describe the two arches, but they were greatly embellished. They had two fronts, in the Tuscan order. The pediment of one was adorned with naval trophies, and the other with military ones.

Major André, who wrote a description of it (although his name is concealed), calls it " the most splendid entertainment ever given by an army to its general." The whole expense was borne by twenty-two field officers. The managers were Sir John Wrotlesby, Colonel O'Hara, Majors Gardiner and Montressor. This splendid pageant blazed out in one short night! Next day the enchantment was dissolved; and in exactly one month, all these knights and the whole army chose to make their march from the city of Philadelphia!

When I think of the few survivors of that gay scene who now exist (of some whose sprightliness and beauty are gone), I cannot but feel a gloom succeed the recital of the fête. I think, for instance, of one who was then "the queen of the Meschianza," since Mrs. L., now blind, and fast waning from the "things that be." To her I am indebted for many facts of illustration. She tells me that the unfortunate Major André was the charm of the company. Lieutenant André, his esquire, was his brother, a youth of about nineteen, possessing the promise of an accomplished gentleman. Major André and Captain Oliver Delancey, painted, themselves, the chief of the decorations. The Siena marble, for instance, on the apparent side walls, was on canvas, in the style of stage-scene painting. André also painted the scenes used at the theater, at which the British officers performed. The proceeds were given to the widows and orphans of their soldiers. The waterfall scene, drawn by him, was still in the building when it lately burnt. She assures me that, of all that was borrowed for the entertainment, nothing was injured or lost. They desired to pay double if accidents occurred. The general deportment of the officers was praiseworthy therein. There were no ladies of British officers, save Miss Auchmuty, the new bride of Captain Montressor. The American young ladies present were not numerous — not exceeding fifty. The others were married ladies. Most of our ladies had gone from the city, and what remained were of course in great demand. The American gentlemen present were aged non-combatants. Our young men were Whigs generally, and were absent.

No offense was offered to the ladies afterwards for their acceptance of this instance of an enemy's hospitality. When the Americans returned, they got up a great ball, to be given to the officers of the French army, and to the American officers of Washington's command. When the managers came to invite their guests, it was made a question whether the "Meschianza ladies" should be invited. It was found they could not make up their company without them; they were therefore included. When they came, they looked differently habited from those who had gone to the country, "they having assumed the high headdress, etc.," of the British fashion, and so the characters, unintentionally, were immediately perceived at a glance through the hall. But lots being cast for partners, they were soon fully intermixed, and conversation ensued as if nothing of jealousy had ever existed, and all umbrage was forgotten.

A NEW ENGLAND THANKSGIVING DINNER
IN 1779

BY JULIANA SMITH

DEAR COUSIN BETSEY: —

When Thanksgiving Day was approaching our dear Grandmother Smith (née Jerusha Mather, great-granddaughter of the Rev. Richard Mather of Dorchester, Mass.,) who is sometimes a little desponding of Spirit as you well know, did her best to persuade us that it would be better to make it a Day of Fasting and Prayer in view of the Wickedness of our Friends &c. the Vileness of our Enemies. I am sure you can hear Grandmother say that and see her shake her cap border. But indeed there was some occasion for her remarks, for our resistance to an unjust authority has cost our beautiful Coast Towns very dear the last year & all of us have had much to suffer. But my dear Father brought her to a more proper frame of Mind, so that by the time the Day came she was ready to enjoy it almost as well as Grandmother Worthington did, & she, you will remember, always sees the bright side. In the mean while we had all of us been working hard to get all things in readiness to do honor to the Day.

This year it was Uncle Simeon's turn to have the dinner at his house, but of course we all helped them as they help us when it is our turn, & there is always enough for us all to do. All the baking of pies & cakes was done at our house & we had the big oven heated & filled twice each day for three days before it was all done, & everything was Good, though we did have to do without something that ought to be used. Neither Love nor Money could buy Raisins, but our good red cherries dried without the pits, did almost as well & happily Uncle Simeon still had some spices in store. The tables were set in the Dining Hall and even that big room had no space to spare when we were all seated. The Servants had enough ado to get around the Table & serve us all without over-setting things. There were our two Grandmothers side by side. They are always handsome old Ladies, but now, many thought, they were handsomer than ever, & happy they were to look around upon so many of their descendants. Uncle & Aunt Simeon preside at one Table, & Father & Mother at the other. Besides us five boys & girls there were two of the Gales & three Elmers, besides James Browne & Ephriam Cowles. We had them at our table because they could be best supervised there. Most of the students had gone to their own homes for the weeks, but Mr. Skiff and Mr. — were too far away from their homes. They sat at Uncle Simeon's table & so did Uncle Paul and his family, five of them in all, & Cousins Phin & Poll. Then there were six of the Livingston family next door. They had never seen a Thanksgiving Dinner before, having been used to keep Christmas Day instead, as is the wont in New York & Province. Then there were four Old Ladies who have no longer Homes or Children of their own & so came to us. They were invited by my Mother, but Uncle and Aunt Simeon wished it so.

Of course we could have no Roast Beef. None of us have tasted Beef this three years back as it all must go to the Army, & too little they get, poor fellows. But, Mayquittymaw's Hunters were able to get us a fine red Deer, so that we had a good haunch of Venisson on each Table. These were balanced by huge Chines of Roast Pork at the other ends of the Tables. Then there was on one a big Roast Turkey & on the other a Goose, & two big Pigeon Pasties. Then there was an abundance of good Vegetables of all the old Sorts & one which I do not believe you have yet seen. Uncle Simeon had imported the Seede from England just before the War began & only this Year was there enough for Table use. It is called Sellery & you eat it without cooking. It is very good served with meats. Next year Uncle Simeon says he will be able to raise enough to give us all some. It has to be taken up, roots & all & buried in earth in the cellar through the winter & only pulling up some when you want it to use.

Our Mince Pies were good although we had to use dried Cherries as I told you, & the meat was shoulder of Venisson, instead of Beef. The Pumpkin Pies, Apple Tarts & big Indian Puddings lacked for nothing save Appetite by the time we had got around to them.

Of course we had no Wine. Uncle Simeon has still a cask or two, but it must all be saved for the sick, & indeed, for those who are well, good Cider is a sufficient Substitute. There was no Plumb Pudding, but a boiled Suet Pudding, stirred thick with dried Plumbs & Cherries, was called by the old name & answered the purpose. All the other spice had been used in the Mince Pies, so for this Pudding we used a jar of West India preserved Ginger which chanced to be left of the last shipment which Uncle Simeon had from there, we chopped the

Ginger small and stirred it through with the Plumbs and Cherries. It was extraordinary goods. The Day was bitter cold & when we got home from Meeting, which Father did not keep over long by reason of the cold, we were glad eno' of the fire in Uncle's Dining Hall, but by the time the dinner was one-half over those of us who were on the fire side of one Table was forced to get up & carry our plates with us around to the far side of the other Table, while those who had sat there were glad to bring their plates around to the fire side to get warm. All but the Old Ladies who had a screen put behind their chairs.

' Uncle Simoen was in his best mood, and you know how good that is! He kept both Tables in a roar of laughter with his droll stories of the days when he was studying medicine in Edinborough, & afterwards he & Father & Uncle Paul joined in singing Hymns & Ballads. You know how fine their voices go together. Then we all sang a Hymn and afterwards my dear Father led us in prayer, remembering all Absent Friends before the Throne of Grace, & much I wished that my dear Betsey was here as one of us, as she has been of yore.

We did not rise from the Table until it was quite dark, & when the dishes had been cleared away we all got around the fire as close as we could, & cracked nuts, & sang songs, & told stories. At least some told, & others listened. You know nobody can exceed the two Grandmothers at telling tales of all the things they have seen themselves, & repeating those of the early years in New England, & even some in the Old England, which they had heard in their youth from their Elders. My Father says it is a goodly custom to hand down all worthy deeds & traditions from Father to Son, as the Israelites were commanded to do about the Passover & as the Indians here have always done, because the Word that is spoken is remembered longer than the one what is written. * * Brother Jack, who did not reach here until late on Wednesday though he left the College very early on Monday Morning & rode with all due diligence considering the snow, brought an orange to each of the Grandmothers, but Alas! they were frozen in his saddle bags. We soaked the frost out in cold water, but I guess they was n't as good as they should have been. . . .

A CALL ON LADY WASHINGTON IN 1780

BY CHARLES D. PLATT

"O Lady Martha Washington
   Has come to Morristown,
And we must go and quickly so,
   Each in her finest gown,
And call at Colonel Ford's to see
   That dame of high renown."

So spake the dames of Hanover
   And put on their array
Of silks to wit, and all that's fit
   To grace a gala day,
And called on Lady Washington
   In raiment bright and gay.

Those were the days of scarcity
   In all our stricken land,
When hardships tried the country-side,
   Want was on every hand;
When they called on Lady Washington
   In fine attire so grand.

"And don't you think! we found her with
   A speckled homespun apron on;
With knitting in hand — that lady so grand —
   That stately Lady Washington!
When we came to Morristown that day
   With all our finest fixin's on!

She welcomed us right graciously
   And then, quite at her ease,
She makes the glancing needles fly
   As nimbly as you please;
And so we found this courtly dame
   As busy as two bees."

"For while our gallant soldiers bear
   The brunt of war," quoth she,
"It is not right that we delight
   In costly finery."
So spake good Martha Washington,
   Still smiling graciously.

"But let us do our part," quoth she,
   "And speedily begin
To clothe our armies on the field
And independence win" —
   "Good-bye! Good-bye!" we all did cry —
   "We're going home to spin!"

HOW PEOPLE TRAVELED IN REVOLUTIONARY TIMES

[1775-1781]

BY JOHN BACH McMASTER

A JOURNEY of any length was beset with innumerable difficulties and delays. Towns and cities between which we pass in an hour were a day's journey apart. For all purposes of trade and commerce two hundred and fifty miles was a greater distance then than twenty-five hundred miles now. A voyage across the ocean to London or Liverpool, a trip across the prairies to the Pacific Coast, is at present performed with more ease and comfort, and with quite as much expedition, as, a hundred years since, a journey from Boston to New York was made. It was commonly by stages that both travelers and goods passed from city to city. Insufferably slow as such a mode of conveyance would seem to an American of this generation, it had, in 1784, but lately come in, and was hailed as a mark of wonderful progress. The first coach and four in New England began its trips in 1744. The first stage between New York and Philadelphia, then the two most populous cities in the colonies, was not set until 1756, and made the run in three days. The same year that the stamp act was passed a second stage was started. This was advertised as a luxurious conveyance, "being a covered Jersey wagon," and was promised to make the trip in three days, the charge being twopence the mile. The success which attended

114

this venture moved others, and in the year following it was announced that a conveyance, described as the "Flying Machine," "being a good wagon, with seats on springs," would perform the whole journey in the surprisingly short time of two days. This increase of speed was, however, accompanied by an increase of fare, the charge being twenty shillings for the through trip and three pence per mile for way passengers.

When the Revolution came, most of these vehicles ceased to ply between the distant cities; horseback traveling was resumed, and a journey of any length became a matter of grave consideration. On the day of departure the friends of the traveler gathered at the inn, took a solemn leave of him, drank his health in bumpers of punch, and wished him God-speed on his way. The Quaker preacher, Hicks, setting out in 1779 for yearly meeting, remarks: "We took a solemn leave of our families, they feeling much anxiety at parting with us on account of the many dangers we were exposed to, having to pass, not only through the lines of the armies, but the deserted and almost uninhabited country that lay between them."

With the return of peace the stages again took the road; but many years elasped before traffic over the highways became at all considerable. While Washington was serving his first term, two stages and twelve horses sufficed to carry all the travelers and goods passing between New York and Boston, then the two great commercial centers of the country. The conveyances were old and shackling; the harness made mostly of rope; the beasts were ill-fed and worn to skeletons. The ordinary's day journey was forty miles in summer; but in winter, when the roads were bad and the darkness came on early in the afternoon, rarely more than twenty-five. In the hot months the traveler was oppressed by the heat and half choked by the dust. When cold weather came, he could scarce keep from freezing. One pair of horses usually dragged the stage some eighteen miles, when fresh ones were put on, and, if no accident occurred, the traveler was put down at the inn about ten at night. Cramped and weary he ate a frugal supper and betook himself to bed, with a notice from the landlord that he would be called at three the next morning. Then, whether it rained or snowed, he was forced to rise and make ready, by the light of a horn-lantern or a farthing candle, for another ride of eighteen hours. After a series of mishaps and accidents such as would suffice for an emigrant train crossing the plains, the stage rolled into New York at the end of the sixth day. The discomforts and trials of such a trip, combined with the accidents by no means uncommon, the great distance from help in the solitary places through which the road ran, and the terrors of ferry-boats on the rivers, made a journey of any distance an event to be remembered to the end of one's days.

Such was the crude state of the science of engineering that no bridge of any considerable length had been undertaken in the States. No large rivers had yet been spanned. While going from Boston to Philadelphia, in 1789, Breck crossed the Connecticut at Springfield, the Housatonic at Stratford, the Hudson at New York, the Hackensack and Passaic between Paulus Hook (now Jersey City) and Newark, the Raritan at New Brunswick, the Delaware at Trenton, and the Neshamung at

Bristol on what were then known as ferry-boats. The crossing of any of these streams was attended by much discomfort and danger; but the wide stretch of water which flowed between Paulus Hook and the city of New York was especially the dread of travelers. There, from December till late in March, great blocks of ice filled the river from either bank far out to the channel. On windy days the waves were high, and when the tide ran counter with the wind, covered with white-caps. Horse-boats had not yet come in; the hardy traveler was, therefore, rowed across in boats such as would now be thought scarcely better than scows. In one of her most touching letters to her husband, Mrs. Burr describes to him the alarm occasioned by his making the danger-ous crossing. How she had anxiously waited for his return, hoping that the dangers of the passage would deter him; how, when she heard that he was really em-barked, she gave herself up to an agony of fear as she thought of him exposed in the little boat to the rough waters and the boisterous winds, and what thankfulness she felt when her son brought word of his safe arrival at Paulus Hook.

Even a trip from Brooklyn to New York, across a river scarce half as wide as that separating the city from New Jersey, was attended with risks and delays that would now be thought intolerable. Then, and indeed till the day thirty years later, when the rude steamboats of Fulton made their appearance on the ferry, the only means of transportation for man and beast were clumsy row-boats, flat-bottomed square-ended scows with sprit-sails, and two-masted boats called periaguas. In one of these, if the day were fine, if the tide were slack, if the watermen were sober, and if the boat did not put back several times to take in belated passengers who were seen running down the hill, the crossing might be made with some degree of speed and comfort, and a landing effected at the foot of the steps at the pier which, much enlarged, still forms part of the Brooklyn slip of the Fulton Ferry. But when the wind blew with the tide, when a strong flood or an angry ebb was on, the boatmen made little headway, and counted themselves happy if, at the end of an hour's hard pulling, the passengers were put ashore opposite Governor's Island, or on the marshes around Wallabout bay.

In summer these delays, which happened almost daily, were merely annoying and did no more harm than to bring down some hearty curses on the boatmen and the tide. But when winter came, and the river began to fill with huge blocks of ice, crossing the ferry was hazardous enough to deter the most daring. Sometimes a rowboat would get in an ice-jam and be held there in the wind and cold for many hours. At others a periagua would go to pieces in the crush, and the passengers, forced to clamber on the ice, would drift up and down the harbor at the mercy of the tide. It is not improbable that the solicitude of Mrs. Burr for the safety of her husband was heightened by the recollection of such an occurrence which took place but a few months before.

Nor were the scows, in the best of weather, less liable to accidents than the row-boats. It was on these that horses, wagons, and cattle were brought over from city to city, for the butchers of the Fly market drew their supplies of beef and mutton from the farms that lay on the hills toward Flatbush and what is now Williamsburg. Every week small herds of steers and flocks of sheep were driven to the ferry, shut up in pens, and brought over the river, a few at a time, on the scows. The calmest days, the smoothest water, and a slack tide, were, if possible, chosen for such trips. Yet even then whoever went upon a cattle-boat took his life in his hands.

If a sudden gust of wind struck the sails, or if one of the half dozen bullocks became restless, the scow was sure to upset. No one, therefore, who was so fortunate as to own a handsome carriage would trust it on the boats if the wind and sea were high, or much ice in the river, but would wait two or three days for a gentle breeze and smooth water.

But it was not solely by coaches and ferry-boats that our ancestors traveled from place to place. Packet sloops plied between important points along the coast and such of the inland cities as stood upon the banks of navigable rivers. The trip from New York to Philadelphia was thus often made by packet to South Amboy, thence by coach to Burlington, in New Jersey, where a packet was once more taken to the Quaker City. A similar line of vessels ran between New York and Providence, where coaches were in waiting to convey travelers to Boston. This mode of conveyance was thought to be far more comfortable than by stage-wagon, but it was, at the same time, far more uncertain. Nobody knew precisely when the sloops would set sail, nor, when once started, how soon they would reach their haven. The wind being favorable and the waters of the sound quite smooth, the run to Providence was often made in three days. But it was not seldom that nine days or two weeks were spent in the trip. On the Hudson were many such sloops, bringing down again timber, and skins from Albany, to be exchanged for broadcloth, half-thicks, and tammies, at New York. They ceased to run, however, when the ice began to form in the river, trade was suspended, and the few travelers who went from one city to the other made the journey on horseback or in the coach. In summer, when the winds were light, two weeks were sometimes spent in sailing the one hundred and fifty miles. The difficulties, indeed, which beset the English traveler, John Maude, on his way to Albany, would now be rarely met with in a canoe on the rivers of the Northwest. Burr, on his way from Albany to attend court, changed from sloop to wagon ere his journey was ended. Travelers by these packets often took boat as the vessel floated slowly down the river, rowed ashore and purchased eggs and milk at the farm-houses near the bank, and overtook their vessel with ease.

The present century had long passed its first decade before any material improvement in locomotion became known. Our ancestors were not wholly unacquainted with the great motive-power which has within the life-time of a generation revolutionized every branch of human industry, and enabled great ships of iron to advance in the face of wind and waves, and long trains of cars to traverse the earth at a speed exceeding the pace of the fleetest horse. Before the close of 1787, Fitch at Philadelphia, and Rumsey at Shepherdstown, Virginia, had both moved vessels by steam. Before 1790, a steamboat company had been organized at Philadelphia, and a little craft built by Fitch had steamed up and down the Delaware to Burlington, to Bristol, to Bordentown, and Trenton. Before 1800, Samuel Morey had gone up the Connecticut River in a steamer of his own construction and design, and Elijah Ormsbee, a Rhode Island mechanic, had astonished the farmers along the banks of the Seekonk River with the sight of a boat driven by paddles. Early in this century, Stevens placed upon the waters of the Hudson a boat moved by a Watt engine. The same year Oliver Evans ran a paddle-wheel vessel on the waters of the Delaware and the Schuylkill. Fulton, in 1807, made his trip to Albany in the famous Clermont, and used it as a passenger-boat till the end of the year. But he met with the same opposition which in our time we have seen expended on the telegraph and the sewing-machine, and which, some time far in the future, will be encountered by inventions and discoveries of which we have not now the smallest conception. No man in his senses, it was asserted, would risk his life in such a fire-boat as the Clermont when the river was full of good packets. Before the year 1820 came, the first boat had steamed down the Mississippi to New Orleans; the first steamboat had appeared upon the Lakes, and the Atlantic had been crossed by the steamship Savannah. But such amazing innovations as these found little favor with men accustomed from boyhood to the stage-coach and the sail-boat. In 1810, nine days were spent in going from Boston to Philadelphia. At the outbreak of the second war with England, a light coach and three horses went from Baltimore to Washington in a day and a half. The mail-wagon, then thought to make the journey with surprising speed, left Pennsylvania Avenue at five in the morning and drew up at the post-office in Baltimore at eleven at night. Ocean travel was scarcely known. Nothing short of the most pressing business, or an intense longing to see the wonders of the Old World, could induce a gentleman of 1784 to leave his comfortable home and his pleasant fields, shut himself up in a packet, and breathe the foul air of the close and dingy cabin for the month or seven weeks spent in crossing the Atlantic. A passage in such a space of time would, moreover, have been thought a short one, for it was no very uncommon occurrence when a vessel was nine, ten, eleven weeks, or even three months, on a voyage from Havre or Madrid to New York. So formidable was this tedious sail, and the bad food and loathsome water it entailed, that fewer men went over each summer to London than now go every month to South America. In fact, an emigrant steamer brings out each passage from Queenstown more human beings than a hundred years ago, crossed the ocean in both directions in the space of a twelvemonth. So late as 1795, a gentleman who had been abroad was pointed out in the streets even of the large cities with the remark, "There goes a man who has been to Europe."

ABRAHAM DAVENPORT

[1780]

BY JOHN G. WHITTIER

In the old days (a custom laid aside
With breeches and cocked hats) the people sent
Their wisest men to make the public laws.
And so, from a brown homestead, where the Sound
Drinks the small tribute of the Mianas,
Waved over by the woods of Rippowams,
And hallowed by pure lives and tranquil deaths,
Stamford sent up to the councils of the State
Wisdom and grace in Abraham Davenport.

'T was on a May-day of the far old year
Seventeen hundred eighty, that there fell
Over the bloom and sweet life of the Spring,
Over the fresh earth and the heaven of noon,
A horror of great darkness, like the night
In day of which the Norland sagas tell, —
The Twilight of the Gods. The low-hung sky
Was black with ominous clouds, save where its rim
Was fringed with a dull glow, like that which climbs
The crater's sides from the red hell below.
Birds ceased to sing, and all the barn-yard fowls
Roosted; the cattle at the pasture bars
Lowed, and looked homeward; bats on leathern wings
Flitted abroad; the sounds of labor died;
Men prayed, and women wept; all ears grew sharp

THE UNITED STATES

To hear the doom-blast of the trumpet shatter
The black sky, that the dreadful face of Christ
Might look from the rent clouds, not as he looked
A loving guest at Bethany, but stern
As Justice and inexorable Law.

Meanwhile in the old State House, dim as ghosts,
Sat the lawgivers of Connecticut,
Trembling beneath their legislative robes.
"It is the Lord's Great Day! Let us adjourn,"
Some said; and then, as if with one accord,
All eyes were turned to Abraham Davenport.
He rose, slow cleaving with his steady voice
The intolerable hush. "This well may be
The Day of Judgment which the world awaits;
But be it so or not, I only know
My present duty, and my Lord's command
To occupy till He come. So at the post
Where He hath set me in his providence,
I choose, for one, to meet Him face to face, —
No faithless servant frightened from my task,
But ready when the Lord of the harvest calls;
And therefore, with all reverence, I would say,
Let God do his work, we will see to ours.
Bring in the candles." And they brought them in.

Then by the flaring lights the Speaker read,
Albeit with husky voice and shaking hands,
An act to amend an act to regulate
The shad and alewive fisheries. Whereupon
Wisely and well spake Abraham Davenport,
Straight to the question, with no figures of speech

ABRAHAM DAVENPORT

Save the ten Arab signs, yet not without
The shrewd dry humor natural to the man:
His awe-struck colleagues listening all the while,
Between the pauses of his argument,
To hear the thunder of the wrath of God
Break from the hollow trumpet of the cloud.

And there he stands in memory to this day,
Erect, self-poised, a rugged face, half seen
Against the background of unnatural dark,
A witness to the ages as they pass,
That simple duty hath no place for fear.

FRIEDLAND, 1807

BY JEAN LOUIS ERNEST MEISSONIER

(*France*, 1815-1891)

IN 1807, Napoleon gained at Friedland a brilliant victory over the Russians, who lost nearly twenty thousand killed and wounded. Eleven days later, Napoleon and the Emperor Alexander met at Tilsit, and there, on a raft in the middle of the Niemen River, peace was concluded between France and Russia. Its terms practically gave to Napoleon the control of western and central Europe; to Russia that of Sweden and Turkey.

Of this picture Meissonier writes: "I did not intend to paint a battle — I wanted to paint Napoleon at the zenith of his glory. I wanted to paint the love, the adoration, of the soldiers for the great Captain in whom they had faith and for whom they were ready to die. . . . The battle, already commenced, was necessary to add to the enthusiasm of the soldiers, and make the subject stand forth, but not to diminish it by saddening details. All such shadows I avoided, and presented nothing but a dismounted cannon, and some growing wheat which would never ripen.

"This was enough.

"The men and the Emperor are in the presence of each other. The soldiers cry to him that they are his, and the impressive Chief, whose imperial will directs the masses that move around, salutes his devoted army. He and they plainly comprehend each other, and absolute confidence is expressed in every face."

Napoleon, mounted on his favorite white charger and surrounded by his generals, returns the salute of a squadron of cuirassiers who are charging at a furious gallop through a field of unripe wheat. With wild enthusiasm the soldiers rise in their stirrups and shouting, "Vive l'Empereur," salute their beloved leader with flashing swords. The battle is already raging and in the distance may be seen the ranks of the French army advancing toward the enemy.

FRANCE

I
IN THE DARK AGES

HISTORICAL NOTE

In 51 B.C., Julius Cæsar went forth from Rome to conquer the almost unknown country called Gaul. This was what is now called France, but it included also the Netherlands and the western part of Germany. Cæsar had to cut roads and build bridges and overcome tribes of tall, strong, independent fighters; but he was successful, and Gaul passed into the hands of the Romans.

The Gauls learned Roman ways. They learned better methods of cultivating the land; they learned how to manufacture linen and silk, how to make armor and weapons, and how to fight in the Roman fashion. They were governed by Roman laws, they had temples and palaces, theaters, baths, aqueducts, schools, and libraries. A forlorn little village called Lutetia, or the town of mud, was situated on an island in the river Seine. It was inhabited by a tribe called the Parisii, and in 508 it became Paris.

Long before the fall of the Roman Empire in the West, her power was weakening. On the shores of the lower Rhine and the Weser dwelt the Franks, and by the time that the fifth century was well begun, they had pushed their way into Gaul. They were invaders, but they had come just in time to aid their unwilling hosts and the Romans to drive away the ferocious Attila and his Huns.[1]

The Franks still came, and in even larger numbers, and pushed farther into northern Gaul. In 486, ten years after the fall of the Empire in the West, Clovis, their chief, led them to Soissons, about sixty miles from Paris, and overcame the Roman governor. They were converted to Christianity; and when the year 732 had come, they were so powerful that they were able to repel the forces of the Mohammedans. Toward the end of the eighth century, Charlemagne became king; and in the year 800 he was crowned by the Pope as Emperor of the Romans. Not many years after Charlemagne's death, France was invaded by the Norsemen. They, too, became Christians, and made their home in Normandy, which took its name from theirs.

[1] See "How the Empire was saved from the Huns," in volume IV.

THE CHRISTMAS OF 496

BY J. C. BATEMAN

[CHLOVIS (or Clovis), King of the Franks, married a Christian princess named Chlotildis. Her one desire was that her husband should also become a Christian, and at length, on going forth to meet the invading Alemanni, he promised her that he would call upon her God. The following selection tells the rest of the story.

The Editor.]

THE eyes of Chlovis blazed with wrath. He stood, his head proudly erect, his forehead resembled a rock of adamant, against which all the wild hordes of the Hercynian forests might dash themselves in vain. Chlotildis had never seen him look more royal. He felt himself the father of his young kingdom, of the companions he was gradually moulding into the people of that kingdom, the sole protector of all that was beginning to take form under the patient exercise of his great sagacity. He was not only determined to hurl back the wave of benighted barbarism, bringing ruin and desolation in its train, but he felt equal to it, and his swelling nostrils, like those of a war horse, scented the war and victory from afar.

"My gracious lord, and great king!" said the queen, rising, her baby prince still cradled in her soft white arms, "you are going to conquest; but in order to be victorious, invoke the God of the Christians. He is the sole Lord of the universe, and is styled the Lord of armies. If you address yourself to Him with confidence, nothing

131

can resist you. Though your enemies were a hundred against one, you would triumph over them."

Chlovis gazed into her face, upturned to his, beaming with fervor, pious enthusiasm, and heavenly faith. Passing his strong arm around her, he drew her gently towards him, and tenderly kissed her.

"I will not forget, sweet wife! Thou art, indeed, my guardian angel. Under the sign of the Cross will I conquer, like the great Constantine of old. I shall return to thee in triumph to be baptized, to make all thy sons kings and thy daughters the wives of kings. Take care of my little one. He is so small, I fear to hurt him. There, lift him thyself to my lips, though I fear my lip fringe may scratch his soft face," he continued, smiling. Chlotildis lifted the infant, her heart filled with rapturous thanksgiving, pouring itself out in mental prayer, whilst the stern warrior, stooping down, kissed the baby cheek with the softness of a woman's touch.

"My dearest wife," he said, rising again to his height, "thou wilt depart for Rheims this day. Only a few guards can I leave in any city or town under my protection. Therefore, thou wilt retire again to the convent, where thou wilt pray to thy God for me, for success to my arms is the sole protection to thee, my dearest. Nay, do not weep. Remember, thou art the wife of a warrior going forth against his enemies and thine, of a king going to do battle for his people. There, that is as it should be; smile on me, beloved. Fare thee well, sweet one, for thou wilt not see me again till I return to thee a conqueror and a Catholic."

Again the streets of Soissons rang with the din of warlike preparation. Chief after chief rode in with his companions or retainers. The Grafs came in with three fourths of their respective guards. The Antrustion Chararic led the king's own body guard, whilst Ethelbert and Athanaric rode at the head of a large body recruited from the southern frontiers. The place of meeting was in the Field of Mars, and there Chlovis received and welcomed his friends and allies as they came up "to the feast of battle." There were the usual names, Ragnacair of Cambray, Regnomer of Mans, Carnaric of Dispargum, and his son, Chlodomir, Chilperic the Merovingian, with a goodly number of armed followers. It was a splendid army, well appointed, well equipped, which filed along the road to Laon, on their way to join King Siegbert at Cologne. At the head of the army rode Chlovis, triumph already in his eyes, and by his side, Aurelian, ever ready to support him with his arm or his counsel. Arrived at Cologne, the king was met by his cousin Siegbert. From him he learned the number and situation of the enemy.

"A goodly mustering," he answered; "let us go forth to meet them. Thou sayest the plain of Tolbiac is a fair battle-field. So be it. Siegbert, take thou the command of the infantry, they are chiefly thine own men; they will obey thee more implicitly. Myself will lead my valiant horsemen. Eight leagues from hence, is it? Right glad am I it is so little distant. When the men and horses are refreshed, we will proceed at once."

Four-and-twenty miles from Cologne, Chlovis and his allies arrived in the close neighborhood of the plains of Tolbiac, and here they found their ancient foes already drawn up. Proudly passed on the Franks, defiling on to the plain before the king, who smiled on them as they passed with words of commendation, encouragement, and assurances of victory.

And now face to face stood two of the fiercest nations of Germany, mutually animated by the memory of past exploits and prospect of future greatness. The Alemanni covered two good thirds of the field of battle with their innumerable hosts, whilst Chlovis and Siegbert drew up their troops, well disciplined, well armed, and trained in many a glorious battle-field, but certainly outnumbered by their adversaries. Chlovis rode along the front of his army, encouraging his men.

"Fight for victory," he 'said, 'and it will alight on our banner. Fight, comrades, for your wives and little ones. Think on the walls of Soissons; think on our fair and smiling plains. Shall they be the prey of the rude Alemanni? No; we will utterly destroy these howling wolves who would ravage our fair country, assuage their hunger with our harvests and cattle. Comrades, the only passage to Soissons is over our dead bodies. But the gods of our country fight on our side. They lead us on to victory!"

The shock of the two contending armies was terrible. The noise of it was like to the roar of thunder. They fought hand to hand and foot to foot. Chlovis had dashed upon the Alemanni with the flower of his cavalry, and had routed and put to flight the right wing of his enemy. But their left wing pressed hard upon Siegbert at the head of his Ripuarians and the rest of the Frank infantry, and gaining ground, steadily drove them back. In vain Chlovis charged at their close ranks; in vain Aurelian, supported by Chararic at the head of his chosen body guard, brought up fresh supplies of cavalry.

Still the Alemanni pressed onward, onward, and all that the valor of the Franks of Soissons could achieve was to force themselves into their midst by dint of fierce fighting. Chlovis fought like a lion, covered with dust and blood, but still the enemy poured on, their number seeming never to diminish. At one moment of the battle, Ethelbert, fighting near to the king, saw Siegbert of Cologne borne off the field desperately wounded.

"Even so," said Chlovis, to whom he spurred with the news. "Seek Athanaric: thou and he force a passage to the Ripuarians, and charge the enemy back before them."

This charge was in vain. Chlovis, wielding his fatal francisque with a power that cleared a path before him, now saw with dismay that his own cavalry, at whose head rode Chararic, began to waver and give way before the Alemanni. All seemed lost. Ragnacair of Cambray was down, Regnomer of Mans was severely wounded, the Antrustion fell bravely, fighting to the last, and many of the best warriors from the frontiers of Gaul were in bad or similar plight.

Then Chlovis suddenly remembered the words which Chlotildis had spoken to him. Smitten to the heart, he acknowledged that, in the absorbing nature of his duties as leader and organizer in such a battle, he had not only forgotten his promise to her, but in the fervor of his address to his warriors had even promised them victory in the name of their own gods. Lifting up his eyes to heaven, in this his dire extremity, he said, the tears of earnest prayer filling his eyes: —

"O Christ! Whom Chlotildis invokes as Son of the living God, I implore thy succor! I have called upon my gods, and find they have no power. I therefore invoke Thee! I believe in Thee! Deliver me from mine enemies, and I will be baptized in thy Name!"

At this moment Aurelian rode up with a fresh troop of horse, which he had succeeded in gathering together, persuading them to follow him. Chlovis put himself at their head, and swooped afresh upon the enemy, at the precise spot where the last King of the Alemanni was fighting at the head of his people. Loudly shouting his war cry, as much to animate his men as to cause panic to his enemy, Chlovis rushed upon him, and after a short but severe struggle, felled him to the ground. The Alemanni, dismayed with this disaster and the pertinacity of a foe who did not know when he was beaten, but returned again and again to the struggle, gave way. Many fled in different directions, whilst others, closely pressed by the cavalry led by Ethelbert and his foster brother, threw down their arms and begged for quarter. A general slaughter took place in other parts of the field, and a hot pursuit of the fugitives, Chlovis having sworn to rout them so entirely they should never rally again.

The news of this great victory was sent to the queen by the triumphant Chlovis, as well as the manner in which it had been obtained. She sent to tell Remigius the important tidings, asking him to celebrate a Mass of Thanksgiving, at which she would be present. At the interview which she held with the holy prelate after these first fruits of gratitude had been offered, she told him of her wish to be the first to go and meet the returning king, as she should like to be the first to congratulate him on his double victory.

"It is well said, my daughter. I myself will accompany thee on such an occasion of joy to the whole Church of Christ. We will go out to meet him with religious pomp and sacred hymns of triumph. It is meet that a conqueror so favored by the Most High should be honored by the Spouse of Christ, whose obedient son he will soon become."

It was in Champagne that the meeting of the loving wife and the victorious warrior-king took place. Chlovis, riding up to her chariot in the long procession of priests and people coming to meet him, said to her:—

"Chlovis has vanquished the Alemanni, and thou hast vanquished Chlovis. The business thou hast so much at heart is done: my baptism can no longer be delayed."

"Thanks be to God," devoutly answered the queen. "To the Lord of Hosts are both these triumphs due!"

On his arrival at Soissons, the first care of Chlovis was to assemble all the chiefs and warriors in a Mallum, where he laid before them the step which he was about to take, and his motives for it.

"It was," he said, "when the battle was well-nigh lost; when my bravest warriors and brethren in arms were falling before the enemy, that I made the vow to worship henceforth only the Lord God of the Catholic Church. Judge, my valiant comrades, whether such a vow, at such a moment, followed by such fortunate results to us all, ought not to be paid most rigorously and without loss of time."

Loud acclamations greeted this speech, and the shouts "for the Lord Christ," were heard by the queen in her oratory, whither she had repaired to supplicate God for her lord and king in this important meeting. When the shouts died away, they cried out with unanimous voice: —

"My lord king, to thy valor and thy piety we owe the victory. We abandon our mortal gods, and are ready to follow thy example and worship the immortal God whom Remigius teaches!"

This was, indeed, an answer to the prayers of the pious queen, and great were now the preparations for the important ceremony which it was thought best should take place on Christmas Day, rather than defer it till Easter. Remigius and Vedast of Toul instructed and prepared the catechumens, whilst many bishops repaired to Rheims in order to be present at this fulfillment of their most fervent prayers.

The efforts of their spiritual teachers were unremitting to prepare the hearts of these fierce warriors and soften them with sentiments of Christian meekness and humility. A great blessing attended their pious work. The king set them all an example of compunction and devotion, induced thereto by the gentle influence of his religious queen, laying aside his regal state and prostrating himself, clothed in sackcloth, imploring day and night the divine mercy. Such conduct on the part of a chief for whom his warriors felt such enthusiastic devotion, had a great effect on them, calming their spirits and giving greater weight to the words of the holy ecclesiastics.

The long-expected day at length drew near. The weather was so clear and bright it seemed as if even the elements had agreed to second the efforts of the queen to give a great external pomp to the sacred rite which should strike the senses of a barbarous people, and implant an awe and respect in their minds befitting the administration of a sacrament so important in its results to the future destinies of the great kingdom fast rising under the auspices of Chlovis. It was a double festival to celebrate — the glorious Nativity of Christ, the birth of the Sun of Justice, spreading light and life in the midst of darkness and death, and the birth to this light and life of those hitherto lost in the darkness of heathendom. All Rheims was alive with joyful anticipation. Never since the first Christmas Day, four hundred and ninety-six years before, had the great festival of the Nativity been more anxiously expected.

The streets leading from the palace — where the king had taken up his abode for the last few weeks — to the door of the cathedral, were hung with rich tapestry and carpets of various colors. The forests had been rifled to supply scarlet berries to twine with lustrous evergreens, hung everywhere in festoons and wreaths, or woven into myriads of sacred devices by the Gauls, to whose taste were always allotted the decorations on these occasions.

These decorations were in themselves a splendid sight in the bright morning sunshine of this long-desired day. It was cold but dry. Snow had fallen in the night, and its myriad crystals sparkled in the sun, its virgin purity contrasting with the bright colors of the tapestries and the glossy green of the wreaths and garlands. The streets through which the procession was to pass were kept clear of foot passengers, but scaffolds and platforms, here and there erected, were crowded with spectators, as well as the tops of the houses, where the most daring had contrived to post themselves.

"It is a most beautiful sight," said the Lady Marcia,

all wrapped in furs, to a friend sitting beside her on a balcony overlooking the whole length of a street opening on the cathedral. "But have you been in the cathedral? It is lovely! it is gorgeous! I was admitted as an especial favor early this morning. All the pillars and arches are twined with holly and ivy, and the high altar is one mass of gold and jewels! As for the baptistery, it passes all description! It is carpeted with lovely green moss, kept down by branches of ivy fastened across. Ivy runs up all the pillars as if it grew there, and here the perfumed wax tapers are put, winding in the other direction. It will be like a wreath of fire when they are lit, before the procession enters. They say that the water in the font comes all the way from the Jordan, from the very spot where our Lord Christ was baptized. It was sent by the Princess Llantildis for the king's baptism, and arrived here last night."

"Who are those going down the street?" asked the Lady Julia, sitting not far from her sister.

"Those," said another lady, "are the people who are to let the birds loose. Such a quantity of pigeons, all white, and some white doves. There would have been more doves, but the people who were bringing them from the south could not get through the snow. I am glad we have not so much snow as it appears they have at Lyons and Vienne."

"Hark! I hear the music of the procession," said the Lady Marcia. "Yes; here they come. What a fine view we have right down the street. I do so like a grand sight like this!"

And grand it certainly was in every sense. Three thousand catechumens marched in procession, all dressed in white, carrying crosses in their hands, and singing litanies. A body of clergy walked at their head, with cross and banner displayed, sacred music swelling as they advanced in the sharp morning air. Then came the king, led by the right hand by the venerable archbishop, clad in his robes and carrying his crozier, a true shepherd, leading his flock into the fold of his Master and Lord. The queen followed, leading the young Prince Theodoric, and then the rest of the catechumens two and two, whilst on each side of them walked a long line of priests in white surplices and scarlet cassocks.

As they were about to enter the door of the cathedral, the archbishop turned to the king and laid the end of his richly embroidered stole, symbol of the yoke of Christ, on his arm, that strong right arm, so often uplifted to fight the battles of the Church, now adopting him as her true son, whilst he addressed to him words of holy exhortation to "enter the temple of the Lord." Followed by Chlovis and the rest, he preceded them to the holy font, amidst the soft strains of sacred music, and entered the baptistery, now as well as the interior of the cathedral a blaze of light, and redolent of the richest perfumes.

The ceremonies of the Church proceeded in the midst of a solemn silence pervading the vast assemblage, and the rapt attention of the Frank warriors, subdued into reverent awe. This feeling increased in intensity as the archbishop, about to pour the consecrated water on the head of Chlovis, addressed to him these ever-memorable words: "Lower thy head, meek Sicambrian! Burn what thou hast adored, and adore what thou hast burned"; whilst Chlovis was bending his head over the

141

sacred font, the archbishop poured over it the regenerating water which cleansed his soul from sin.

At this moment a beautiful white dove — escaped perhaps before the time from its keepers — flew through the open window of the baptistery, and swooping down upon the altar, to which the archbishop turned for the vial containing the holy chrism, rose again, and soaring on high through the chancel, disappeared from view. Scarcely interrupted by this slight incident, Remigius took the consecrated oil and anointed the king, singeing him on the forehead as he knelt before him, thus enlisting him into the ranks of the army of the Lord of Hosts.

After the sacred rites had been administered to all the catechumens, they returned up the church in long procession, the triumphant chants of the clergy answered by the loud shouts of the multitude without, waving branches and flags, whilst martial music swelled high, and those who held the birds in cages set them free, saying, —

"Soar towards heaven! souls of the redeemed of the Lord! Captives of sin no longer, washed in the pure water of Baptism, ransomed by His precious Blood!"

The Sacrifice of the Mass was then offered; wreaths of incense ascended in clouds, whilst the pealing strains of the *Gloria in excelsis* rose to the lofty arches, and the threefold *Sanctus* of the heavenly choir was reëchoed upon earth.

THE FAMOUS VICTORY OF CHARLES MARTEL

[732]

BY A. W. GRUBE

[OWING to a succession of weak sovereigns in France, the real power of the crown fell more and more completely into the hands of the mayors of the palace. Charles Martel held this office. He was succeeded by his son Pepin, who determined to have the title as well as the power of king. Thereupon he appealed to the Pope: "Say, father of Christendom, who ought to be king of the Franks, he who merely bears the name, or he who makes his people great by his counsel and power?" The Holy Father answered: "He alone should wear the crown who deserves it." And Pepin was crowned king of France.

The Editor.]

PEPIN was succeeded by Charles Martel, in whose time Abderrahman was the leader of the Moors in Spain. Abderrahman, in accordance with the aspirations of his nation, formed a design of extending the Arab empire to the north of the Pyrenees, and then advancing through Europe from west to east till he should again reach the Arab empire in the east. With an immense army he crossed the Pyrenees, destroying as he went, defeated Eudes, Duke of Aquitaine (southern France), and bore down all resistance. He then advanced to the Rhone in order to take Arles. Here Eudes encountered him again, but in vain; the waters of the Rhone washed the bodies of the slaughtered Franks down to the sea in thousands. Once more Eudes assembled an army, but his defeat was so crushing that the Franks said with sorrow that God alone could have counted the slain. The churches and monasteries were in ashes, the fields lay waste; in the great Frankish kingdom there was none to help and save except Charles, the mayor of the palace.

The Frankish nobles accordingly came to him, and even Eudes forgot the enmity which he had formerly shown towards Charles, and begged him now to help him. Charles's answer to the petition was: "Let the Moors first march unopposed, and do not be in too great hurry to attack them, for they are like a stream, which can only be impeded in its course at a great risk. Let them first satiate their thirst for riches, and encumber themselves with booty; then they will be disunited, and will make the victory easier for you!"

Charles spoke thus, having regard to the difficulty of speedily assembling a great army; for Austrasia was tardy in raising a levy, as it did not realize the danger to which Neustria had almost succumbed. But when at length the army had, with great trouble, been collected, Charles marched with a stout heart against the robbers whose bands were busy with pillage in the neighborhood of Tours and Poitiers. Then the nations of the remote East and West encountered each other. It was a hard-fought and terrible battle, and lasted seven days. The Arabs were superior to the Franks in cavalry and in the quickness of their archers; the German tribes, on the other hand, had stouter bodies and stronger limbs, and had the advantage when it came to fighting at close quarters.

Charles had chosen a strong position, for a chain of hills protected the flank of his army, and made it difficult for the Moors to attack with cavalry on that side. But after the battle had lasted six days they advanced nearer, and the Arabs were terrified by the broad limbs and fierce looks of the Germans. Abderrahman himself fell on the seventh day, and at evening the Moors withdrew into their camp.

Quite late in the evening the Franks heard a great uproar in the Moorish camp, but they did not know the reason, and prepared to continue the battle on the following day. Morning dawned and the sun rose higher and higher in the heavens, but all remained silent in the camp of the Moors. The Christians were surprised at this, and Charles suspected a stratagem. But scouts reported that the whole camp was empty and deserted, so the Franks advanced. They found in the camp a quantity of plundered treasures and valuables. But Charles allowed the Arabs themselves to escape unmolested, for his army was fatigued with seven days' fighting.

Three hundred and fifty thousand Moorish corpses are said to have covered the battle-field; and Charles's fame resounded through Christendom, which he and his Franks had saved by this victory. From this battle he acquired the surname of "Martel" (hammer), because he had shattered the power of the Moors like a hammer.

THE LAMENT OF CHARLEMAGNE FOR ROLAND

[About 780]

TRANSLATED BY ISABEL BUTLER

[CHARLEMAGNE, the one great figure of his age, came to the throne in 768. Then followed one campaign after another, against the Lombards, the Saracens, and the Saxons. When in pursuit of the Saracens, he crossed the Pyrenees, took possession of the northeastern corner of Spain, and then started triumphantly on his return. His rear forces were commanded by Roland, a knight of marvelous achievements, and while marching through a narrow pass in the mountains these troops were attacked by the wild Gascons and Basques and were cut down before Charlemagne could come to them. Poems without number have been written on this episode; but the most famous is the "Song of Roland," from which the following extract is taken. This pictures the coming of Charlemagne to take vengeance upon his heathen foes.

The Editor.]

CHARLES is come into Roncevals. He begins to weep because of the dead he finds there, and he saith to the Franks: "Barons, ride softly, for I would go on before, to seek my nephew, whom I myself would find. Once at Aix, at the feast of Christmas, when my good knights were boasting of great battles and fierce onsets, I heard Roland speak his mind, saying, that if he should hap to die in a strange land, it would be at the head of his men and his peers, and his face would be turned to the land

of his foes, and he would die as a conqueror, the baron."
And farther than a man may throw a staff, before all the
rest Charles rides on up the mountain.

As the Emperor went seeking his nephew, he found
the grass and the flowers of the field bright red with the
blood of his barons. Great pity he has thereof, and he
may not help but weep. He has come up the hill to the
two trees, full well he knew Roland's blows on the three
stairs, and he sees his nephew lying stretched on the
greengrass. No wonder is it that Charles is full of wrath.
He lights down from his horse, and runs to Roland and
gathers him in his arms; and he swoons over him, so
great is his grief.

The Emperor has recovered from his swoon; and
Naymes the Duke and Count Acelin, Geoffrey of Anjou,
and his brother Thierry take the king and help him to sit
up under a pine tree. He looks to the ground and sees
his nephew lying there, and begins softly to lament him:
"Dear Roland, may God have mercy upon thee! For
the arraying and winning of great battles, never has the
world seen thy like. My glory is near to its setting."
And Charles cannot help but swoon again.

Charles the King has recovered from his swoon, four
of his barons hold him in their arms; he looks to the
ground and sees his nephew lying dead, still strong and
gallant of seeming, but his color is gone, and his eyes,
which have turned upwards, are darkened. Charles
makes lament for him in all faith and love: "Dear
Roland, may God bring thy soul among the flowers of
Paradise, among the glorious. Woe worth the day thou
camest into Spain, Baron! Never shall the day dawn
whereon I shall not grieve for thee. Now my pride and

my power will pass; for who henceforth will uphold my kingdom? In all the world I do not think to have a single friend; though I have other kindred, none are valiant as thou wert." With both his hands he plucks the hair of his head; and so great is the dole of the Franks, that of a hundred thousand men there is not one that doth not weep.

"Dear Roland, I shall go back to France, and when I am come to Laon, to my great hall there, strange men will come to me from many lands, and they will ask of me where is the Count, the great chieftain, and I shall say to them that he lies dead in Spain. Thenceforth in sorrow shall I maintain my kingdom; never shall the day dawn whereon I shall not mourn for thee.

"Dear Roland, brave captain, fair youth, when I am come to Aix, to my chapel there, men will come to me asking news, and I shall tell them marvelous and heavy news: 'My nephew, who has conquered many lands for me, is dead.' Then the Saxons will rise up against me, and the Hungarians and the Bulgarians, and many hostile people, the Romans and the Apulians, and all those of Palermo, and those of Africa, and those of Californe; then my woes and troubles will increase; for who will lead my armies against such a host when he is dead who was ever our champion? Ah, fair France, how art thou made desolate! So great is my sorrow that gladly would I lay down my life." With both hands the king plucks his white beard and the hairs of his head. And a hundred thousand Franks fall swooning to the ground.

"Dear Roland, woe worth thy life days! May thy soul be brought into Paradise. He who slew thee wrought shame to sweet France. Now is my grief so great that I would not outlive those of my household who lie dead for my sake. May God, the son of Mary, grant that before I am come to the pass of Cizre, my soul may part from my body, and follow their souls, and that my body may be laid in the earth beside their bodies." And the king weeps and plucks his white beard. "Now great is the wrath of Charles," quoth Naymes the Duke.

"My lord and Emperor," then saith Geoffrey of Anjou, "make ye not such great dole; rather let the field be searched and our dead, whom those of Spain have slain in battle, be brought together in a common grave." "Now, blow thy horn," the king makes answer.

Geoffrey of Anjou has sounded his horn; and the Franks light down from their horses, so Charles hath bidden it. And all their comrades which they find dead they straightway bring to the fosse. Many a bishop and abbot is there, and monks and canons and tonsured priests, and they have absolved the dead, and blessed them in God's name. And they kindled myrrh and sweet spices, and richly they perfumed them with incense, and buried them with great honor; and then they left them — how else should they do?

CHARLEMAGNE, EMPEROR OF THE WEST

[800]

BY A. W. GRUBE

THE presence [at Rome] of the powerful King of the Franks, and of many nobles of his kingdom, gave additional splendor to the [Christmas] festival, and attracted an immense multitude to Rome. Clad in a purple mantle, Charlemagne knelt on the steps of the high altar to offer up his prayer. As he rose up, and was about to depart, the Holy Father approached him, followed by a procession of ecclesiastical dignitaries, with a crown of gold in his hand, which he set on the head of the King of the Franks, and anointed him with oil as Emperor of the Romans, and temporal lord of the whole of Catholic Christendom. The people cheered, and cried aloud three times, "Long life and victory to Charlemagne, the peace-bringing Emperor, crowned of God!" The trumpets at once struck up, clear music mingled with the repeated cheers of the multitude, and an immense chorus joined in the coronation hymn. Universal rapture pervaded the city.

The imperial dignity had been in abeyance for three hundred and twenty-four years, ever since Odoacer had dethroned Romulus Augustulus. As the Empire of the Romans was then overthrown by a German, so it was now restored by a German, to the great vexation of the Emperor of the East, who was now called simply the Greek Emperor.

CHARLEMAGNE, EMPEROR OF THE WEST

If Charlemagne had been merely a conqueror he would have done but little good, for soon after his death the edifice of his kingdom, which was composed of so many incongruous elements, tumbled to pieces. But his efforts were directed towards something higher and nobler. Those whom he, as hero, had conquered with the sword, he would make happy by his fatherly love.

He was incessantly laboring to civilize his people, and to make them wiser and better. The most learned men of his time lived at his court, and enjoyed his esteem and friendship. With their aid he established many schools to provide a better education for youth.

He had more regard for knowledge acquired by study, which ennobles the poorest, than for the hereditary advantages of rank. He once found, on visiting a school, that the children of the higher ranks were far inferior in diligence and good manners to those of the common citizens. He had the industrious placed on his right hand, and the lazy on his left, and then spoke thus to the poor but clever children: "I thank you, my children; you have behaved according to my wishes: honor and permanent usefulness will be yours." Then he turned angrily to the high-born children: "But you, sons of noblemen, you well-dressed dolls, who have been idle and disobedient to my commands, do not rely on the rank and wealth of your parents; if you do not mend, none of you shall ever come into my sight again. By the King of Heaven, I will punish you as you deserve."

He was devoted to Christianity with his whole heart. He was therefore careful to provide good priests, and forbade them to do anything inconsistent with the dignity of their calling — as, for example, hunting. The monasteries were richly endowed, for within their quiet walls not only was the education of youth promoted, but the sick and poor were provided for, and strangers were hospitably entertained; for in those days inns were but little known. The churches were adorned with images of the saints, for Charlemagne thought it good that the lives and deeds of pious men should awaken pious memories in the Christian congregations. To make the church service more impressive, he brought singers and organists from Italy; for his Franks had such harsh and untrained voices, that their singing almost resembled the roaring of wild beasts. The more refined Romans compared this music to the rumbling of a wagon over the pavement.

Charlemagne loved his mother tongue above everything. He himself labored, in conjunction with the learned men of his court, at the compilation of a German grammar, and had a collection made of ancient German heroic lays. Unfortunately nothing of the praiseworthy efforts of the great man has come down to us except the German names which he gave to the winds and months.

January he called Winter-month; February, Horning (perhaps because in that month stags cast their horns); March, Spring-month; April, Easter-month; May, Joy-month; June, Fallow-month; July, Hay-month; August, Harvest-month; September, Autumn-month; October, Wine-month; November, Wind-month; December, Christ-month.

He bestowed particular care on the administration of justice. For this purpose he appointed respectable men, distinguished by their age and experience, who bore the name of "Graves," i.e., "Gray-beards," for most of them, being old men, had gray hair. These Graves had different titles, according to their functions. Those who were set over a province (gau) were called Gaugraves; those who were set over a castle (burg) were styled Burgraves; the Pfalzgraves, or Counts Palatine, had the charge of the Emperor's palaces — *pfalz* meaning palace. The Margraves guarded the Marches or borders.

He, moreover, made strict inquiries as to whether his servants were faithful to their duties. To this end he from time to time sent special judges into the provinces, who were to render exact information about everything.

In the midst of the great affairs of the empire he did not forget the little ones of his household. He examined with the greatest strictness his steward's account of receipts and expenditure. Some written directions which he had sketched out for them are still extant. He prescribed exactly, like an experienced farmer, how butter and cheese, honey and wax, were to be prepared, how grapes were to be pressed and beer brewed, and how many eggs, geese, ducks, and fowls were to be sold.

Charlemagne had no fixed residence. He was now here, now there; but was most partial to Aix-la-Chapelle, on account of the warm baths, which had been held in high estimation by the Romans; he also favored Ingelheim, near Mayence, and lastly Nimeguen.

Charlemagne was a true German, strongly built and slender. He had a high, open forehead, and extremely large, keen eyes, which seemed friendly to friends and suppliants, but formidable to enemies. In early youth, according to the custom of the Franks, he exercised his bodily powers, and excelled in fighting and swimming. He especially delighted in the chase, and when he wished to prepare a feast for his court, a battue was organized. Every one mounted his horse, and then, amid the winding of horns and the barking of countless hounds, they went forth with shouts of joy into the depths of the forest, where each of the young nobles strove to surpass the rest in skill and courage. Charlemagne in their midst endured many an arduous conflict with wild boars, bears, and buffaloes.

Charlemagne had a large appetite, but was not luxurious in eating or drinking. Roast venison brought to table by a huntsman on the spit was his favorite dish. Drunkenness was hateful to him.

He often rose from his couch at night, took writing-tablets and style, and practiced the art of writing, which he had neglected in his early years; or he prayed, or set himself at the window to survey the starry heavens with reverence and admiration for the Creator.

His simple mode of life wonderfully increased the strength of the powerful man, and he became so strong that he could lift a man in full armor like a child.

His dress was simple, according to the German custom. His clothes were the work of his wife's busy fingers; he wore stockings and linen trousers crossed with colored stripes, a linen waistcoat, and over it a plain coat striped with silk; occasionally a square cloak of a white or green color. But a great sword, with a golden hilt and belt, hung ever by his side. Only at diets and great festivals did he appear in full majesty, with a golden crown glittering with diamonds on his head, dressed in a long flowing robe, decked with golden bees.

Up to his latest years Charlemagne always enjoyed good health. Not until four years before his death did it begin to fail, when continual attacks of fever shattered him. He was deeply affected by the deaths of his two favorite sons, Pepin and Charles, who died within a year of each other. He continued, nevertheless, to study the welfare of his empire.

Feeling himself to be growing weaker and weaker, he summoned his only remaining son, Louis, who had for some time been King of Aquitaine, to a State Council at Aix-la-Chapelle (813). Here he exhorted the nobles of his empire to show themselves loyal to his son, and then asked each of them from the greatest to the least whether he approved of his making over a share in the government and the imperial title to Louis. With one accord they answered: "Such is the will of God!"

The next Sunday Charlemagne proceeded with his son to the Church of St. Mary at Aix, which he had built. He himself appeared in royal attire, with a crown on his head, and had another crown placed on the altar. Both father and son prayed in silence for a long time before the altar. Then the venerable old man arose, and in presence of the whole people exhorted his son "to fear and love God, and obey His commandments in all things, to provide for the Church and protect it against evil-doers, always to show himself kind to his kinsmen, to honor the priests as fathers, and to love like children the nations who were committed to his care, to appoint faithful and God-fearing officers, and to deprive no one of his fiefs or dignities without sufficient cause." After this exhortation, Charlemagne asked his son whether he was resolved to live in conformity to it. "Gladly," replied Louis; "gladly will I obey, and by God's help fulfill the commands which you have given me." Charlemagne now enjoined him, as if in token that he owed the empire to God alone, to take the crown from the altar and to set it on his own head. Louis did as he was ordered.

After the ceremony was over, Charlemagne went back, supported by his son, to the imperial palace. Here he bestowed splendid presents upon him and sent him back to Aquitaine. At parting they embraced and kissed each other, and shed tears of love and sorrow. They felt that this was their last meeting; and, in fact, they never saw each other again.

In January of the following year (814), Charlemagne was again attacked by a violent fever. He tried to cure himself by fasting, as he was wont to do; but in vain: his body was too much enfeebled; his end was at hand. On the seventh day of his illness he sent for his trusty friend Bishop Hildbald, in order to receive the sacrament from his hand. After he had partaken of it his weakness increased. The following morning he saw that his end was near. He crossed himself, folded his hands on his breast, closed his eyes, and prayed in a low voice, saying, "Lord, into Thy hands I commend my spirit!" Thus he passed away peacefully and happily on the 28th of January, 814, when he had reached the age of seventy-two years, and had governed his great kingdom with honor for forty-seven years.

ROLLO THE VIKING

[885]

BY EVA MARCH TAPPAN

THE story is told that while Charlemagne was sitting one day at dinner, a fleet of long, narrow boats came swiftly toward the land. "Those must have come from Brittany," some one declared; and another said, "No, they are surely Jewish merchantmen." But Charlemagne had noted the vessels, that they had only one sail, that bow and stern were shaped alike and were gilded and carved to represent the head or tail of a dragon, and that a row of shields was ranged along the gunwale. "Those bring nothing to sell," he said. "They are most cruel foes, they are Northmen." Then there was a hurrying and scurrying to put on armor, snatch up swords and spears, and hasten down to the shore to drive away the pirates. But the Northmen had heard of the prowess of Charlemagne, and as soon as they knew he was there they rowed away as fast as their boats could be made to carry them. The Franks had much to say about these enemies, but Charlemagne stood silent, gazing at the sea. At length he turned toward his friends. His eyes were full of tears, and he said, "I am not afraid that the Northmen will harm me, but I weep to see that they have ventured so near our shore, and to think of the evils that they will bring upon my children and their people."

Charlemagne was right, for it was not many years after his death before one hundred and twenty pirate vessels were rowed swiftly up the River Seine, and a mass of Northmen, or Vikings, poured into the little city of Paris, ready to kill, burn, and steal, as usual. But suddenly a heavy fog hid them from one another. There was some enchantment about it, they thought, and made their way back to their ships as best they might. But they came again and again. Sometimes they were met with arms, sometimes with tribute. Still they came. "Did not we promise you twelve thousand pounds of silver if you would leave us in peace?" demanded the Franks in despair. "The king promised it," was the insolent reply, "and we left him in peace. He is dead now, and what we do will not disturb him."

The following year the famous leader Rollo led the Vikings in an attack upon Paris. They hammered at the walls of the city with battering-rams. With great slings they hurled stones and leaden balls. They dug a mine under one of the walls, leaving wooden props. Then they set fire to these and scrambled out of the narrow passage as fast as they could. The beams burned and the earth fell in, but the walls did not crumble as the Vikings had hoped. Then they built a fire close to the wooden walls, but a sudden rain put it out. There were thirty or forty thousand of the Vikings, and only two hundred of the Franks in the besieged city; but the Franks had wise leaders, and all this time they were boiling oil and pitch and pouring them down upon the besiegers. The blazing Northmen leaped into the river to extinguish the flames, but they never thought of giving up. They collected food and encamped near the city. Month after month the siege went on, and still the king did not come to help his brave people.

ROLLO THE VIKING

At last the valiant Eudes, or Odo, one of the chief
leaders of the Parisians, determined to go in search of
aid, and one stormy night he managed to slip through
the gate of the city and the lines of the Northmen, and
gallop off to the king. Pretty soon the king came with
his army, — and went into camp! After he had dawdled
a month away, news came that more Vikings were at
hand. The king was so frightened that he offered the
Northmen seven hundred pounds of silver if they would
depart, and told them they might go farther up the river
and plunder Burgundy as much as they chose. The
brave defenders of Paris were indignant. They rushed
out of the city and struck one fierce blow at their departing foes. The following year the cowardly king was de-
posed, and at his death they chose the valiant Eudes for
their ruler.

The Northmen were bright, shrewd people; and, wild
as they were, they could not help seeing that the Frankish way of living was better than theirs, and that the
worship of the Christian God was better than that of
Odin and Thor. Rollo led them again to France some
years later, and this time the Vikings ranged themselves
on one side of a little river, and the king with his Franks
stood on the other side, to talk about peace. Rollo was
willing to give up his pirate life, be baptized, and live in
the Frankish country if the king would give him land.
"I will give you Flanders," said the king; but Rollo replied, "No. that is too swampy." "Then you may have
the parts of Neustria nearest to the shore." "No,"
declared Rollo, "that is nothing but forest land." At
length it was agreed that he and his followers should
have the land which afterward took its name from them

and to this day is called Normandy. They were to hold it by what is known as a feudal tenure, that is, it was to be theirs so long as they were faithful to the king and gave him loyal military service.

There is a story that the bishops told Rollo he must kiss the king's foot in token of his having received this great gift and having become the king's vassal. The haughty Northman had no idea of doing any such thing; but when the bishops insisted, he motioned to one of his warriors to do it for him. The warrior was as proud as his lord. The old account says that he would not kneel, but lifted the royal foot so high that the king fell backward. The Franks were angry, but the Northmen roared with laughter.

The Northmen, or Normans, as they were afterwards called, went into their new domain. Rollo ruled them strictly, for he was as anxious to be a successful ruler as he had been to be a successful pirate. The same story is told of him that is related of Alfred the Great and several other kings, that one might leave a golden bracelet hanging on a tree in perfect safety anywhere in his possessions. Whether that is true or not, it is true that any robber who fell into the hands of Rollo was promptly hanged. It is also true that it was exceedingly difficult for a criminal to escape, because Rollo made the whole land responsible for him. Whenever any one committed a trespass, the first man who found it out must cry "Haro!" and the cry must go through the whole kingdom until the man was captured.

So it was that the Vikings who had come to France to plunder gave up their wild, savage life and became permanent dwellers in that country.

SAINT LOUIS OPENING THE PRISONS OF HIS REALM

BY LUC OLIVIER MERSON
(*French painter*, 1846–

Saint Louis, or Louis IX, came to the throne of France at the age of twelve. His mother, Blanche of Castile, brought him up with the utmost strictness. "I should rather have him dead," said she, "than to have him commit sin." He seems to have been a gentle, kindly boy, but with a keen sense of justice and, moreover, with a very decided will of his own. Even when the pope himself urged him to undertake war with the German emperor, he refused because he thought it unjust. The young king fasted, he wore sackcloth, and he made pilgrimages barefooted. Every Friday he was, by his own command, severely scourged by his confessor. When he was criticized for spending so much time in hearing mass, he replied, "If I spent twice as much time in dice and hawking, should I be so rebuked?" In an illness Louis commanded the crusader's cross to be placed upon his shoulder, and on his recovery he kept his vow to go on a crusade, in spite of his mother, his ministers, nobles, and clergy. In battle he showed himself a hero as a soldier, but a failure as a general. He was captured, released, and returned to France. In 1270 he insisted upon undertaking a second crusade; and on this one he died. In 1296 he was canonized by Pope Boniface VIII.

The illustration shows Louis as a child, throwing open a prison. Behind him stands his mother, at his side a bishop. Thronging out from the prison is the crowd of prisoners. One of them is kissing the hem of his robe. At the right is the mother of a young captive, gazing into his face as if to say, "And can it really be you?" The little dog at his feet has no questionings, but springs upon him joyfully.

II
STORIES OF THE HUNDRED YEARS' WAR

HISTORICAL NOTE

THE Salic Law, a law of some of the ancient Franks, forbade the wearing of the French crown by a woman; and therefore in 1328 it was given to a cousin of the dead king, Charles IV, instead of to Isabella, daughter of Charles. Edward III of England, son of Isabella, claimed it on the ground that he could wear it even if his mother could not. This, together with the aid given by the French to the Scotch during a recent Scottish war with England, brought about the Hundred Years' War, which with occasional breaks raged for a century.

The first great battle was that of Crécy, in which, as well as in the battle of Poictiers, the English were successful. By 1377, however, Edward and his valiant son, the Black Prince, were both dead, a child was on the throne, and the English had lost nearly all their possessions in France. A long truce followed. In 1415, Henry V of England invaded France, won the battle of Agincourt, and held practically the whole country. France was in despair, when suddenly the whole situation was changed by one of the strangest occurrences in history.

There was an old prophecy current in France that at some time when the country should be in the depths of trouble, it should be delivered by a maiden of Domremy; and a peasant girl, Joan of Arc, now declared that she was the maiden of the prophecy. She had heard supernatural voices, she said, bidding her to raise the siege of Orléans, one of the few towns still faithful to Charles, the French claimant to the throne, and to conduct that prince to Rheims to be crowned king of France. Her services were accepted, and Orléans was saved. This was the beginning of French success. In 1453, the war came to an end, leaving not a rod of French soil in the hands of the English except Calais and a small district adjoining. This they held until 1558.

THE BATTLE OF CRÉCY

[1346]

BY SIR JOHN FROISSART

THE English, who were drawn up in three divisions and seated on the ground, on seeing their enemies advance, rose undauntedly up and fell into their ranks. That of the prince was the first to do so, whose archers were formed in the manner of a portcullis or harrow, and the men-at-arms in the rear. The earls of Northampton and Arundel, who commanded the second division, had posted themselves in good order on his wing, to assist and succor the prince if necessary.

You must know that these kings, earls, barons, and lords of France did not advance in any regular order, but one after the other, or any way most pleasing to themselves. As soon as the King of France came in sight of the English, his blood began to boil, and he cried out to his marshals, "Order the Genoese forward and begin the battle, in the name of God and St. Denis." There were about fifteen thousand Genoese crossbowmen; but they were quite fatigued, having marched on foot that day six leagues, completely armed, and with their crossbows. They told the constable they were not in a fit condition to do any great things that day in battle. The Earl of Alençon, hearing this, said, "This is what one gets by employing such scoundrels, who fall off when there is any need for them." During this time a heavy rain fell, accompanied by thunder and a very terrible

165

eclipse of the sun; and before this rain a great flight of crows hovered in the air over all those battalions, making a loud noise. Shortly afterwards it cleared up, and the sun shone very bright; but the Frenchmen had it in their faces, and the English in their backs. When the Genoese were somewhat in order, and approached the English, they set up a loud shout, in order to frighten them; but they remained quite still, and did not seem to attend to it. They then set up a second shout, and advanced a little forward; but the English never moved.

They hooted a third time, advancing with their cross-bows presented, and began to shoot. The English archers then advanced one step forward, and shot their arrows with such force and quickness that it seemed as if it snowed. When the Genoese felt these arrows, which pierced their arms, heads, and through their armor, some of them cut the strings of their crossbows, others flung them on the ground, and all turned about and retreated quite discomfited. The French had a fine body of men-at-arms on horseback, richly dressed, to support the Genoese. The King of France, seeing them thus fall back, cried out, "Kill me those scoundrels; for they stop up our road without any reason." You would then have seen the above-mentioned men-at-arms lay about them, killing all they could of these runaways.

The English continued shooting as vigorously and quickly as before; some of their arrows fell among the horsemen, who were sumptuously equipped, and, killing and wounding many, made them caper and fall among the Genoese so that they were in such confusion they could never rally again. In the English army there were some Cornish and Welsh men on foot, who had armed themselves with large knives: these advancing through the ranks of the men-at-arms and archers, who made way for them, came upon the French when they were in this danger, and falling upon earls, barons, knights, and squires slew many, at which the King of England was afterwards much exasperated.

The valiant King of Bohemia was slain there. He was called Charles of Luxembourg; for he was the son of the gallant king and Emperor, Henry of Luxembourg: having heard the order of the battle, he inquired where his son, the Lord Charles, was: his attendants answered that they did not know, but believed he was fighting. The king said to them: "Gentlemen, you are all my people, my friends and brethren at arms this day: therefore, as I am blind, I request of you to lead me so far into the engagement that I may strike one stroke with my sword." The knights replied, they would lead him forward; and in order that they might not lose him in the crowd, they fastened all the reins of their horses together, and put the king at their head, that he might gratify his wish, and advanced toward the enemy. The Lord Charles of Bohemia, who already signed his name as King of Germany and bore the arms, had come in good order to the engagement; but when he perceived that it was likely to turn out against the French, he departed, and I do not well know what road he took. The king, his father, had ridden in among the enemy, and made good use of his sword; for he and his companions had fought most gallantly. They had advanced so far that they were all slain; and on the morrow they were found on the ground with their horses all tied together.

The Earl of Alençon advanced in regular order upon

the English, to fight with them; as did the Earl of Flanders, in another part. These two lords with their detachments coasting, as it were, the archers, came to the prince's battalion, where they fought valiantly for a length of time. The King of France was eager to march to the place where he saw their banners displayed, but there was a hedge of archers before him. He had that day made a present of a handsome black horse to Sir John of Hainault, who had mounted on it a knight of his, called Sir John de Fusselles, that bore his banner: which horse ran away with him, and forced his way through the English army and, when about to return, stumbled and fell into a ditch and severely wounded him: he would have been dead if his page had not followed him round the battalions, and found him unable to rise: he had not, however, any other hindrance than from his horse; for the English did not quit the ranks that day to make prisoners. The page alighted, and raised him up; but he did not return the way he came, as he would have found it difficult from the crowd. This battle, which was fought on the Saturday between La Broyes and Crécy, was very murderous and cruel; and many gallant deeds of arms were performed that were never known. Toward evening, many knights and squires of the French had lost their masters: they wandered up and down the plain, attacking the English in small parties: they were soon destroyed; for the English had determined that day to give no quarter or hear of ransom from any one.

Early in the day, some French, Germans, and Savoyards had broken through the archers of the prince's battalion, and had engaged with the men-at-arms; upon which the second battalion came to his aid, and it was time, for otherwise he would have been hard pressed. The first division, seeing the danger they were in, sent a knight in great haste to the King of England, who was posted upon an eminence near a windmill. On the knight's arrival, he said, "Sir, the Earl of Warwick, the Lord Reginald Cobham, and the others who are about your son are vigorously attacked by the French; and they entreat that you would come to their assistance with your battalion, for, if their numbers should increase, they fear he will have too much to do." The king replied, "Is my son dead, unhorsed, or so badly wounded that he cannot support himself?" "Nothing of the sort, thank God," rejoined the knight; "but he is in so hot an engagement that he has great need of your help." The king answered, "Now, Sir Thomas, return back to those that sent you, and tell them from me not to send again for me this day or expect that I shall come, let what will happen, as long as my son has life; and say that I command them to let the boy win his spurs, for I am determined, if it please God, that all the glory and honor of this day shall be given to him and to those into whose care I have entrusted him." The knight returned to his lords and related the king's answer, which mightily encouraged them, and made them repent they had ever sent such a message. . . .

When, on the Saturday night, the English heard no more hooting or shouting, nor any more crying out to particular lords or their banners, they looked upon the field as their own, and their enemies as beaten. They made great fires and lighted torches because of the obscurity of the night. King Edward then came down from his post, who all that day had not put on his helmet, and with his whole battalion advanced to the Prince of Wales, whom he embraced in his arms and kissed, and said, "Sweet son, God give you good perseverance: you are my son, for most loyally have you acquitted yourself this day: you are worthy to be a sovereign." The prince bowed down very low, and humbled himself, giving all the honor to the king his father.

HOW QUEEN PHILIPPA SAVED THE BURGHERS

[1347]

BY SIR JOHN FROISSART

[THE town of Calais resisted the siege of Edward until its people were on the point of perishing of hunger. Then they asked for a parley, and when the envoys of the English king had come, they begged that he would be satisfied with the treasures of the town and castle and would allow them to depart in safety.

The Editor.]

THE two lords returned to the king and related what had passed. The king said he had no intentions of complying with the request, but should insist that they surrender themselves unconditionally to his will. Sir Walter replied: "My lord, you may be to blame in this, as you will set us a very bad example; for if you order us to go to any of your castles, we shall not obey you so cheerfully if you put these people to death; for they will retaliate upon us in a similar case." Many barons who were then present supported this opinion. Upon which the king replied: "Gentlemen, I am not so obstinate as to hold my opinion alone against you all: Sir Walter, you will inform the governor of Calais that the only grace he must expect from us is, that six of the principal citizens of Calais march out of the town with bare heads and feet, with ropes around their necks, and the keys of the town and castle in their hands. These six persons shall be at my absolute disposal, and the remainder of the inhabitants pardoned."

Sir Walter returned to the Lord de Vienne, who was waiting for him on the battlements, and told him all that he had been able to gain from the king. "I beg of you," replied the governor, "that you would be so good as to remain here a little, while I go and relate all that has passed to the townsmen; for, as they have desired me to undertake this, it is but proper they should know the result of it." He went to the market-place and caused the bell to be rung; upon which all the inhabitants, men and women, assembled in the town hall. He then related to them what he had said, and the answers he had received; and that he could not obtain any conditions more favorable, to which they must give a short and immediate answer. This information caused the greatest lamentations and despair; so that the hardest heart would have had compassion on them; even the Lord de Vienne wept bitterly.

'After a short time, the most wealthy citizen of the town, by name Eustace de St. Pierre, rose up and said: "Gentlemen, both high and low, it would be a very great pity to suffer so many people to die through famine, if any means could be found to prevent it; and it would be highly meritorious in the eyes of our Saviour if such misery could be averted. I have such faith and trust in finding grace before God if I die to save my townsmen that I name myself as first of the six." When Eustace had done speaking, they all rose up and almost worshiped him: many cast themselves at his feet with tears and groans. Another citizen, very rich and respectable, rose up and said he would be the second to his companion Eustace; his name was John Daire. After him, James Wisant, who was very rich in merchandise and lands, offered himself as companion to his two cousins, as did Peter Wisant, his brother. Two others then named themselves, which completed the number demanded by the King of England.

The Lord John de Vienne then mounted a small hackney, for it was with difficulty that he could walk, and conducted them to the gate. There was the greatest sorrow and lamentation all over the town; and in such manner were they attended to the gate, which the governor ordered to be opened, and then shut upon him and the six citizens, whom he led to the barriers, and said to Sir Walter Manny, who was there waiting for him, "I deliver up to you, as governor of Calais, with the consent of the inhabitants, these six citizens; and I swear to you that they were, and are to this day, the most wealthy and respectable inhabitants of Calais. I beg of you, gentle sir, that you would have the goodness to beseech the king that they may not be put to death." "I cannot answer for what the king will do with them," replied Sir Walter, "but you may depend that I will do all in my power to save them." The barriers were opened, when these six citizens advanced toward the pavilion of the king, and the Lord de Vienne rendered the town.

When Sir Walter Manny had presented these six citizens to the king, they fell upon their knees, and with uplifted hands said, "Most gallant king, see before you six citizens of Calais, who have been capital merchants, and who bring you the keys of the castle and of the town. We surrender ourselves to your absolute will and pleasure, in order to save the remainder of the inhabitants of Calais, who have suffered much distress and misery. Condescend, therefore, out of your nobleness of mind, to have mercy and compassion upon us."

All the barons, knights, and squires that were assembled there in great numbers, wept at this sight. The king eyed them with angry looks (for he hated much the people of Calais, for the great losses he had formerly suffered from them at sea), and ordered their heads to be stricken off. All present entreated the king that he would be more merciful to them, but he would not listen to them. Then Sir Walter Manny said, "Ah, gentle king, let me beseech you to restrain your anger: you have the reputation of great nobleness of soul, do not therefore tarnish it by such an act as this, nor allow any one to speak in a disgraceful manner of you. In this instance, all the world will say you have acted cruelly if you put to death six such respectable persons, who, of their own free will, have surrendered themselves to your mercy in order to save their fellow-citizens." Upon this, the king gave a wink, saying, "Be it so," and ordered the headsman to be sent for; for that the Calesians had done him so much damage, it was proper they should suffer for it. The Queen of England fell on her knees and with tears said, "Ah, gentle sir, since I have crossed the seas with great danger to see you, I have never asked you one favor: now, I most humbly ask you as a gift, for the sake of the Son of the Blessed Mary, and for your love to me, that you will be merciful to these six men." The king looked at her for some time in silence, and then said; "Ah, lady, I wish that you had been anywhere else than here: you have entreated me in such a manner that I cannot refuse you; I therefore give them to you, to do as you please with them." The queen conducted the six citizens to her apartments, and had the halters taken from round their necks, after which she new clothed them, and served them with a plentiful dinner: she then presented each with six nobles,[1] and had them escorted out of the camp in safety.

[1] The noble was a gold coin of the value of about $5.96.

THE COMING OF THE MAID OF ORLÉANS

[1428]

BY JOHANN CHRISTOPH FRIEDRICH VON SCHILLER

[IN the early days of the fifteenth century, France was in a sad condition. Not only were there dissensions, uprisings, and even civil war, but the king, Charles VI, had become insane. It was a favorable time to make an invasion, and this was done by Henry V of England. Isabel, wife of Charles VI, had small regard for the rights of her son Charles, and in 1420 she willingly signed the Treaty of Troyes, by which Henry was recognized as the heir of the insane sovereign. At the death of the kings of both France and England, in 1422, the little boy, Henry VI, now King of England, was brought to Paris by the English and crowned King of France.

Some of the French people stood by Charles VII as their lawful sovereign, but he had little of either hope, or skill in warfare. The town of Orléans was one of the few that remained true to him, and the English had laid siege to that. But now a strange thing came to pass, for a simple village maiden came to the camp and asked to speak with the king. Stories had preceded her that she regarded herself as chosen of God to raise the siege of Orléans and to conduct Charles to Rheims to be crowned. The following scene, from Schiller's play, "The Maid of Orléans," pictures the interview. To test her power, Charles has bidden the Earl Dunois to occupy the royal seat, while he himself stands amongst the courtiers.

The Editor.]

JOHANNA, *accompanied by the Councilors and many Knights, who occupy the background of the scene; she*

176

advances with noble bearing, and slowly surveys the
company.

Dunois (after a long and solemn pause). Art thou the
wond'rous Maiden —

Johanna (interrupts him, regarding him with dignity).
Thou wilt tempt thy God!
This place abandon, which becomes thee not!
To this more mighty one the Maid is sent.

> [*With a firm step she approaches the* KING, *bows*
> *one knee before him, and, rising immediately,*
> *steps back. All present express their astonish-*
> *ment;* DUNOIS *forsakes his seat, which is occu-*
> *pied by the* KING.

Charles. Maiden, thou ne'er hast seen my face before.
Whence hast thou then this knowledge?

Johanna.   Thee I saw
When none beside, save God in heaven, beheld thee.

> [*She approaches the* KING *and speaks myste-*
> *riously.*

Bethink thee, Dauphin, in the bygone night!
When all around lay buried in deep sleep,
Thou from thy couch didst rise and offer up
An earnest prayer to God. Let these retire
And I will name the subject of thy prayer.

Charles. What I to Heaven confided need not be
From men conceal'd. Disclose to me my prayer,
And I shall doubt no more that God inspires thee.

Johanna. Three prayers thou offer'dst, Dauphin; lis-
ten now
Whether I name them to thee! Thou didst pray
That if there were appended to this crown
Unjust possession, or if heavy guilt,

Not yet atoned for, from thy father's times,
Occasion'd this most lamentable war,
God would accept thee as a sacrifice,
Have mercy on thy people, and pour forth
Upon thy head the chalice of his wrath.

    Charles (steps back with awe). Who art thou, mighty
        one? Whence comest thou?

                          [*All express their astonishment.*

    Johanna. To God thou offeredst this second prayer:
That if it were His will and high decree
To take away the scepter from thy race,
And from thee to withdraw whate'er thy sires,
The monarchs of this kingdom, once possess'd,
He in his mercy would preserve to thee
Three priceless treasures — a contented heart,
Thy friend's affection, and thine Agnes' love.

        [*The* KING *conceals his face: the spectators express their astonishment.*

Thy third petition shall I name to thee?

    Charles. Enough — I credit thee! This doth surpass
Mere human knowledge: thou art sent by God!

    Archbishop. Who art thou, wonderful and holy maid?
What favor'd region bore thee? What blest pair.
Belov'd of Heaven, may claim thee as their child?

    Johanna. Most reverend father, I am nam'd Johanna,
I am a shepherd's lowly daughter, born
In Dom Remi, a village of my King,
Included in the diocese of Toul,
And from a child I kept my father's sheep.
— And much and frequently I heard them tell
Of the strange islanders, who o'er the sea

THE COMING OF THE MAID OF ORLÉANS

Had come to make us slaves, and on us force
A foreign lord, who loveth not the people;
How the great city, Paris, they had seized,
And had usurp'd dominion o'er the realm.
Then earnestly God's Mother I implor'd
To save us from the shame of foreign chains,
And to preserve to us our lawful King.
Not distant from my native village stands
An ancient image of the Virgin blest,
To which the pious pilgrims oft repair'd;
Hard by a holy oak, of blessed power,
Standeth, far-fam'd through wonders manifold.
Beneath the oak's broad shade I lov'd to sit,
Tending my flock — my heart still drew me there
And if by chance among the desert hills
A lambkin strayed, 't was shown me in a dream,
When in the shadow of this oak I slept.
— And once, when through the night beneath this tree
In pious adoration I had sat,
Resisting sleep, the Holy One appear'd,
Bearing a sword and banner, otherwise
Clad like a shepherdess, and thus she spake: —
" 'T is I; arise, Johanna! leave thy flock.
The Lord appoints thee to another task!
Receive this banner! Gird thee with this sword!
Therewith exterminate my people's foes;
Conduct to Rheims thy royal master's son,
And crown him with the kingly diadem!"
And I made answer: "How may I presume
To undertake such deeds, a tender maid,
Unpractic'd in the dreadful art of war!"
And she replied. "A maiden pure and chaste

179

FRANCE

Achieves whate'er on earth is glorious,
If she to earthy love ne'er yields her heart.
Look upon me! a virgin, like thyself;
I to the Christ, the Lord divine, gave birth,
And am myself divine!" — Mine eyelids then
She touch'd, and when I upward turn'd my gaze,
Heaven's wide expanse was fill'd with angel-boys,
Who bore white lilies in their hands, while tones
Of sweetest music floated through the air.
— And thus on three successive nights appear'd
The Holy One, and cried — "Arise, Johanna!
The Lord appoints thee to another task!"
And when the third night she reveal'd herself,
Wrathful she seem'd, and chiding spake these words:
"Obedience, woman's duty here on earth;
Severe endurance is her heavy doom;
She must be purified through discipline;
Who serveth here, is glorified above!"
While thus she spake, she let her shepherd garb
Fall from her, and as Queen of Heaven stood forth
Enshrined in radiant light, while golden clouds
Upbore her slowly to the realms of bliss.

> [*All are moved;* AGNES SOREL, *weeping, hides her
> face on the bosom of the* KING.

Archbishop (*after a long pause*). Before divine creden-
    tials such as these
Each doubt of earthly prudence must subside.
Her deeds attest the truth of what she speaks,
For God alone such wonders can achieve.

Dunois. I credit not her wonders, but her eyes,
Which beam with innocence and purity.

Charles. Am I, a sinner, worthy of such favor?

THE COMING OF THE MAID OF ORLÉANS

Infallible, All-searching eye, thou seest
Mine inmost heart, my deep humility!

Johanna. Humility shines brightly in the skies:
Thou art abased, hence God exalteth thee.

Charles. Shall I indeed withstand mine enemies?

Johanna. France I will lay submissive at thy feet!

Charles. And Orléans, say'st thou, will not be surrender'd?

Johanna. The Loire shall sooner roll its waters back.

Charles. Shall I in triumph enter into Rheims?

Johanna. I through ten thousand foes will lead thee
there.

> [*The knights make a noise with their lances and
> shields, and evince signs of courage.*

Dunois. Appoint the Maiden to command the host!
We follow blindly whereso'er she leads.
The holy one's prophetic eye shall guide,
And this brave sword from danger shall protect her!

Hire. A universe in arms we will not fear,
If she, the mighty one, precede our troops.
The God of battle walketh by her side;
Let her conduct us on to victory!

> [*The knights clang their arms and press forward.*

Charles. Yes, holy Maiden, do thou lead mine host;
My chiefs and warriors shall submit to thee.
This sword of matchless temper, proved in war
Sent back in anger by the Constable,
Hath found a hand more worthy. Prophetess,
Do thou receive it, and henceforward be —

Johanna. No, noble Dauphin! conquest to my Liege
Is not accorded through this instrument
Of earthly might. I know another sword

181

Wherewith I am to conquer, which to thee,
I, as the Spirit taught, will indicate;
Let it be hither brought.

    Charles.   Name it, Johanna.

    Johanna. Send to the ancient town of Fierbois;
There in Saint Catherine's churchyard is a vault
Where lie in heaps the spoils of bygone war.
Among them is the sword, which I must use.
It, by three golden lilies may be known,
Upon the blade impress'd. Let it be brought,
For thou, my Liege, shalt conquer through this sword.

    Charles. Perform what she commands.

    Johanna.   And a white banner,
Edg'd with a purple border, let me bear.
Upon this banner let the Queen of Heaven
Be pictur'd, with the beauteous Jesus child,
Floating in glory o'er this earthly ball.
For so the Holy Mother show'd it me.

    Charles. So be it as thou sayest.

    Johanna (to the ARCHBISHOP). Reverend Bishop
Lay on my head thy consecrated hands!
Pronounce a blessing, Father, on thy child!

                          [She kneels down.

    Archbishop. Not blessings to receive, but to dispense
Art thou appointed. — Go, with power divine!
But we are sinners all and most unworthy.

182

CORONATION OF CHARLES VII AT RHEIMS

BY JULES EUGÈNE LENEPVEU

(From a painting in the Pantheon at Paris)

BEFORE the coming of Joan of Arc, all France seemed destined to fall into the hands of the English, but the faith of this girl saved the land. Fired by her enthusiasm the country rallied about its king. Steadily the English were driven back until but one town remained to them.

This picture was selected from the many that have been inspired by the life of Joan of Arc, because it shows her at the summit of her wonderful career. Charles VII is at last crowned King of France, and the vow that led Joan from the peaceful meadows of Domremy to face death before the walls of Orleans, is now fulfilled.

Every face is turned toward the king, who kneels to receive the crown of his fathers. But it is the Maid who is the real center of the picture. She is in armor, but the robe over it produces the effect of graceful womanly attire. In one hand she grasps the ancient sword whose hiding place she had divined; in the other she bears the sacred lily-embroidered standard of her own designing, pure white and with the image of God on one side and a representation of the Annunciation on the other.

Her face, lifted in solemn ecstasy, is illumined by the sunlight that streams in through the high windows as a symbol of divine approval, and in her gratitude to heaven she seems, for a moment, to have forgotten the scene of which she is a part. Does she see the end that is so near — the capture by the English, the trial for sorcery, the scaffold high above the crowded square at Rouen?

THE DEATH OF JEANNE D'ARC

[1431]

BY MARY ROGERS BANGS

[AFTER the coronation of Charles VII, Joan of Arc pleaded to be allowed to return to her home. Even though she declared that her Voices had given her no commands to do more and that her power had ended, the French had no idea of giving up such a leader, and Charles insisted upon her remaining with the army. From that hour she met little but failure, and in 1430 she was captured by the Duke of Burgundy and given up to the English. She was brought before the Inquisition and tried as a sorceress in the Church Court, was declared guilty, and was burned at the stake. This was in 1431. In 1875, the question of her canonization was considered. In 1902, she was proclaimed "Venerable," a step on the way to being accepted as a "Saint."

The Editor.]

AT about nine o'clock, she mounted the tumbril which should bear her to the Old Market, a square not far from the river. She wore a long black robe and a woman's coif; Massieu and Ladvenu rode with her, and several scores of English soldiers, armed with battle-axes and swords, formed the guard.

The story goes that Loiselleur jumped on the cart as it was moving and begged her forgiveness, weeping bitterly, and that the guards drove him off and would have slain him later if Warwick had not interfered. That may have been part of the legend which grew up at Rouen after her death, when those who had part in it

185

were pointed out with hatred, and men said that all who were so guilty came to some shameful end. And an Englishman who had sworn to give a fagot to her burning was stricken down as he saw a dove ascending from the flames and the name *Jesus* written there, and was borne off by his companions to a neighboring tavern. Another Englishman had declared her soul was in the hands of God; and Canon Alépée, an assessor, was heard to say: "God grant that my soul may be where the soul of that woman is." Manchon was so disturbed that he was terrified for a month, and bought a missal with his clerk's pay that he might pray for her soul. And that same afternoon the executioner had come to the Dominican convent, and told Brother Martin Ladvenu that he feared much he should be damned, for he had burned a saint; never had he been so afraid at any burning. He had cast her ashes into the Seine, but her heart — that great heart that had held all France — would not burn. And forthwith he made his confession; he had erred and repented of what he had done, for he held her to be a good woman.

Three scaffolds had been erected in the old Market Place: one for the lords, lay and clerical; one for the accused and her preacher — for she must hear yet another exhortation; one built high that all might see, with the stake for her burning. The executioner said this was cruelly done, and placed her beyond his reach, so that he could not shorten her suffering, as was the custom. Upon the pyre was a great placard, bearing the inscription: "Jeanne, self-styled the Maid, liar, mischief-maker, deceiver of the people, diviner, superstitious, blasphemer of God, presumptuous, false to the faith of Christ, boaster, idolater, cruel, dissolute, invoker of devils, apostate, schismatic, heretic."

Nicolas Midi preached the sermon that day from the text: "If one member suffer, all the members suffer with it."

The square was filled to suffocation, windows, balconies, roofs, were crowded, the great lords in steel and scarlet, the prelates in rich robes, pushed and jostled on their scaffold. Jeanne sat quietly through the sermon, gazing out over the throng to the pure and lovely line of low hill in the street's vista, looking her last on the France for which she died. Cauchon read his sentence, and recommended her to the counsel of Martin Ladvenu and Isambard de la Pierre, who attended her. Then, weeping, the Maid knelt in her last supplication. She invoked her saints and all the company of heaven to aid her, "with devotion, lamentation, and true confession of faith." Very humbly, she begged forgiveness of all men, whether of her party or the other, asking their prayers and pardoning the evil they had done her. She begged the priests each to say a mass for her soul, and again she declared that for what she had done, good or bad, she alone was to answer.

Many wept with her, Beaufort and Louis de Luxembourg were greatly moved, Cauchon shed tears, — he had good cause to weep. English soldiers, here and there, laughed, others shouted that time was passing. "How now, priests, would you have us dine here?" The crowd surged back and forth, hustling the guards about the scaffold. Without formal sentence, the bailiff hurriedly waved his hand to the executioner, with the words, "Do thy duty." A paper miter with the words, "Heretic, Relapsed, Apostate, Idolater," was set on her head, and two sergeants of the king gave her over to the executioner. Ladvenu and La Pierre never left her; to the end Massieu stood at the foot of the scaffold.

She climbed the height to her last battleground, with no more thought of fear than in the warfare of other days. *"Ayez bon courage! sus! sus!*[1]*"* But this foe she met alone. As she faced the city, she sighed: —

"Ah, Rouen, I have great fear that you shall suffer for my death."

She asked for a cross, and an Englishman broke a stick and fashioned one which she kissed devoutly and slipped into her bosom next her heart. They fetched a Crucifix from the neighboring church, and she embraced it "close and long" until she was fastened to the stake.

"Hold it on high before me until the moment of death, that the Cross on which God is hanging may be continually before my eyes."

Cauchon and one of his men came to the foot of the scaffold, and once more the terrible indictment rang out: —

"Bishop, I die by you!"

If he had hoped, in her extremity, to hear an arraignment of king, or lord, or priest, he got his desert; she had for him only the just sentence of his own damnation.

As the executioner set the fagots alight, she cried once for "Water, holy water!" and as the flames ascended, she bade Brother Isambard, who always bore aloft the Cross before her eyes, to leave her lest he come to harm. She called on St. Michael and her saints. "My Voices, my Voices, they have never deceived me."

[1] Be of good courage! on! on!

188

THE DEATH OF JEANNE D'ARC

Through the gate of fire she saw the paradise they had never ceased to promise. As the flames wrapped her from the world, she cried upon the Holy Name of Jesus, and again as her head drooped to her breast, and once more, with a loud voice: "Jesus." "By a great victory" had she been delivered.

III
FRANCE UNDER THE VALOIS KINGS

HISTORICAL NOTE

FOR two centuries and a half the kings of the House of Valois were on the throne. During the first century of this period the land was torn by the struggles of the Hundred Years' War. At its close, in 1453, France recuperated rapidly, but in the reign of Louis XI the old strife between king and aristocracy became more savage than ever. By picking quarrels with his nobles, giving them up to the executioner, and seizing their domains, by inheritance, and by royal marriages the boundaries of his land were widely enlarged by King Louis. Foreign conquest was tempting, and invasions of Italy were made, but to no permanent advantage. In 1519, Maximilian, Emperor of Germany, died, and both Francis I of France and Charles V, then King of Spain, were eager for the imperial crown, — Charles winning the prize, — and their reigns were full of hostilities.

During the early and middle part of the sixteenth century science and literature flourished, and also painting, sculpture, and architecture, to such an extent that this became one of the most brilliant periods in the history of the country. The coming of the Reformation was greeted with joy by some and with horror by others, and the latter part of the century was stained with massacres and the barbarities of civil wars.

WHERE LOUIS XI SAID HIS PRAYERS

[About 1483]

BY VICTOR HUGO

[THE following extract is not only interesting in itself, but is worthy of special note in its vivid illustration of those qualities by which Louis XI stripped the nobles of their power, and perhaps altered the course of all subsequent French history. It is impossible to estimate exactly the value of the coins mentioned in this selection. Roughly speaking, a livre was equal to about $1.40 and a livre parisis to about $1.75. A sou was one twentieth of a livre, and a denier one twelfth of a sou.

The Editor.]

THE king (Louis XI) had actually been for two days past in Paris. He was to leave it again on the day after the morrow for his fortress of Montilz les Tours. His visits to his good city of Paris were rare and short; for there he felt that he had not trap-doors, gibbets, and Scottish archers enough about him.

He had come that day to sleep in the Bastile. He disliked the great chamber which he had at the Louvre, five fathoms square, with its great chimney-piece adorned with twelve great beasts and thirteen great prophets, and its great bed, twelve feet by eleven. He was lost amid all this grandeur. This burgher king gave the preference to the Bastile, with a humble chamber and suitable bed. Besides, the Bastile was stronger than the Louvre.

This chamber which the king had reserved for himself

in the famous state-prison was spacious, and occupied the topmost floor of a turret in the keep. It was an apartment of circular form, the floor covered with shining straw-matting, the rafters of the ceiling adorned with fleurs-de-lis of pewter gilt, the spaces between them colored, wainscoted with rich woods, sprinkled with rosettes of tin, painted a fine lively green composed of orpine and wood.

There was but one long and pointed window, latticed with brass wire and iron bars, and somewhat darkened besides by beautiful stained glass, exhibiting the arms of the king and those of the queen, each pane of which cost twenty-two sous.

There was but one entrance, a modern door, with elliptic arch, covered on the inside with cloth, and having without one of those porches of Irish wood, frail structures of curious workmanship, which were still very common in old buildings one hundred and fifty years ago. "Though they disfigure and encumber the places," says Sauval peevishly, "yet will not our ancient folk put them away, but they preserve them in spite of every one."

In this chamber was to be seen none of the furniture of ordinary apartments, neither tables upon trestles, nor benches, nor forms, nor common stools in the shape of a box, nor those of a better sort, standing upon pillars and counter-pillars, at four sous apiece. Nothing was to be seen there, save a very magnificent folding armchair. The woodwork was adorned with roses painted on a red ground, and the seat was of scarlet Spanish leather, garnished with silk fringe, and studded with a thousand golden nails. This solitary chair indicated that one person only had a right to sit down in that apartment. Near the chair and close to the window was a table covered with a cloth, on which were the figures of birds. On this table were a portfolio spotted with ink, sundry parchments, pens, and a chased silver mug. At a little distance stood a chafing-dish, and a desk for the purpose of prayer, covered with crimson velvet embossed with studs of gold. Lastly, at the farthest part of the room there was a simple bed, of yellow and flesh-colored damask, without lace or any trimming but plain fringe. This bed, famed for having witnessed the sleep or the sleeplessness of Louis XI, was to be seen two hundred years ago in the house of a councilor of state.

Such was the chamber commonly called "The place where Louis of France said his prayers."

At the moment of our ushering the reader into this retreat it was very dark. An hour had elapsed since the tolling of the curfew; it was night, and there was only one flickering wax candle upon the table, to light five persons who formed several groups in the chamber.

The first on whom the light fell was a personage superbly dressed in hose, scarlet close-bodied coat striped with silver, and a surtout of cloth of gold with black designs, and trimmed with fur. This splendid costume, upon which the light played, seemed to be braided with flame at all its folds. The wearer had his arms embroidered at the breast in gaudy colors; a chevron, with a deer passant in the base of the shield. The escutcheon was supported on the dexter side by an olive branch, and on the sinister by a buck's horn. This personage carried in his belt a rich dagger, the hilt of which, of silver gilt, was chased in the form of a crest, and terminated in a count's coronet. He carried his head high, had a haughty bearing, and an ill-natured look. At the first glance you discovered in his countenance an expression of arrogance; at the second, of cunning.

He stood bareheaded, with a long paper in his hand, before the armchair, on which was seated a person, shabbily dressed, his body ungracefully bent, one knee crossed over the other, and his elbow upon the table. Figure to yourself, on the seat of rich Cordova leather, a pair of slender thighs and spindle-shanks, appareled in black knitted woolen stuff; a body wrapped in a surtout of fustian trimmed with fur, which showed much more leather than hair; lastly, to crown all, an old greasy hat of the coarsest black cloth, in the band of which were stuck a number of small leaden figures. This, with a dirty skull-cap, which suffered scarcely a hair to struggle from beneath it, was all that could be seen of the seated personage. His head was so bent forward upon his breast as to throw into the shade the whole of his face, excepting the tip of his nose, on which a ray of light fell; it was evidently a long one. The wrinkled, attenuated hand indicated that he was old. It was Louis XI.

At some distance behind the two persons we have described, two men, dressed in the Flemish fashion, were conversing in a low voice. It was not so dark where they stood but that one who attended the representation of Gringoire's mystery would have recognized in them two of the principal Flemish envoys, Guillaume Rym, the sagacious pensionary of Ghent, and Jacques Coppenole, the popular hosier. It will be recollected that these two persons were mixed up with the secret politics of Louis XI.

Lastly, at the opposite end of the room, near the door, stood, motionless as a statue, a short, thick-set man in military attire, with coat of arms embroidered on the breast, whose square face without brow, eyes on a level with the top of the head, and ears hidden by two large pent-houses of straight hair, partook at once of the dog's and the tiger's.

All were uncovered excepting the king.

The nobleman standing near the king was reading to him a long memorial, to which his majesty seemed to listen attentively. The two Flemings were whispering together.

" By the Rood!" muttered Coppenole, "I am tired of standing. Are no chairs allowed here?"

Rym answered by a shake of the head, accompanied by a discreet smile.

"By the mass!" resumed Coppenole, who was quite miserable to be obliged to speak in so low a tone, "I have a good mind to clap myself down on the floor, as I might do at home."

"Nay, Master Jacques, prithee do no such thing."

"Hey-day, Master Guillaume! must one keep on one's legs all the while one is here, then?"

"Even so, or on your knees," replied Rym.

At that moment the king raised his voice. They were silent.

" Fifty sous the gowns of our serving men, and twelve livres the cloaks of the clerks of our crown! Why, 't is throwing gold away by tons! Are you distraught, Olivier?"

As he thus spoke, the old king raised his head. About his neck might then be seen glistening the golden balls

of the collar of St. Michael. The rays of the candle fell
full upon his skinny and morose face. He snatched the
paper from the hands of the reader.

"You will ruin us!" he cried, running his hollow eye
over it. "What means all this? What need have we for
such prodigious establishment? Two chaplains, at the
rate of ten livres each per month, and a clerk of the
chapel at one hundred sous! A valet-de-chambre, at
ninety livres by the year! Four esquires of the kitchen,
at six score livres by the year, each! An overseer of the
roast, another of the vegetables, another of the sauces, a
head cook, a butler, and two assistants, at ten livres each
per month! Two scullions at eight livres! A groom and
his two helpers at twenty-four livres the month! A porter, a pastry cook, a baker, two carters, at sixty livres
by the year each! And the marshal of the forges, six
score livres! And the master of the chamber of our
exchequer, twelve hundred livres! And the controller,
five hundred! And I know not how many more! 'T is
enough to drive one mad! To pay the wages of our servants, France is plundered. All the ingots in the Louvre
will melt away before such a fire of expense! We will sell
our plate! And next year, if God and our Lady" (here
he lifted his hat) "grant us life, we will take our diet-
drink out of a pewter pot."

As he thus spoke he cast a look at the silver mug
which glistened upon the table. He coughed and then
proceeded: "Master Olivier, the princes who rule over
great countries, such as kings and emperors, ought never
to suffer habits of expense to creep into their households;
for that fire runs further and catches the provinces. Give
me not occasion to repeat this, Master Olivier. Our ex-

penditure increases every year. The thing likes us not. Why, Pasque Dieu! till '79 it never exceeded thirty-six thousand livres; in '80 it amounted to forty-three thousand six hundred and nineteen livres — I have the exact sum in my head; in '81, to sixty-six thousand six hundred and eighty; and this year, by the faith of my body, it will not be under eighty thousand! Doubled in four years; monstrous!"

He paused to take breath, and then began again with warmth: "I see about me none but people who fatten upon my leanness. Ye suck crowns out of me at every pore!"

All present maintained profound silence. It was one of those paroxysms which must be left to themselves. He continued:—

"It is like that petition in Latin from the nobles of France, that we would reëstablish what they call the great charges of the crown! Charges, in good sooth! crushing charges! Ah, gentlemen, ye say that we are not a king to reign *dapifero nullo, buticalario nullo!* [1] We will show you, Pasque Dieu! whether we are not a king."

Here he smiled in the feeling of his power: his wrath was softened, and he turned toward the Flemings.

"Look you, Compère Guillaume, the grand master of the pantry, the grand chamberlain, the grand seneschal, are of less use than the meanest serving-man. Remember that, Compère Coppenole! They are good for nothing. Such useless attendants on a king are very like the four evangelists about the dial of the great clock of the palace, which Philip Brille has lately beautified.

[1] Without serving man, without butler.

They are gilt, but they mark not the hour, and the hand can go without them."

For a moment he appeared thoughtful, and then, shaking his old head, he added: "No, no; by our Lady, I am not Philip Brille, and I will not new-gild the grand vassals. Go on, Olivier." The person to whom he spoke took up the paper, and began reading again with a loud voice: —

"To Adam Tenon, clerk to the keeper of the seals of the provosty of Paris, for silver, making and engraving said seals, which have been new made, because the former could no longer be used, by reason of their being old and worn out — twelve livres parisis.

"To Guillaume Frère, the sum of four livres four sous parisis, as his salary and wages for feeding the pigeons in the two dove-cotes of the Hôtel des Tournelles, in the months of January, February, and March of this present year; and for this there have been given seven quarters of barley.

"To a Gray Friar, for confessing a criminal, four sous parisis."

The king listened in silence. He coughed from time to time; he would then lift the mug to his lips and swallow a mouthful, at the same time making a wry face.

"In this year there have been made by order of justice, by sound of trumpet, in the public places of Paris, fifty-six proclamations — the account to be settled.

"For having made quest and search in certain places, both in Paris and elsewhere, after moneys which were said to be concealed there, but none found, forty-five livres parisis."

"Bury a crown to dig up a sou!" said the king.

WHERE LOUIS XI SAID HIS PRAYERS

"For putting six panes of white glass in the place where the iron cage is at the Hôtel des Tournelles, thirteen sous.

"For two new sleeves to the king's old doublet, twenty sous.

"For a pot of grease to grease the king's boots, fifteen deniers.

"For new-making a sty for the king's black hogs, thirty livres parisis.

"For sundry partitions, planks, and doors, made to shut up the lions at St. Pol, twenty-two livres."

"Costly beasts those!" said Louis XI. "No matter: 't is a seemly magnificence in a king. There is a great red lion which I am very fond of for his engaging ways. Have you seen him, Master Guillaume? It is right that princes should keep extraordinary animals. We kings ought to have lions for our dogs and tigers for our cats. What is great befits crowns. In the time of Jupiter's pagans, when the people offered to the churches a hundred oxen and a hundred sheep, the emperors gave a hundred lions and a hundred eagles. That was proud and magnificent. The kings of France have always had these bellowings around their thrones: nevertheless, people must do me the justice to say that I spend less money in that way than my predecessors, and that I am exceedingly moderate on the score of lions, bears, elephants, and leopards. Go on, Master Olivier. We wished to say thus much to our Flanders friends."

Guillaume Rym made a profound obeisance, while Coppenole, with his sulky mien, looked like one of those bears which his majesty had been talking of. The king did not notice this. He sipped at the mug, and spitting

out the drink, exclaimed: "Faugh! the horrid ptisan!"
The reader proceeded:—

"For the feed of a vagabond knave shut up for these
six months in the lodge of the slaughter-house, till it is
settled what to do with him, six livres, four sous."

"What is that?" said the king—"feed what ought
to hang! Pasque Dieu! not another sou will I give for
that feed. Olivier, settle that business with Monsieur
d'Estouteville, and this very night make me the needful
preparations for wedding this gallant with the gallows.
Go on."

Olivier made a mark with his thumb-nail against the
last item, and proceeded: —

"To Henriet Cousin, master executioner of Paris, the
sum of sixty sous parisis, to him adjudged and ordered
by Monseigneur the Provost of Paris, for that he did
buy, at the command of the said Sieur the Provost, a
great sword for executing and beheading persons condemned by justice for their misdeeds, and did provide
a sheath and all thereunto appertaining, and likewise did
get the old sword ground and repaired, by reason that it
was broken and notched in doing justice upon Messire
Louis of Luxembourg, as may more fully appear —"

The king interrupted the reader. "That is enough; I
order that sum with all my heart. Those are expenses
which I think not of. I never grudge moneys so laid out.
Go on."

"For new-making a great cage —"

"Ah!" said the king, grasping the arms of his chair
with both hands, "I knew that I had come to this
Bastile for something. Stop, Master Olivier; I will look
at that cage myself. You shall read the items while I

examine it. Gentlemen of Flanders, come and look at it — 't is a curious thing."

He then rose, leaned upon the arm of the reader, motioned to the kind of mute standing before the door to precede him, and the two Flemings to follow, and left the chamber.

The royal party was reinforced at the door of the retreat by men at arms encumbered with iron, and slender pages bearing torches. It pursued its way for some time through the interior of the somber keep, perforated with staircases and corridors even into the substance of the walls. The captain of the Bastile went first, to get the wickets opened for the old king, who, bent with age and infirmity, coughed as he walked along. At each wicket every head was obliged to stoop excepting that of the old monarch. " Hum!" muttered he between his gums — for he had lost all his teeth — "we are already not far from the door of the tomb. At a low door the passenger must stoop."

At length, having passed the last wicket, so encumbered with locks and fastenings that it took nearly a quarter of an hour to open it, they entered a lofty and spacious hall in the middle of which was discovered by the light of the torches a massive cube of masonry, iron, and timber. The interior was hollow. It was one of those famous cages for prisoners of state which were called " the king's daughters." In the sides of it were two or three small windows, so closely latticed with thick iron bars that the glass could not be seen. The door was a large stone slab, like those which are laid upon graves, one of those doors which are never used but to enter: only in this case the buried person was yet living.

FRANCE

The king began to walk slowly round the little edifice, examining it with care, while Master Olivier, who followed him, read aloud to this effect: "For having new-made a great wooden cage of thick joists, girders, and planks, being nine feet long by eight wide, and seven feet from floor to ceiling, planed and clamped with strong iron clamps, the which hath been set in a chamber situate in one of the towers of the Bastile St. Antoine, in which cage is put and kept, by command of our lord the king, a prisoner who aforetime dwelt in a cage that was old, crazy, and decayed. There were used for the said new cage ninety-six joists, fifty-two uprights, ten girders, three fathoms in length; and there were employed nineteen carpenters in squaring, cutting, and working all said timber in the court of the Bastile for twenty days —"

"Capital heart of oak!" said the king, rapping the wood with his knuckle.

"There were used for this cage," continued the reader, "two hundred and twenty thick iron clamps of nine and eight feet, the rest of middling length, with the screws, nuts, and bands to the said clamps; the whole of the said iron weighing three thousand seven hundred and thirty-five pounds; besides eight stout holdfasts to fasten the said cage, with the nails, weighing together two hundred and eighteen pounds; without reckoning the iron grating to the windows of the chamber in which the cage is placed, the iron door of that chamber, and other things—"

"A great deal of iron," said the king, "to repress the levity of one mind!"

"The whole amounts to three hundred and seventeen livres, five sous, seven deniers."

WHERE LOUIS XI SAID HIS PRAYERS

"Pasque Dieu!" exclaimed the king. At this impreca-
tion, which was the favorite oath of Louis XI, some
person appeared to rouse within the cage. Chains were
heard trailing upon the floor, and a faint voice, which
seemed to issue from a tomb, cried, "Mercy, sire!
mercy!" The person who thus spoke could not be seen.

"Three hundred and seventeen livres, five sous, seven
deniers!" repeated Louis XI.

The lamentable voice which issued from the cage had
thrilled all present, including Master Olivier himself.
The king alone appeared not to have heard it. At his
command, Master Olivier began reading again, and His
Majesty coolly continued his examination of the cage.

"Besides the above, there has been paid to a mason
who made the holes to receive the bars of the windows,
and the floor of the chamber where the cage is, because
the floor could not have borne this cage by reason of its
weight — twenty-seven livres, fourteen sous parisis."

The voice again began moaning: "Mercy, for Heav-
en's sake, sire! I assure Your Majesty that it was the
Cardinal of Angers who did the treason, and not I."

"The mason is high," said the king. "Proceed."

Olivier continued: —

"To a joiner for windows, bedstead, and other things,
twenty livres, two sous parisis."

The voice likewise continued: "Alas! sire! will you
not hear me? I protest that it was not I who wrote that
thing to Monseigneur de Guyenne, but Cardinal Balue!"

"The joiner is dear," observed the king. "Is that
all?"

"No, sire. To a glazier, for the windows of the said
chamber, forty-six sous, eight deniers parisis."

"Pardon, sire! pardon! Is it not enough that all my goods have been given to my judges, my plate to Monsieur de Torcy, my library to Master Pierre Doriolle, my tapestry to the Governor of Roussillon? I am innocent. For fourteen years I have pined in an iron cage. Mercy, sire! mercy! You will be rewarded for it in heaven."

"Master Olivier," said the king, "the total?"

"Three hundred and sixty-seven livres, eight sous, three deniers parisis."

"By our Lady!" exclaimed the king, "an extravagant cage."

Snatching the paper from the hand of Master Olivier, he looked by turns at the account and at the cage, and began to reckon up himself upon his fingers. Meanwhile, the prisoner continued wailing and sobbing. It was truly doleful in the dark. The bystanders looked at one another and turned pale.

"Fourteen years, sire! fourteen long years! ever since the month of April, 1469. In the name of the Blessed Mother, sire, hearken to me. Your Majesty has all this time been enjoying the warmth of the sun. Am I never more to see the daylight? Be merciful, sire! Clemency is a right royal virtue which turneth aside the current of wrath. Doth Your Majesty believe that at the hour of death it is a great consolation to a king not to have any offense unpunished? Besides, sire, it was not I, but Monsieur d'Angers, who was guilty of the treachery against Your Majesty. Would that you saw the thick chain fastened to my leg, and the great iron ball at the end of it, much heavier than it need be! Ah! sire! take pity on me!"

"Olivier," said the king, shaking his head, "I perceive that I am charged twenty sous by the load for lime, though it may be bought for twelve. Send back this account."

Turning from the cage, he began to move toward the door of the chamber. The wretched prisoner judged from the receding torches and noise that the king was going. "Sire! sire!" cried he, in tones of despair. The door shut. He saw nothing, he heard nothing save the husky voice of the jailer chanting a stanza of a song of that day on the subject of his own misfortunes: —

> "Maître Jehan Balue
> Has lost out of view
> His good bishoprics all:
> Monsieur de Verdun
> Cannot now boast of one;
> They are gone, one and all."

The king returned in silence to his retreat, followed by his train, who were thrilled by the last heart-rending wailings of the prisoner. His Majesty turned abruptly toward the governor of the Bastile.

"By the bye," said he, "was there not some one in that cage?"

"In good sooth, sire, there was," replied the governor, astonished at the question.

"Who, then?"

"The Bishop of Verdun."

The king knew that better than anybody else, but this was his way.

"Ah!" said he, as naturally as if he had but just thought of it; "Guillaume de Harancourt, a friend of Monsieur de Balue. A good fellow of a bishop!"

FRANCE

The door of the retreat presently opened and again closed upon the five personages to whom the reader was introduced at the beginning of this chapter, and who resumed their places, their whispering conversation, and their attitudes.

ANNE OF BRITTANY AND HER COURT

[1476–1514]

BY CATHERINE CHARLOTTE

[ANNE was the daughter and heiress of the Duke of Brittany, and her suitors were many, all eager to win the fair land of Brittany with its hundred leagues of seacoast, and its sturdy people. Finally, she became the wife of Charles VIII, King of France. The French had no idea of loosening their grasp on Anne's noble dowry, and it was made a condition of the marriage settlement that if Charles died without a son, she should never marry any one except his successor. This successor was Louis XII, and she became his wife.

The Editor.]

IN the course of her double reign of twenty-two years, Anne initiated many changes in the social régime of the court. Not only was she a patroness of learning, but was herself one of the learned ladies of her day. She read the ancient Greek and Latin authors, and had a considerable acquaintance with modern languages. To eminent men of letters she gave a very gracious reception, and was fond of conversing with them. The poets of the period—poets certainly of no great fame, yet a pleiad of twinkling luminaries, precursor of one of brighter lights—found a patroness in the queen. Amongst them was Jean Marot, father of the more famous Clement; the youthful Clement being also her protégé, and his earlier productions read in the queen's apartment, while she and "ses filles" worked at their point lace or tapestry.

A number of young ladies of noble birth, whom at first she was accustomed to call "ses filles," but afterwards gave them the title of "filles d'honneur," or maids of honor, resided in the palace under the queen's protection. They were carefully trained and educated to become her and her daughters' companions. Some were orphans, but all were slenderly provided for. When opportunity offered, however, advantageously to marry her maids, she either added considerably to their own small fortune, or, when none was forthcoming, generously gave one.

Before the time of "Madame Anne, the duchess-queen," one might have well supposed that the Salic law not only rigidly excluded woman from the succession to the throne, but was as jealously intolerant of her presence at court — if court it could be called, where no queen presided, no ladies attended.

The king, princes, courtiers, and nobility generally, when not actually engaged in war, which was seldom, or occupied with public affairs, — which meant chiefly devising new wars and new taxes, — found the relaxation best suited to their tastes and habits in rough sports and games. There was the mimic warfare of jousts and tournaments, by which the ancient spirit of chivalry was supposed to be sustained. There were the great hunts in the Forests of Chaumont, Fontainebleau, Saint-Germain, or Vincennes; and when the day's exciting sport was ended, there was the amply spread supper-table to repair to, where jesting, practical joking, and boisterous mirth — partly inspired by goblets of Hypocras, champagne, or the potent old wines of the Juraçon — gave a keener zest to the viands killed in the chase.

Conspicuous amongst these were the roebuck, roasted whole and served with a sauce of balm-mint and fennel (recently imported into France, with many other of the vegetable products of Italy), the highly-flavored haunch, and the wild boar's head—royal dishes all of them, and substantial ones too, on which only the great ones of the earth might then presume to feast. Italian cookery as yet scarcely satisfied the hearty appetites of these robust cavaliers, whose pleasures and amusements were all external, and who took but two meals a day.

To the calmer enjoyments of domestic life the men of this period, and especially those of the upper ranks, were utterly strangers. But a change in manners began, and, as regards social life, the step that may be "considered as signalizing the passage from the Middle Ages to modern times, and from ancient barbarism to civilization," was taken when, at the close of the fifteenth century, Anne of Brittany — the first queen-consort of France who held a separate court — desired the ministers of State and foreign ambassadors who attended to offer their congratulations on her marriage with Louis XII, to bring their wives and daughters with them when next they paid their respects to her. To the ladies themselves she sent her invitation, or royal command, to leave their gloomy feudal abodes, where they were sometimes immured for years together, and repair to the court of their sovereign lady at the Palais des Tournelles or Château de Blois.

The moment was well chosen. It was a festive occasion, and the fair châtelaines were by no means reluctant to obey the summons of their queen. But the lords of those ladies, and especially the more elderly ones, murmured greatly at the attempted startling innovation. Hitherto they were accustomed to expend their revenues chiefly on themselves. They must have gay court dresses, picturesque hunting costumes, horses and dogs, and all the paraphernalia of the chase. Besides these, there was the splendid panoply of war — the burnished helmets, the polished steel armor in which they were wont to encase themselves when, attended each by a suite of four or five horsemen similarly equipped, they went forth to fight their foes. Naturally, then, they were little disposed to incur any new outlay for wives and daughters that necessitated curtailment of their own.

By the younger courtiers Louis XII was considered rather penurious. But, in fact, he was so unwilling to burden his people with taxes, that beyond greatly embellishing his châteaux of Amboise and Blois (for which he employed native artists, under the direction of the great architect Fra Giocondo), he refrained from gratifying any expensive tastes. But Anne disbursed with a more liberal hand, and kept up great state at her separate court of Blois and Des Tournelles. She also dressed with great elegance and magnificence, and required the ladies who attended her to do likewise.

"What she has in her mind to do," writes at this time the Ambassador Contarini, "she will certainly accomplish, whether it be by tears, smiles, or entreaties." And quietly but firmly, wholly disregarding the opposition of the elderly nobles, she effected the revolution she had long desired, in the social régime of the court. The younger nobility and the élite of the world of art and letters entered readily into her views, and the receptions in the queen's apartment soon became a center of great attraction. There, following the Italian fashion — which Charles VIII and Louis XII, it appears, had both found much to their taste — sorbets and iced lemonade were served. Her banquets, too — for the duchess-queen had her banquets as well as the king — were arranged with more order and with especial regard to what was due to the ladies. Each lady had now her cavalier, which had not always been the case. Each guest had also a separate plate — for Anne would not dip in another's dish, though it were even the king's. Doubtless, the forks, long in use in Italy, would soon have been introduced at her table, had the reforming queen been spared. But they had yet to wait a century before finding in France a patron in the Duc de Montausier. *En attendant*, rose-water was handed round in silver basins.

The senior nobles, however, made no scruple of strongly hinting to the king that he would do well in this and other matters to yield less readily to the queen's dominion.

To this he replied, "Some indulgence should be conceded to a woman who loves her husband and is solicitous both for his honor and her own."

Yet, sometimes he did resist her wishes, and by fables and parables — notably his favorite one of the does which had lost their antlers because they desired to put themselves on an equality with the stags — showed her that it was not seemly that woman's will should always prevail over her husband's. This mild method of administering reproof to "his Bretonne," as he was accustomed to call his queen, seems to have often

213

FRANCE

amused, if it did not always convince her. However, to the Bretonne queen the merit undoubtedly belongs of setting the ladies of her court, in an age of lax morality, a much needed example of virtuous conduct and conjugal fidelity, as well as of the useful employment of time and the cultivation of their minds.

THE DEATH OF THE CHEVALIER BAYARD

[1524]

FROM THE OLD CHRONICLES

[LOUIS XII conquered Lombardy; but Germany, Spain, and England were afraid that France was becoming too powerful, and by their united forces Louis was driven out of Italy. When Francis I came to the throne, he succeeded in recovering the lost Italian possessions. He tried his best to get more, for Charles V was ruling both Germany and Spain; and now it was Charles who was becoming too powerful. The turn of France to make an attack had come. This attack was made upon the holdings of Charles in Italy. Francis won neither land nor glory; and he lost the famous Chevalier Bayard, the knight "without fear and without reproach."

The Editor.]

BAYARD, last as well as first in the fight, according to his custom, charged at the head of some men-at-arms upon the Imperialists who were pressing the French too closely, when he was himself struck by a shot from an arquebus, which shattered his reins. "Jesus, my God," he cried, "I am dead!" He then took his sword by the handle, and kissed the cross-hilt of it as the sign of the cross, saying aloud as he did so, "Have pity on me, O God, according to thy great mercy (*Miserere mei, Deus, secundum magnam misericordiam tuam*);" thereupon he became incontinently quite pale, and all but fell; but he still had heart enough to grasp the pommel of the saddle, and remained in that condition until a young gentleman, his own house-steward, helped him to dismount and set him down under a tree, with his face to the enemy. The poor gentleman burst into tears, seeing his good master so mortally hurt that remedy there was none; but the good knight consoled him gently, saying, "Jacques, my friend, leave off thy mourning; it is God's will to take me out of this world; by His grace I have lived long therein, and have received therein blessings and honors more than my due. All the regret I feel at dying is that I have not done my duty so well as I ought. I pray you, Jacques, my friend, let them not take me up from this spot, for, when I move, I feel all the pains that one can feel, short of death which will seize me soon."

The Constable de Bourbon, being informed of his wound, came to him, saying, "Bayard, my friend, I am sore distressed at your mishap; there is nothing for it but patience; give not way to melancholy; I will send in quest of the best surgeons in this country, and, by God's help, you will soon be healed."

"My lord," answered Bayard, "there is no pity for me; I die, having done my duty; but I have pity for you, to see you serving against your king, your country, and your oath." Bourbon withdrew without a word.

The Marquis of Pescara came passing by. "Would to God, gentle Sir Bayard," said he, "that it had cost me a quart of my blood, without meeting my death, that I had been doomed not to taste meat for two years, and that I held you safe and sound my prisoner, for, by the treatment I showed you, you should have understanding of how much I esteemed the high prowess that was in you." He ordered his people to rig up a tent over Bayard, and to forbid any noise near him, so that he might die in peace.

THE DEATH OF THE CHEVALIER BAYARD

Bayard's own gentlemen would not, at any price, leave him. "I do beseech you," he said to them, "to get you gone; else you might fall into the enemy's hands, and that would profit me nothing, for all is over with me. To God I commend you, my good friends; and I recommend to you my poor soul; and salute, I pray you, the king our master, and tell him that I am distressed at being no longer able to do him service, for I had good will thereto. And to my lords the princes of France, and all my lords my comrades, and generally to all gentlemen of the most honored realm of France when ye see them."

He lived for two or three hours yet. There was brought to him a priest to whom he confessed, and then he yielded up his soul to God; whereat all the enemy had mourning incredible. Five days after his death, on the 5th of May, 1524, Beaurain wrote to Charles V, "Sir, albeit Sir Bayard was your enemy's servant, yet was it pity of his death, for 't was a gentle knight, well beloved of every one, and one that lived as good a life as ever any man of his condition. And in truth he fully showed it by his end, for it was the most beautiful that I ever heard tell of." By the chiefs of the Spanish army certain gentlemen were commissioned to bear him to the church, where solemn service was done for him during two days. Then, by his own servitors was he carried into Dauphiny, and, on passing through the territory of the Duke of Savoy, where the body rested, he did it as many honors as if it had been his own brother.

When the news of his death was known in Dauphiny, I trow that never for a thousand years died there gentleman of the country mourned in such sort. He was borne from church to church, at first near Grenoble, where all my lords of the parliament-court of Dauphiny, my lords of the exchequer, pretty well all the nobles of the country and the greater part of all the burgesses, townsfolk, and villagers came half a league to meet the body: then into the Church of Notre Dame, in the aforesaid Grenoble, where a solemn service was done for him; then to a house of *Minimes*, which had been founded aforetime by his good uncle the Bishop of Grenoble, Laurens Alment; and there he was honorably interred. Then every one withdrew to his own house, but for a month there was a stop put to festivals, dances, banquets, and all other pastimes. 'Las! they had good reason; for greater loss could not have come upon the country.

FRANCIS I AND CHARLES V IN ST. DENIS

BY ANTOINE JEAN GROS

(French artist, 1771–1835)

THE enmity between Charles V and Francis I kept Europe in a turmoil throughout their reigns. By the efforts of Cardinal Wolsey, Henry VIII of England, Charles, and the Pope united against Francis. At Pavia, in 1525, he was defeated and captured, and was released by Charles only after making the most humiliating promises. The Pope absolved him from these promises, and Charles in wrath sacked Rome and imprisoned the Pope. There was an occasional interval of peace, the most noted being in 1540, when Charles became the guest of Francis and was entertained sumptuously for six days.

The scene represented in the picture portrays the visit of the two sovereigns, made at the request of Charles, to the Church of St. Denis, the mauosleum of the rulers of France. Francis is pointing out the tomb of Louis XII, which is not visible in this part of the picture. On the right of Charles stands Henri, Dauphin of France. On the left of Francis is his son Charles of Orleans. In the extreme right of the foreground, attended by two priests, is the Cardinal de Bourbon, Abbot of St. Denis, with miter and crosier. At the left, the Constable de Montmorency, sword in hand, stands between Henri d'Albret and the Duke of Guise. In the tribune at the back are Catharine de' Medici, Diane de Poitiers, la belle Féronnière, the young Montaigne, Rabelais, and other famous persons. Standing just within the arched door of the stairway is a chaplain holding two lights, ready to guide the monarchs to the royal vaults.

KING FRANCIS I AND THE GOLDSMITH

[1540]

BY BENVENUTO CELLINI

[THROUGH the wiles of his enemies, the Italian goldsmith, Benvenuto Cellini, was imprisoned by the Pope. He escaped once, but was soon captured and thrown back into his dungeon. Francis I, King of France, succeeded, through Cardinal Ferrara, in bringing about his release, and sent for him to come immediately to France.

The Editor.]

WE found the court of the French monarch at Fontaine-bleau, where we directly waited on the cardinal, who caused apartments to be assigned us: we spent the night very agreeably, and were well accommodated. The next day the wagon came up, so we took out what belonged to us, and the cardinal having informed the king of our arrival, he expressed a desire to see me directly. I waited on His Majesty accordingly, with the cup and basin so often mentioned: being come into his presence I kissed his knee, and he received me in the most gracious manner imaginable. I then returned His Majesty thanks for having procured me my liberty, observing that every good and just prince like His Majesty was bound to protect all men eminent for any talent, especially such as were innocent like myself; and that such meritorious actions were set down in the books of the Almighty before any other virtuous deeds whatever.

The good king listened to me until I had made an end

of my speech, and expressed my gratitude in terms worthy of so great a monarch. When I had done, he took the cup and basin, and said: "It is my real opinion that the ancients were never capable of working in so exquisite a taste. I have seen all the masterpieces of the greatest artists of Italy, but never before beheld anything that gave me such high satisfaction." This the king said in French to the Cardinal of Ferrara, at the same time paying me several other compliments greater even than this. He then turned about and said to me in Italian: "Benvenuto, indulge yourself and take your pleasure for a few days; in the mean time I shall think of putting you into a way of making some curious piece of work for me." The Cardinal of Ferrara soon perceived that His Majesty was highly pleased with my arrival, and that the specimens he had seen of my abilities had excited in him an inclination to employ me in other works of greater importance.

Whilst we followed the court, we may justly be said to have been in great straits, and the reason is that the king travels with upwards of twelve thousand horses, his retinue in time of peace being eighteen thousand. We sometimes danced attendance in places where there were hardly two houses, were often under the necessity of pitching very inconvenient tents, and lived like gypsies. I frequently solicited the cardinal to put the king in mind of employing me: he made answer that it was best His Majesty should think of it himself, advising me to appear sometimes in his presence, when he was at table. This advice I followed, and the king one day called me to him whilst he was at dinner. He told me in Italian that he proposed I should soon undertake some pieces of great importance; that he would soon let me know where I was to work, and provide me with tools and all things necessary; at the same time he conversed with me in a free and easy manner, on a variety of different subjects.

The Cardinal of Ferrara was present, for he almost always dined with the king: the conversation being over, His Majesty rose from the table, and the cardinal said in my favor, as I was informed afterwards: "May it please Your Majesty, this Benvenuto has a great desire to be at work, and it would be a pity to let such a genius lose his time." The king answered that he was very right, and desired him to settle with me all that concerned my subsistence. The cardinal, who had received the commission in the morning, sent for me that night after supper, and told me from the king that His Majesty had resolved I should immediately begin to work; but that he desired first to know my terms. To this the cardinal added, "It is my opinion that if His Majesty allows you a salary of three hundred crowns a year, it will be abundantly sufficient. Next I must request of you that you would leave the whole management of the affair to me, for every day I have opportunities of doing good in this great kingdom, and I shall be always ready to assist you to the best of my power." I answered, "Without my ever soliciting Your Reverence, you promised, upon leaving me behind you in Ferrara, never to let me quit Italy or bring me into France without first apprising me upon what terms I was to be with His Majesty. But instead of acquainting me with the terms, you sent me express orders to ride post, as if riding post was my business. If you had then mentioned three hundred crowns as a salary, I should not have thought it worth my while to stir for double the sum. I notwithstanding return thanks to Heaven and to Your Reverence, since God has made you the instrument of so great a blessing as my deliverance from a long imprisonment I therefore declare that all the hurt you can do me is not equal to a thousandth part of the great blessing for which I am indebted to you. I thank you with all my heart, and take my leave of you, and in whatever part of the world I shall abide I shall always pray for Your Reverence." The cardinal then said in a passion, "Go wherever you think proper, for it is impossible to serve any man against his will." Some of his niggardly followers then said: "This man must have high opinion of his merit, since he refuses three hundred crowns"; others amongst the connoisseurs replied: "The king will never find another artist equal to this man, and yet the cardinal is for abating his demands as he would bargain for a fagot of wood." It was Signor Luigi Alamanni that said this, the same who at Rome gave the model of the salt-cellar, a person of great accomplishments and a favorer of men of genius. I was afterwards informed that he had expressed himself in this manner before several of the noblemen and courtiers. This happened at a castle in Dauphiny, the name of which I cannot recollect; but there we lodged that evening.

Having left the cardinal, I repaired to my lodging, for we always took up our quarters at some place not far from the court, but this was three miles distant. I was accompanied by a secretary of the Cardinal of Ferrara, who happened to be quartered in the same place. By the way, this secretary, with a troublesome and impertinent curiosity, was continually asking me what I intended to do with myself when I got home, and what salary I had expected. I, who was half angry, half grieved, and highly provoked at having taken a journey to France, and being afterwards offered no more than three hundreds crowns a year, never once returned him any answer: I said nothing more to him than that I knew all. Upon my arrival at our quarters, I found Paolo and Ascanio, who were waiting for me. I appeared to be in great disorder, and they, knowing my temper, forced me to tell them what had happened. Seeing the poor young men terribly frightened, I said to them, "To-morrow morning I will give you money enough to bear your charges home, for I propose going by myself about some business of importance: it is an affair I have long revolved in my mind, and there is no occasion for your knowing it."

Our apartments was next to that of the secretary, and it seems very probable that he acquainted the cardinal with all that I intended, and was firmly resolved to do; though I could never discover whether he did or not. I lay restless the whole night, and was in the utmost impatience for the approach of day, in order to put my design in execution. As soon as morning dawned, I ordered my horses should be in readiness, and having got myself ready likewise, I gave the young men all that I had brought with me, with fifty gold ducats over, and kept as many for myself, together with the diamond which the duke had made me a present of; taking with me only two shirts and some very indifferent clothes to travel in, which I had upon my back. But I could not get rid of the two young men, who were bent upon going with me by all means. I did my utmost to dissuade them, and said, "One of you has only the first down upon his cheeks and the other has not even that; I have instructed you to the utmost of my poor abilities, insomuch that you are become the two most expert young men in your way in Italy. Are you not then ashamed that you cannot contrive to help yourselves, but must be always in leading-strings? This is a sad affair, and if I were to dismiss you without money, what would you say? Be gone directly, and may God give you a thousand blessings! so farewell."

I thereupon turned my horse about, and left them both bathed in tears. I took a delightful path through a wood, intending to ride at least forty miles that same day, to the most remote corner I could possibly reach. I had already ridden about two miles, and in the little way I had gone formed a resolution to work at no place where I was known; nor did I ever intend to work upon any other figure but a Christ, about three cubits high, willing to make as near an approach as possible to that extraordinary beauty which he had so often displayed to me in visions. Having now settled everything in my own mind, I bent my course towards the Holy Sepulcher, thinking I was not got to such a distance that nobody could overtake me.

Just at this time I found myself pursued by some horsemen, which occasioned me some apprehensions, for I had been informed that these parts were infested by numbers of freebooters, called *Venturieri*, who rob and murder passengers, and who, though many of them are hanged almost every day, do not seem to be in the least intimidated. Upon the near approach of the horsemen,

I perceived them to be one of the king's messengers accompanied by Ascanio. The former upon coming up to me said, "I command you, in the king's name, to repair to him directly." I answered, "You come from the Cardinal of Ferrara, for which reason I am resolved not to go with you." The man replied that, since I would not go by fair means, he had authority to command the people to bind me hand and foot like a prisoner. Ascanio at the same time did his utmost to persuade me to comply, reminding me that whenever the King of France caused a man to be imprisoned, it was generally five years before he consented to his release. The very name of a prison revived the idea of my confinement at Rome, and so terrified me that I instantly turned my horse the way the messenger directed, who never once ceased chattering in French till he had conducted me to court: sometimes he threatened me, sometimes he said one thing and sometimes another, by which I was almost vexed to death.

On our way to the king's quarters, we passed before those of the Cardinal of Ferrara, who being at his door called me to him and said, "Our most Christian King has of his own accord assigned you the same salary that he allowed Leonardo da Vinci the painter, namely, seven hundred crowns a year. He will pay you over and above for whatever you do for him: he likewise makes you a present of five hundred crowns for your journey; and it is his pleasure that they should be paid you before you stir from hence." When the cardinal ceased speaking, I answered that these indeed were offers worthy of so great a monarch. The messenger, who did not know who I was, seeing such great offers made me in the king's name, asked me a thousand pardons. Paolo and Ascanio said, "It is to God we owe this great good fortune."

The day following, I went to return His Majesty thanks, who ordered me to make him models of twelve silver statues, which he intended should serve as candlesticks round his table. He desired they should be the figures of six gods and six goddesses, made exactly of his own height, which was very little less than three cubits. When he had given me this order, he turned to his treasurer and asked him whether he had paid me five hundred crowns: the treasurer answered that he had heard nothing at all of the matter: at this the king was highly offended, as he had commanded the cardinal to speak to him about it. He at the same time desired me to go to Paris and look out for a proper house to work at my business, telling me I should have it directly. I received the five hundred gold crowns and repaired to Paris, to a house of the Cardinal of Ferrara's, where I began to work zealously, and made four little models two thirds of a cubit high, in wax, of Jupiter, Juno, Apollo, and Vulcan.

IV
THE HOUSE OF BOURBON

HISTORICAL NOTE

THE rule of the House of Bourbon began in 1589 with the reign of Henry IV of Navarre. In 1598, the Edict of Nantes was passed, which granted religious toleration. By the shrewd policy of Henry's minister, Sully, the power of the Crown increased. Richelieu, minister of the succeeding sovereign, Louis XIII, aimed at the same thing; and through this reign, as well as that of Louis XIV, France was governed by a king who firmly believed that the people had no rights which he was bound to respect.

Louis XIV was engaged in many wars, most of them brought on by his desire of conquest. He claimed the Spanish Netherlands, and on this account fell into war with Spain. A second war was with Holland; a third with England and allies because of his claims to the Palatinate. In 1701, he engaged in a war with England, Holland, Austria, and most of the German States in order to win the throne of Spain for his grandson, Philip of Anjou. In most of these struggles he was successful, but his country was impoverished by the severe taxation necessary to carry them on and to support an extravagant court. His revocation of the Edict of Nantes is said to have driven some fifty thousand Huguenot families from the country. During the latter part of his reign, the French armies were defeated again and again, and it is said that if it had not been for the jealousy felt by his opponents for one another, France would have been utterly humiliated.

The more pleasing side of the picture is that culture and refinement prevailed, literature reached its Augustan Age, and the arts of peace flourished.

It was during the reign of Henry IV that the first permanent French settlements in America were established.

THE BATTLE OF IVRY

[1590]

BY THOMAS BABINGTON MACAULAY

[WHEN Henry of Navarre, a Protestant, inherited the French
crown, he was opposed by the Catholic Party, led by the
Duke of Mayenne and aided by Spain and Savoy. In 1590,
Henry gained a decisive victory over the Duke at Ivry.
Just before the battle, he said to his troops, "My children,
if you lose sight of your colors, rally to my white plume —
you will always find it in the path to honor and glory." In
1593, Henry abjured Protestantism and was crowned king.

The Editor.]

Now glory to the Lord of Hosts, from whom all glories
    are!
And glory to our Sovereign Liege, King Henry of Na-
    varre!
Now let there be the merry sound of music and the dance,
Through thy cornfields green, and sunny vines, oh pleas-
    ant land of France!
And thou, Rochelle, our own Rochelle, proud city of the
    waters,
Again let rapture light the eyes of all thy mourning
    daughters.
As thou wert constant in our ills, be joyous in our joy,
For cold, and stiff, and still are they who wrought thy
    walls annoy.
Hurrah! hurrah! a single field hath turned the chance of
    war;
Hurrah! hurrah! for Ivry and King Henry of Navarre.

FRANCE

Oh! how our hearts were beating, when at the dawn of
day,
We saw the army of the League drawn out in long
array;
With all its priest-led citizens, and all its rebel peers,
And Appenzel's stout infantry, and Egmont's Flemish
spears.
There rode the brood of false Lorraine, the curses of our
land!
And dark Mayenne was in the midst, a truncheon in his
hand;
And, as we looked on them, we thought of Seine's em-
purpled flood,
And good Coligny's hoary hair all dabbled with his
blood;
And we cried unto the living God, who rules the fate of
war,
To fight for his own holy name, and Henry of Navarre.

The king is come to marshal us, in all his armor drest,
And he has bound a snow-white plume upon his gallant
crest:
He looked upon his people, and a tear was in his eye;
He looked upon the traitors, and his glance was stern
and high.
Right graciously he smiled on us, as rolled from wing to
wing,
Down all our line, in deafening shout, "God save our
lord, the King."
"And if my standard-bearer fall, as fall full well he
may —
For never saw I promise yet of such a bloody fray —

THE BATTLE OF IVRY

Press where ye see my white plume shine, amidst the
    ranks of war,
And be your oriflamme, to-day, the helmet of Navarre."

  Hurrah! the foes are moving! Hark to the mingled
    din
Of fife, and steed, and trump, and drum, and roaring
    culverin!
The fiery Duke is pricking fast across Saint Andre's
    plain,
With all the hireling chivalry of Guelders and Almayne.
Now by the lips of those ye love, fair gentlemen of
    France,
Charge for the golden lilies now, upon them with the
    lance!
A thousand spurs are striking deep, a thousand spears
    in rest,
A thousand knights are pressing close behind the snow-
    white crest;
And in they burst, and on they rushed, while, like a
    guiding star,
Amidst the thickest carnage blazed the helmet of Na-
    varre.

  Now God be praised, the day is ours! Mayenne hath
    turned his rein,
D'Aumale hath cried for quarter — the Flemish Count
    is slain,
Their ranks are breaking like thin clouds before a Biscay
    gale;
The field is heaped with bleeding steeds, and flags, and
    cloven mail;

And then we thought on vengeance, and all along our
      van,
"Remember St. Bartholomew," was passed from man
      to man;
But out spake gentle Henry then, "No Frenchman is
      my foe;
Down, down with every foreigner; but let your brethren
      go."
Oh! was there ever such a knight, in friendship or in war,
As our sovereign lord, King Henry, the soldier of Na-
      varre!

Ho! maidens of Vienna! Ho! matrons of Lucerne!
Weep, weep, and rend your hair for those who never
      shall return:
Ho! Philip, send for charity, thy Mexican pistoles,
That Antwerp monks may sing a mass for thy poor
      spearmen's souls!
Ho! gallant nobles of the League, look that your arms
      be bright!
Ho! burghers of St. Genevieve, keep watch and ward to-
      night!
For our God hath crushed the tyrant, our God hath
      raised the slave,
And mocked the counsel of the wise and the valor of the
      brave.
Then glory to his holy name, from whom all glories are;
And glory to our sovereign lord, King Henry of Navarre.

HENRI IV AND MARIE DE MÉDICI

BY PETER PAUL RUBENS

(Flemish painter, 1574–1642)

Two of the worst queens of France came from the famous Medici family of Florence. The first was Catharine, wife of Henri II. After his death she became regent in behalf of her son, afterwards Charles IX. She schemed with the Huguenots to overthrow the Catholics; then, as the influence of the Protestants increased, she made a treaty with Spain for the destruction of heretics. Later, she planned the murder of the Protestant leaders and induced her son to give the command which brought about the terrible massacre of St. Bartholomew, resulting in the murder of from twenty to thirty thousand Protestants.

Marie de Médici became the wife of Henri IV of France. After his death, in 1610, she became the head of perhaps the worst government from which France has ever suffered. At length she was exiled, and made her way to England. In the days of her prosperity, she commissioned Rubens to portray her life in a series of twenty-four pictures, half literal and half allegorical. The reproduction here given is one of these, representing Henri when about to depart for the war in Germany. This was in 1610, when, owing to the troubles among the three confessions, — Catholic, Lutheran, and Calvinistic, — the Protestant princes interfered, and Henri took up their cause. Marie was to be regent during his absence, and he is here shown presenting her with the orb of sovereignty.

CARDINAL RICHELIEU AND HIS ENEMY

[About 1640]

BY SIR EDWARD BULWER-LYTTON

[CARDINAL RICHELIEU was the minister of Louis XIII. He had two aims: first, to make the will of the king supreme in France; second, to make France the most powerful country in Europe. To bring about the first, he crushed the Huguenots, who then held considerable power; and he broke down the pride and independence of the nobles. The Thirty Years' War was now going on in Germany, practically a struggle between the Catholic and the Protestant German princes. Richelieu had crushed the Huguenot Protestants in his own country; but now, he aided the Protestants of Germany, because their success would divide Germany and humble Austria, and thus the power of France would be increased. The great cardinal died before the close of this war; but the carrying out of his plans resulted in giving to his country the proud position that he had sought for her.

In Bulwer's play, "Richelieu," "Julie" is the cardinal's beloved ward. "Joseph" is a Capuchin monk, his confidant. "De Mauprat" had before this joined in a revolt, but had been exempted from the general pardon and left by Richelieu with the threat, "Beware the axe! — 't will fall one day."

The Editor.]

Richelieu. That's my sweet Julie! why, upon this face
Blushes such daybreak, one might swear the Morning
Were come to visit Tithon.

Julie (placing herself at his feet). Are you gracious?
May I say "Father"?

Rich. Now and ever!

Julie. Father!

A sweet word to an orphan.

    Rich. No; not orphan

While Richelieu lives; thy father loved me well;

My friend, ere I had flatterers (now, I 'm great,

In other phrase, I 'm friendless) — he died young

In years, not service, and bequeathed thee to me;

And thou shalt have a dowry, girl, to buy

Thy mate amid the mightiest. Drooping? — sighs? —

Art thou not happy at the court?

    Julie. Not often.

    Rich. (*aside*). Can she love Baradas? Ah! at thy
       heart

There 's what can smile and sigh, blush and grow pale,

All in a breath! — Thou art admired — art young;

Does not His Majesty commend thy beauty!

Ask thee to sing to him? — and swear such sounds

Had smooth'd the brows of Saul?

    Julie. He 's very tiresome,

Our worthy king.

    Rich. Fie! kings are never tiresome,

Save to their ministers. What courtly gallants

Charm ladies most? — De Sourdiac, Longueville, or

The favorite Baradas?

    Julie. A smileless man —

I fear and shun him.

    Rich. Yet he courts thee?

    Julie. Then he 's more tiresome than His Majesty.

    Rich. Right, girl, shun Baradas. Yet of these flowers

Of France, not one, on whose more honeyed breath

Thy heart hears summer whisper?

Enter HUGUET.

Huguet. The Chevalier
De Mauprat waits below.
 Julie (starting up). De Mauprat!
 Rich. Hem!
He has been tiresome too! — Anon. [*Exit* HUGUET.
 Julie. What doth he?
I mean — I — Does Your Eminence — that is —
Know you Messire de Mauprat?
 Rich. Well! — and you —
Has he address'd you often?
 Julie. Often! No —
Nine times! nay, ten; — the last time by the lattice
Of the great staircase. (*In a melancholy tone.*) The
  Court sees him rarely.
 Rich. A bold and forward royster!
 Julie. He? nay, modest,
Gentle, and sad, methinks.
 Rich. Wears gold and azure?
 Julie. No; sable.
 Rich. So you note his colors, Julie?
Shame on you, child, look loftier. By the mass,
I have business with this modest gentleman.
 Julie. You're angry with poor Julie. There's no cause.
 Rich. No cause — you hate my foes?
 Julie. I do!
 Rich. Hate Mauprat?
 Julie. Not Mauprat. No, not Adrien, father.
 Rich. Adrien!
Familiar! — Go, child; no, not *that* way; wait
In the tapestry chamber; I will join you, — go.

239

Julie (aside). His brows are knit; I dare not call
    him father!
But I *must* speak. — Your Eminence —
  Rich. (sternly). Well, girl!
  Julie. Nay,
Smile on me — one smile more; there, now I'm happy.
Do not rank Mauprat with your foes; he is not,
I know he *is* not; he loves France too well.
  Rich. Not rank De Mauprat with my foes? So be it.
I'll blot him from that list.
  Julie. That's my own father.   [*Exit* JULIE.
  Rich. (ringing a small bell on the table). Huguet!
De Mauprat struggled not, nor murmur'd?
  Huguet. No: proud and passive.
  Rich. Bid him enter. — Hold:
Look that he hide no weapon. Humph, despair
Makes victims sometimes victors. When he has enter'd,
Glide round unseen; place thyself yonder (*pointing to
    the screen*); watch him;
If he show violence (let me see thy carbine;
So, a good weapon); if he play the lion,
Why, the dog's death.
            [*Exit* HUGUET; RICHELIEU *seats himself at the
            table, and slowly arranges the papers before
            him. Enter* DE MAUPRAT, *preceded by*
            HUGUET, *who then retires behind the screen*.
  Rich. Approach, sir. Can you call to mind the hour,
Now three years since, when in this room, methinks,
Your presence honored me?
  De Mauprat.   It is, my lord,
One of my most —
  Rich. (dryly).   Delightful recollections.

CARDINAL RICHELIEU AND HIS ENEMY

De Maup. (aside). St. Denis! doth he make a jest of
    axe
And headsman?
    Rich. (sternly). I did then accord you
A mercy ill requited — you still live? .

                Messire de Mauprat,
Doom'd to sure death, how hast thou since consumed
The time allotted thee for serious thought
And solemn penance?
    De Maup. (embarrassed). The time, my lord?
    Rich. Is not the question plain? I'll answer for thee.
Thou hast sought nor priest nor shrine; no sackcloth
    chafed
Thy delicate flesh. The rosary and the death's-head
Have not, with pious meditation purged
Earth from the carnal gaze. What thou hast *not*
    done
Brief told; what done, a volume! Wild debauch,
Turbulent riot: — for the morn the dice-box —
Noon claim'd the duel — and the night the wassail:
These, your most holy, pure preparatives
For death and judgment! Do I wrong you, sir!
    De Maup. I was not always thus: — if changed my
    nature,
Blame that which changed my fate. — Alas, my lord,
There is a brotherhood which calm-eyed Reason,
Can wot not of betwixt Despair and Mirth.
My birthplace mid the vines of sunny Provence,
Perchance the stream that sparkles in my veins
Came from that wine of passionate life, which erst,
Glow'd in the wild heart of the Troubadour:

241

And danger, which makes steadier courage wary,
But fevers me with an insane delight;
As one of old who on the mountain-crags
Caught madness from a Mænad's haunting eyes.
Were you, my lord, — whose path imperial power,
And the grave cares of reverent wisdom guard
From all that tempts to folly meaner men, —
Were you accursed with that which you inflicted —
By bed and board, dogg'd by one ghastly specter —
The while within you youth beat high, and life
Grew lovelier from the neighboring frown of death —
The heart no bud, nor fruit — save in those seeds
Most worthless, which spring up, bloom, bear, and
     wither
In the same hour — Were this your fate, perchance,
You would have erred like me!
  Rich. I might, like you,
Have been a brawler and a reveler; — not,
Like you, a trickster and a thief. —
  De Maup. (*advancing threateningly*). Lord Cardinal!—
Unsay those words. —
      [HUGUET *deliberately raises his carbine.*
  Rich. (*waving his hand*). Not quite so quick, friend
    Huguet;
Messire de Mauprat is a patient man,
And he can wait! —
      You have outrun your fortune; —
I blame you not, that you would be a beggar —
Each to his taste! — but I do charge you, sir,
That, being beggar'd, you would coin false moneys
Out of that crucible called DEBT. — To live
On means not yours — be brave in silks and laces,

CARDINAL RICHELIEU AND HIS ENEMY

Gallant in steeds, splendid in banquets; — all
Not *yours* — ungiven — uninherited — unpaid for; —
This is to be a trickster; and to filch
Men's art and labor, which to them is wealth,
Life, daily bread, — quitting all scores with — "Friend,
You're troublesome!" — Why this, forgive me,
Is what — when done with a less dainty grace —
Plain folks call "*Theft!*" — You owe eight thousand
      pistoles,
Minus one crown, two liards! —
   De Maup. (*aside*). The old conjurer! —
'Sdeath, he'll inform me next how many cups
I drank at dinner! —
   Rich. This is scandalous,
Shaming your birth and blood. — I tell you, sir,
That you must pay your debts —
   De Maup. With all my heart,
My lord. Where shall I borrow, then, the money?
   Rich. (*aside and laughing*). A humorous dare-devil! —
      The very man
To suit my purpose — ready, frank, and bold!
               [*Rising, and earnestly.*
Adrien de Mauprat, men have called me cruel; —
I am not; I am *just!* — I found France rent asunder, —
The rich men despots, and the poor banditti; —
Sloth in the mart, and schism within the temple;
Brawls festering to Rebellion; and weak Laws
Rotting away with rust in antique sheaths. —
I have re-created France; and, from the ashes
Of the old feudal and decrepit carcass,
Civilization on her luminous wings
Soars, phœnix-like, to Jove! — what was my art?

FRANCE

Genius, some say, — some, Fortune, — Witchcraft,
 some:
Not so; my art was JUSTICE! — Force and fraud
Misname it cruelty — you shall confute them!
My champion YOU! — You met me as your foe.
Depart, my friend — you shall not die — France needs
 you.
You shall wipe off all stains, — be rich, be honor'd,
Be great.
> [DE MAUPRAT *falls on his knee* — RICHELIEU
> *raises him.*

I ask, sir, in return, this hand,
To gift it with a bride, whose dower shall match,
Yet not exceed, her beauty.
 De Maup.   I, my lord, — [*Hesitating.*
I have no wish to marry.
 Rich.   Surely, sir,
To die were worse.
 De Maup. Scarcely; the poorest coward
Must die, — but knowingly to march to marriage —
My lord, it asks the courage of a lion!
 Rich. Traitor, thou triflest with me! — I know *all!*
Thou hast dared to love my ward — my charge.
 De Maup.   As rivers
May love the sunlight — basking in the beams,
And hurrying on! —
 Rich.   Thou hast told her of thy love?
 De Maup. My lord, if I had dared to love a maid,
Lowliest in France, I would not so have wrong'd her,
As bid her link rich life and virgin hope
With one the deathman's gripe might, from her side,
Pluck at the nuptial altar.

Rich.   I believe thee;
Yet since she knows not of thy love, renounce her;
Take life and fortune with another! — Silent?

   De Maup. Your fate has been one triumph. You
       know not
How bless'd a thing it was in my dark hour
To nurse the one sweet thought you bid me banish.
Love hath no need of words; — nor less within
That holiest temple — the heaven-builded soul —
Breathes the recorded vow. — Base knight, — false lover
Were he, who barter'd all that brighten'd grief,
Or sanctified despair, for life and gold.
Revoke your mercy; I prefer the fate
I look'd for!

   Rich.   Huguet! to the tapestry chamber
Conduct your prisoner.
(*To* MAUPRAT.)   You will there behold
The executioner: — your doom be private —
And Heaven have mercy on you!

   De Maup.   When I 'm dead,
Tell her I loved her.

   Rich.   Keep such follies, sir,
For fitter ears; — go —

   De Maup.   Does he mock me?

             [*Exeunt* DE MAUPRAT *and* HUGUET.

   Rich.   Joseph,
Come forth.

Enter JOSEPH.

        Methinks your cheek has lost its rubies;
I fear you have been too lavish of the flesh;
The scourge is heavy.

Joseph.   Pray you, change the subject.

Rich. You good men are so modest! — Well, to
    business!
Go instantly — deeds — notaries! — bid my stewards
Arrange my house by the Luxembourg — *my* house
No more! — a bridal present to my ward,
Who weds to-morrow.

Joseph.   Weds, with whom?

Rich.   De Mauprat.

Joseph. Penniless husband!

Rich.   Bah! the mate for beauty
Should be a man, and not a money-chest!
When her brave sire lay on his bed of death,
I vow'd to be a father to his Julie; —
And so he died — the smile upon his lips! —
And when I spared the life of her young lover,
Methought I saw that smile again! — Who else,
Look you, in all the court — who else so well,
Brave, or supplant the favorite: — balk the King —
Baffle their schemes? — I have tried him: — he has
    honor
And courage; — qualities that eagle-plume
Men's souls, — and fit them for the fiercest sun
Which ever melted the weak waxen minds
That flutter in the beams of gaudy Power!
Besides, he has taste, this Mauprat: — When my play
Was acted to dull tiers of lifeless gapers,
Who had no soul for poetry, I saw him
Applaud in the proper places; trust me, Joseph,
He is a man of an uncommon promise!

Joseph. And yet your foe.

Rich.   Have I not foes enow? —

CARDINAL RICHELIEU AND HIS ENEMY

Great men gain doubly when they make foes friends.
Remember my grand maxims! — First employ
All methods to conciliate.
    Joseph.   Failing these?
    Rich. (*fiercely*). All means to crush; as with the open-
        ing, and
The clenching of this little hand, I will
Crush the small venom of these stinging courtiers.
So, so, we've baffled Baradas.
    Joseph.   And when
Check the conspiracy?
    Rich.   Check, check? Full way to it.
Let it bud, ripen, flaunt i' the day, and burst
To fruit — the Dead Sea's fruit of ashes; ashes
Which I will scatter to the winds.
                        Go, Joseph;
When you return, I have a feast for you —
The last great act of my great play; the verses,
Methinks are fine, — ah, very fine. — *You* write
Verses! — (*aside*) *such* verses! You have wit, discern-
        ment.
    Joseph (*aside*). Worse than the scourge! Strange
        that so great a statesman
Should be so bad a poet.
    Rich.   What dost say?
    Joseph. That it is strange so great a statesman should
        be so sublime a poet.
    Rich. Ah, you rogue;
Laws die; books never. Of my ministry
I am not vain; but of my muse, I own it.
Come, you shall hear the verses now.
                  [*Takes up a manuscript.*

FRANCE

Joseph.　　　　　　　　　　My lord,
The deeds, *the notaries!*
　Rich.　　　　　　　True, I pity you;
But business first, then pleasure.

　　　　　　　　　　　　　[*Exit* JOSEPH.

Rich. (*seats himself, and reading*). Ah, sublime!

Enter DE MAUPRAT *and* JULIE.

De Maup. Oh, speak, my lord! I dare not think you
　　mock me.
And yet —
　Rich. Hush, hush — this line must be considered!
　Julie. Are we not both your children!
　Rich.　　　　　　　　What a couplet! —
How now! Oh, sir, — you live!
　De Maup.　　　　　　Why, no, methinks,
Elysium is not life.
　Julie.　　　　He smiles! you smile,
My father! From my heart for ever, now,
I'll blot the name of orphan!
　Rich.　　　　　　　Rise, my children,
For ye are mine — mine both; — and in your sweet
And young delight, your love (life's first-born glory),
My own lost youth breathes musical!
　De Maup.　　　　　　I'll seek
Temple and priest henceforward: — were it but
To learn Heaven's choicest blessings.
　Rich.　　　　　　　Thou shalt seek
Temple and priest right soon; the morrow's sun
Shall see across these barren thresholds pass
The fairest bride in Paris. Go, my children;
Even *I* loved once! — Be lovers while ye may.

CARDINAL RICHELIEU AND HIS ENEMY

How is it with you, sir? You bear it bravely:
You know, it asks the courage of a lion.
>   [*Exeunt* DE MAUPRAT *and* JULIE.
Oh, godlike Power! Woe, Rapture, Penury, Wealth —
Marriage, and Death, for one infirm old man
Through a great empire to dispense — withhold —
As the will whispers! And shall things, like motes
That live in my daylight; lackeys of court wages,
Dwarf'd starvelings; manikins, upon whose shoulders
The burthen of a province were a load
More heavy than the globe on Atlas — cast
Lots for my robes and scepter? France, I love thee!
All earth shall never pluck thee from my heart!
My mistress, France; my wedded wife, sweet France;
Who shall proclaim divorce for thee and me!
>   [*Exit* RICHELIEU.

IN THE DAYS OF THE FRONDE

[1648]

BY ALEXANDRE DUMAS

[AFTER the death of Louis XIII, his widow, Anne of Austria, became regent, and appointed Cardinal Mazarin prime minister. The people were called upon for such severe taxes that Parliament refused to register them, and therefore several of the members were imprisoned. A strong party called the Fronde was formed against the Mazarin Government, and was led by Jean François Paul de Gondi, the Coadjutor, or assistant Bishop of Paris.

Broussel was a leader of Parliament and a popular idol. D'Artagnan was captain of the king's guard, and Porthos, his comrade, served under him.

The Editor.]

THE queen was standing, pale from anger; yet her self-control was so great that she showed no signs of emotion. Behind her were Comminges, Villequier, and Guitant; behind them the ladies. Before her was the Chancellor Seguier, the same who twenty years before had so greatly persecuted her. He was telling her how his carriage had been broken, he had been pursued, and had taken refuge in the mansion of O——; that this had been immediately entered and pillaged. Fortunately he had had time to reach a closet hidden in the tapestry, where an old woman had shut him up along with her brother, the Bishop of Meaux. There the danger was so real, the mad crowd had approached this cabinet with such threats, that the chancellor thought his hour had come; and he had confessed to his brother, that he might be ready to die if he was discovered. Happily he had not been; the people, believing that he had escaped through some rear door, retired and left his retreat open. He had then disguised himself in the clothes of Marquis d'O——, and had come out of the hotel, stepping over the bodies of his officer and of two guards slain in defending the street-door.

During this narrative Mazarin had come in, and quietly taking a place near the queen was listening.

"Well," the queen asked, when the chancellor ended, "what do you think of that?"

"I think it a very serious matter, Madame."

"But what advice can you give me?"

"I could give very good advice to Your Majesty, but I do not dare."

"Dare, dare, Monsieur," said the queen, with a bitter smile; "you have, indeed, dared other things."

The chancellor blushed, and stammered out a few words.

"The question is not of the past, but of the present," said the queen. "You say you can give me some good advice; what is it?"

"Madame," said the chancellor, hesitating, "it is to set Broussel at liberty."

The queen, although very pale, visibly became paler, and her face contracted.

"Set Broussel at liberty!" said she; "never!"

Just then some steps were heard in the adjoining room, and without being announced Maréchal de la Meilleraie appeared at the door.

"Ah, it's you, Maréchal!" exclaimed Anne of Austria

joyfully. "I hope you have brought all that rabble to reason."

"Madame, I have left three men on Pont Neuf, four at the public markets, six at the corner of the Rue de l'Arbre Sec, and two at the gate of your palace, — fifteen in all. I have brought back ten or twelve wounded. My hat has gone, I know not where, carried off by a bullet, and most probably I should have been where my hat is, but for Monsieur the Coadjutor, who arrived in time to rescue me."

"Ah, indeed!" said the queen; "I should have felt astonished if that bandy-legged turnspit had not been mixed up in it all."

"Madame," said La Meilleraie, laughing, "do not say too much evil about him in my presence, for the service he has done me is still in my mind."

"It is right that you should be grateful to him as much as you please, but that does not bind me. Here you are safe and sound, — that is all I could desire; count yourself not only welcome, but safely returned to us."

"Yes, Madame; but I am the latter only on one condition, — that I transmit to you the will of the people."

"Their will!" said Anne, knitting her eyebrows. "Oh, oh, Monsieur the Marshal; you must have been in very great danger to take upon yourself such a strange embassy." And these words were said with a tone of irony which did not escape the marshal.

"Pardon me, Madame, I am not an advocate, but a soldier; and consequently I perhaps imperfectly understand the significance of words. I should have said the *desire*, not the *will*, of the people. As for the reply with which you have honored me, I believe you meant that I felt afraid."

The queen smiled.

"Well, yes, Madame, I did feel afraid; this is the third time in my life that that has been the case, and yet I have been in a dozen pitched battles, and I do not know how many fights and skirmishes. Yes, I did feel afraid; and I prefer being in the presence of Your Majesty, however menacing your smile, to that of those demons of hell who accompanied me back here, and who come from I cannot say where."

"Bravo!" said D'Artagnan, in a low voice to Porthos, "a capital answer."

"Well," said the queen, biting her lips, while the courtiers looked at one another with astonishment, "what is the desire of my people?"

"The release of Broussel, Madame."

"Never!" said the queen, "never!"

"Your Majesty is mistress," said La Meilleraie, bowing and stepping backwards.

"Where are you going, Marshal?" said the queen.

"I am going to take Your Majesty's reply to those awaiting it."

"Stay, Marshal! I do not like to have the appearance of treating with rebels!"

"Madame, I have pledged my word to them," said the marshal.

"Which means —"

"That if you do not cause me to be arrested, I am compelled to go down to them."

Anne of Austria's eyes flashed like lightning.

"Oh, don't let that make any difference, Monsieur,"

said she; "I have arrested many of greater importance then you. Guitant!"

Mazarin stepped forward.

"Madame," said he, "may I venture in my turn to give you my opinion?"

"Is it yours also that I should release Broussel, Monsieur? In that case you may spare yourself the trouble."

"No," said Mazarin; "although that may be perhaps as good as any."

"What, then, is it?"

"My advice is to summon Monsieur the Coadjutor."

"The Coadjutor!" exclaimed the queen, "that frightful mischief-maker! He it is who has caused the whole revolt."

"The greater reason," said Mazarin; "if he caused it, he can quell it."

"And stay, Madame," said Comminges, who was keeping close to a window through which he was looking, — "stay, the occasion is favorable, for I see him giving his blessing on the Place Palais-Royal."

The queen hurried to the window. "It is true; the arch-hypocrite! Look at him."

"I see," said Mazarin, "that every one kneels before him, although he is only the Coadjutor; yet if I were in his place they would pull me to pieces, although I am a cardinal. I persist, then, in my *desire* [Mazarin emphasized the word] that Your Majesty receive the Coadjutor."

"And why do you not as well say, *in your will?*" replied the queen, in a low voice.

Mazarin bowed. The queen remained thoughtful a

short time. Then, raising her head, "Monsieur the Marshal," said she, "go and bring Monsieur the Coadjutor to me."

"And what shall I say to the populace?"

"To have patience," said the queen; "I have had much of it."

There was in the voice of the haughty Spaniard such imperativeness that the marshal made no observation; he bowed and went out.

D'Artagnan turned towards Porthos.

"How is this going to end?" said he.

"We shall see," said Porthos, with his usual tranquillity.

During this time Anne of Austria was talking in a low tone to Comminges.

Mazarin, feeling anxious, looked in the direction of D'Artagnan and Porthos. The rest were conversing together in a low tone. The door opened; the marshal appeared, followed by the Coadjutor.

"Madame, here is M. de Gondy, who hastens to receive Your Majesty's commands."

The queen advanced a few paces towards him, then stopped, looking cold, severe, unmoved, with her lower lip scornfully projecting.

Gondy bowed respectfully.

"Well, Monsieur, what do you say about this riot?"

"That it is no longer a riot, Madame, but a revolt."

"The revolt is on the part of those who think that my people can revolt!" exclaimed Anne, unable to hide her real feelings from the Coadjutor, whom she regarded, with good reason, perhaps, as the promoter of this movement. "A revolt is the name those give it who desire the tumult of which they have been the cause; but wait, wait! the king's authority will put it straight."

"Is it simply to tell me that, Madame," coolly replied Gondy, "that Your Majesty has admitted me to the honor of your presence?"

"No, my dear Coadjutor," said Mazarin, "it was to ask your advice in the present difficult situation."

"Is it true," asked Gondy, putting on an astonished look, "that Her Majesty has summoned me to ask my advice?"

"Yes," said the queen. "They have wished it."

The Coadjutor bowed.

"Her Majesty desires, then, —"

"That you should tell her what you would do if you were in her place," Mazarin hastened to reply.

The Coadjutor looked at the queen, who signified her assent.

"If I were in Her Majesty's place," said Gondy coldly, "I should not hesitate; I should release Broussel."

"And if I do not release him, what do you think will happen?"

"I think that by to-morrow there will not be one stone left upon another in Paris," said the marshal.

"I am not questioning you, but M. de Gondy," the queen said in a dry tone, and without even turning round.

"Since it is I whom Your Majesty questions," replied the Coadjutor, with the same calmness, "I say in reply that I am entirely of the marshal's opinion."

The color rose to the queen's face; her beautiful blue eyes seemed starting from her head; her carmine lips, compared by all the poets of the time to pomegranates in flower, turned pale, and trembled with rage. She almost frightened Mazarin himself, who was, however, used to the domestic bursts of rage in this disturbed household. "Release Broussel!" she said at last, with a frightful smile; "fine advice, upon my word! It is very clear that it comes from a priest."

Gondy held firm. The insults of the day seemed to glide from him like the sarcasm of the previous evening; but hatred and vengeance were gathering silently and drop by drop at the bottom of his heart. He looked coldly at the queen, who touched Mazarin to get him also to say something.

Mazarin, as was his habit, thought much, but said little.

"Eh, eh!" said he, "good advice, friendly counsel. I also would release this good man Broussel, dead or alive, and all would be ended."

"If you were to release him dead. all would be at an end, as you say, Monseigneur, but in a different way from what you mean."

"Did I say dead or alive?" replied Mazarin. "It is a form of speech. You know I do not understand French well, and that you speak and write it wonderfully well, Monsieur the Coadjutor."

"Here 's a Council of State," said D'Artagnan to Porthos; "but we have held better ones at Rochelle with Athos and Aramis."

"In the bastion St. Gervais," said Porthos.

"There and elsewhere."

The Coadjutor suffered the shower to pass, and continued, always with the same coldness, "Madame, if

Your Highness does not like the advice which I submit to her, it is without doubt because she has better guidance. I know too well the wisdom of the queen and that of her councilors to suppose that they will leave the capital city long in a trouble which may lead to a revolution."

"So then, in your opinion," said the Spaniard, with a sneer, and biting her lips with rage, "this riot of yesterday, which has become to-day a revolt, may become to-morrow a revolution?"

"Yes, Madame," the Coadjutor gravely said.

"But if you are right, Monsieur, the nations have then become unmindful of all restraint."

"The times are unfortunate for kings." said Gondy, shaking his head; "look at England, Madame."

"Yes, but fortunately we have no Oliver Cromwell in France," replied the queen.

"Who knows?" said Gondy. "Such men are like thunderbolts; they are known only when they strike."

Every one shuddered, and there was a short silence. Meanwhile the queen had rested her hand against her breast; it was clear that she was checking the hurried beatings of her heart.

"Porthos," whispered D'Artagnan, "look closely at that priest."

"Yes, I see him," said Porthos. "Well?"

"Well, he is a thorough man."

Porthos looked at D'Artagnan with some astonishment; it was clear that he did not fully comprehend his friend's meaning.

"Your Majesty," pitilessly continued the Coadjutor, "is then going to take measures which please yourself.

But I foresee that they will be terrible ones, and such as will irritate the rebels still more."

"Well, then, *you*, Monsieur the Coadjutor, who have such power over them, and who are our friend," said the queen ironically, "will calm them by giving them your blessing."

"Perhaps it will be too late," said Gondy, in his freezing manner, "and perhaps I shall have lost all my influence; while by releasing Broussel Your Majesty will cut the root of the sedition, and acquire the right of punishing severely every new growth of revolt."

"Have I not this right?" exclaimed the queen.

"If you have, use it," replied Gondy.

"Hang it!" said D'Artagnan to Porthos, "that is the sort of character I like. Would that he were minister, and I his D'Artagnan, instead of belonging to this rascal Mazarin. Ah, *mordieu!* what splendid strokes we should make together!"

The queen with a sign dismissed the court, except Mazarin. Gondy bowed, and was about retiring like the rest.

"Stay, Monsieur," said the queen.

"Good," said Gondy to himself; "she is going to yield."

"She is going to have him killed," said D'Artagnan to Porthos; "but by no means will I be the doer of it. I take my oath that, on the contrary, if anything should happen to him I would fall upon those who caused it."

"So would I," said Porthos.

"Good!" muttered Mazarin, taking a seat, "we are going to see something new."

The queen followed with her eyes the persons leaving. When the last had closed the door, she turned round. It was evident that she was making violent efforts to conquer her anger; she fanned herself, she inhaled a perfume, she walked forward and back. Mazarin remained in his seat as if reflecting. Gondy, who began to feel anxious, scanned all the tapestry, sounded the cuirass which he wore under his long robe, and now and then felt under his *camail* to ascertain if the handle of a good Spanish poniard which he had hidden there was well within reach.

"Now," said the queen at last, standing still, — "now we are alone, repeat your advice, Monsieur the Coadjutor."

"This is it, Madame: Profess to have reflected; publicly confess having made a mistake, which is the strength of strong governments; release Broussel from prison, and give him up to the people."

"Oh!" exclaimed Anne of Austria, "thus to humiliate me! Am I queen or am I not? Is this howling mob subject to me or not? Have I friends? Have I guards? Ah! by our Lady, as Queen Catherine used to say, rather than give up this infamous Broussel, I would strangle him with my own hands." And she stretched her clinched fists towards Gondy, who certainly detested her just then as much as Broussel did.

Gondy did not stir, not a muscle of his face moved; only his icy look crossed blades, as it were, with the furious look of the queen.

"He is a dead man, if there is still a Vitry at court, and he were to enter at this instant," said the Gascon. "But I, rather than that should take place, would kill Vitry, and that neatly! Monsieur the Cardinal would be infinitely obliged to me."

"*Chut!*" said Porthos; "listen now."

"Madame!" exclaimed the cardinal, taking hold of Anne of Austria and drawing her back, — "Madame, what are you doing?" Then he added in Spanish, "Anne, are you a fool? You quarrel with the citizens, — you, a queen! And do you not see that you have before you in the person of this priest the whole people of Paris, whom it is dangerous to insult, especially now; and that if this priest wishes it, in an hour you would no longer possess a crown? On another occasion, later on, you may keep firm, but to-day is not the time; to-day flatter and caress, or you are only a vulgar woman."

At the beginning of this appeal, D'Artagnan had seized Porthos's arm, and had squeezed it harder and harder; then when Mazarin was silent, "Porthos," said he, quite in a whisper, "never say in Mazarin's presence that I know Spanish, or you and I are lost men."

"No," said Porthos.

This severe reprimand, impressed with that eloquence which distinguished Mazarin when he spoke Italian or Spanish, and which he entirely lost in speaking French, was spoken with an emotionless countenance which did not permit Gondy, although a skillful physiognomist, to suppose that it was more than a simple warning to be more moderate.

The queen, thus roughly addressed, grew suddenly milder. She allowed the fire in her eyes, so to speak, to expire; the blood left her cheeks, the strong words of anger her lips. She sat down, and with softened tones, and letting her arms fall by her side, "Pardon me, Monsieur the Coadjutor," said she, "and ascribe this outbreak to my sufferings. As a woman, and consequently subject to the weaknesses of my sex, I have a horror of civil war; as a queen, and accustomed to be obeyed, I am enraged at the first provocation."

"Madame," said Gondy, bowing, "Your Majesty deceived herself in qualifying as resistance my sincere advice. Your Majesty has only submissive and respectful subjects. It is not the queen with whom the people feel angry, — they call for Broussel, and that's all; too happy to live subject to Your Majesty's laws, — if Your Majesty at once releases Broussel," added Gondy, with a smile.

Mazarin, who at the words, "It is not the queen with whom the people are angry," had at once paid great attention, thinking that the Coadjutor was going to speak of the cries, "Down with Mazarin!" thought well of Gondy for this omission, and said, in his softest tones and with his most gracious look, "Madame, trust in the Coadjutor, who is one of the most able politicians that we have; the first vacant cardinal's hat seems fit for this noble head."

"Ah! so you want me, you tricky rascal!" thought Gondy.

"And what will he promise us," said D'Artagnan, "on the day when they want to kill him? Hang it, if he gives away hats so liberally, let us get ready our requests, Porthos, and each of us ask for a regiment after to-morrow. Let the civil war last a year only, and I will have the Constable's sword re-gilt for my own use."

"And I," said Porthos.

"You! I will make them give you the *bâton* of Maréchal de la Meilleraie, who does not seem in great favor just at present."

"So, Monsieur," said the queen, "you seriously fear the popular movement?"

"Seriously, Madame," said Gondy, astonished at not having made more progress; "I am afraid that when the torrent has broken its banks it will cause great devastation."

"I," said the queen, "think that in that case new banks must be erected. You can go. I will think it over."

Gondy looked at Mazarin, quite astonished. Mazarin approached to speak to the queen. At that moment a frightful tumult was heard on the Place du Palais-Royal.

Gondy smiled, the queen looked excited, Mazarin became very pale.

"What more is there?" said the cardinal.

At that moment Comminges came hastily into the room.

"Pardon, Madame," said he to the queen; "but the people have crushed the sentinels against the railings, and are now forcing the gates. What orders do you give?"

"Listen, Madame," said Gondy.

The roar of waves, the roar of thunder, the rumblings of a volcano, are not to be compared to the tempest of cries which then arose.

"What orders do I give?"

"Yes; time presses."

"About how many men have you at the Palais-Royal?"

"Six hundred."

"Put a hundred to guard the king, and with the rest sweep away all this mob for me."

"Madame," said Mazarin, "what are you doing?"

"Go!" said the queen.

Comminges went off with a soldier's passive obedience. Just then a terrible crash was heard; one of the gates was giving way.

"Ah, Madame," said Mazarin, "you will ruin us all, — the king, yourself, and me."

Anne of Austria, at this cry of distress from the terrified cardinal, herself felt afraid, and recalled Comminges.

"It is too late!" said Mazarin, tearing his hair, "it is too late!"

The gate gave way, and shouts of joy were heard from the populace. D'Artagnan took his sword in his hand, and made a sign to Porthos to do the same.

"Save the queen!" exclaimed Mazarin, speaking to the Coadjutor.

Gondy sprang to the window and opened it; he recognized Louvières at the head of perhaps three or four thousand men.

"Not a step farther!" cried he; "the queen will sign."

"What do you say?" exclaimed the queen.

"The truth, Madame," said Mazarin, handing her paper and pen; "it must be done." Then he added, "Sign, Anne, I pray you; I wish it!"

The queen sank into a chair, took the pen, and signed.

Restrained by Louvières, the populace had not advanced a step; but the terrible murmur indicating the wrath of the multitude continued.

The queen wrote, "The governor of the prison of St.

Germain will set Councilor Broussel at liberty," and she signed it.

The Coadjutor, who devoured with his eyes her slightest movements, seized the paper as soon as the signature was appended, returned to the window, and waving it in his hand, "This is the order," said he.

The whole of Paris seemed to send forth a great shout of joy; then the cries were heard, "Long live Broussel! Long live the Coadjutor!"

"Long live the queen!" said the latter.

Some responses were made to it, but they were few and feeble. Perhaps the Coadjutor raised the cry simply to make Anne of Austria feel her weakness.

"And now that you have gained what you desired," said she, "retire, M. de Gondy."

"When the queen needs me," said he, bowing, "Her Majesty knows that I am ready to obey her commands."

The queen made a sign with her head, and Gondy retired.

"Ah, you cursed priest!" exclaimed Anne of Austria, stretching out her hand toward the door, then scarcely closed, "I will one day make you drink the dregs of the cup which you have to-day poured out for me."

Mazarin made a movement to approach her.

"Leave me," said she; "you are not a man!" and she went out.

"It is you who are not a woman," muttered Mazarin.

LOUIS XIV AND MOLIÈRE

BY JEAN LÉON GÉRÔME

(French painter, born 1824, *died* 1904)

The story of the famous incident shown in this picture is told by Mme. Campan in her memoirs.

It came to the ears of Louis XIV that certain officers of his household had refused to dine with Molière, the great dramatist, at the house of his majesty's purveyor-in-chief. A day or two later, Molière, with his troupe, happened to be at Versailles, where the court was. Through an ante-chamber crowded with courtiers, Louis, who was just from the hands of his valet, had the comedian introduced into his presence. He was breakfasting lightly, as was his custom, on the luncheon that had been prepared for him in case he had wished to eat in the night. Commanding Molière to sit opposite him, he served him with a wing of his own fowl and ordered the courtiers to be admitted, to whom he said: "You see me, gentlemen, in the act of eating with Molière, whom the people of my house do not find good enough for them."

The scene is laid in one of the smaller state apartments, an interior ornate in the architecture and decoration of the period, with a canopied throne seat at the back. "Every face is full of expression, the king's beaming with malicious enjoyment at the sensation he has just created; Molière, already seated, is bending modestly forward, with his two-pronged fork in his hand, to attack the viands in obedience to the royal will. The pale bishop in the corner, with the violet vestments, is especially indignant, his face white with anger and full of scorn, but the king is not in a humor to be frightened by anybody's cross looks."

THE DEATH OF LOUIS XIV

[1715]

BY JULIA PARDOE

[LOUIS XIV reigned for seventy-two years. Under his rule France rose to her zenith not only in political influence, but in literature and culture as well. But this outward prosperity was purchased at a terrible cost. At his death, France was virtually bankrupt and already enmeshed in the difficulties that led at length to the Revolution.

The Editor.]

THE scene was a touching one: the gray-haired king, half lying, half sitting, in his gorgeous bed, whose velvet hangings, looped back with their heavy ropes and tassels of gold, were the laborious offering of the pupils of St. Cyr, and were wrought with threads of gold and silver, and party-colored silks, representing, in a singular and incongruous mixture, the principal passages of the Scriptures, interspersed with the less holy incidents of the heathen mythology; the groups of princes in their gorgeous costumes, dispersed over the vast apartment; the door opening from the cabinet thronged with courtiers and ladies; and, finally, the court functionaries, who had simultaneously sunk upon their knees as they approached the dying monarch; the gilded cornices, the priceless, the tapestried hangings, the richly-carpeted floor, the waste of luxury on every side, the pride of man's intellect and of man's strength; and in the midst decay and death, a palsied hand and a dimmed eye.

268

THE DEATH OF LOUIS XIV

The most stoical were moved at such a moment; and even when the attendant gentlemen had risen slowly and in silence, and disappeared across the threshold, like a procession of shadows, the stillness of the death-room continued for a time unbroken.

It was the voice of the king by which it was at length dispelled. He first informed the Marshal de Villeroy that he had appointed him governor to the dauphin; and then desired that Duchess de Ventadour would introduce the child who was soon to become his successor; and the little prince had no sooner knelt upon the cushion which had been placed for him near the side of the bed, still holding the hand of his gouvernante firmly grasped in his own, than the monarch, after gazing upon him for a time with an expression of mingled anxiety and tenderness, said, in an impressive voice, —

"My child, you are about to become a great king; do not imitate me either in my taste for building or in my love of war. Endeavor, on the contrary, to live in peace with the neighboring nations; render to God all that you owe him, and cause his name to be honored by your subjects. Strive to relieve the burdens of your people, in which I have been unfortunate enough to fail; and never forget the gratitude that you owe to Madame de Ventadour."

"Madame," he continued, addressing himself to the duchess, "permit me to embrace the prince."

The dauphin was lifted into his arms; and after he had clasped him fondly to his breast, he said, in a less steady voice, —

"I bless you, dear child, with all my heart."

This done, Madame de Ventadour was about to reclaim her charge, but the king did not relax his hold, until, raising his eyes to heaven, he had repeated his solemn benediction.

On the 27th, the king, having commanded all the great dignitaries and officers of the household to meet in his apartment, addressed them in a firm voice, in the presence of Madame de Maintenon and his confessor, saying, —

"Gentlemen, I die in the faith and obedience of the Church. I know nothing of the dogmas by which it is divided; I have followed the advice that I received, and have done only what I was desired to do. If I have erred, my guides alone must answer before God, whom I call upon to witness this assertion."

Toward the afternoon Louis XIV next desired the attendance of the chancellor, to whom he delivered a casket filled with papers, a portion of which he instructed him to burn, giving distinct instructions for the disposal of the remainder: and, in the course of the evening, he sent for M. de Pontchartrain, who still acted as one of the secretaries of state, and when he appeared, said calmly, —

"So soon as I am dead, you will be good enough to issue an order that my heart may be conveyed to the church of the Jesuits in Paris, and cause it to be placed there in precisely the same manner as that of my deceased father."

Then, after a pause, he continued, in a tone of equal placidity, —

"When I shall have breathed my last, and my death has been announced according to custom from the balcony of the state apartment, conduct *the king* to

Vincennes. But as it strikes me that Cavoie has never regulated the distribution of the rooms in that castle, where the court have not resided for the last fifty years, in the casket" (and as he spoke the dying monarch indicated one with his finger) "you will find a plan of the apartments of Vincennes; take it, and carry it to the grand-marshal of the palace, in order that it may assist him in his arrangements."

The night which succeeded was restless and agitated, and was entirely passed by the monarch in prayer; and on the morning of the 28th, immediately that he awoke, the physicians proposed to amputate the leg in which mortification had commenced.

"Will the operation prolong my life?" was the composed inquiry.

"Yes, sire," replied the head surgeon; "certainly, for several days; and perhaps even for several weeks."

"If that be all," said Louis XIV, "the result will not be adequate to the suffering. God's will be done!"

On the morning of the 30th the strength of the king was nearly exhausted.

"All is well-nigh over," he said feebly to the Marshal de Villeroy, who stood at his bedside; "farewell, my friend, we must soon part."

The courage of the dying monarch never forsook him for an instant; neither did he exhibit the slightest emotion. He took leave of every member of his family with a dry eye and a steady voice, merely exhorting them to live, if possible, on terms of friendship, to do their duty to the young king, and to conduct themselves in a Christian spirit; nor was it until the princes and princesses had withdrawn that he at length betrayed a slight degree of feeling as he turned toward Madame de Maintenon, saying, —

"At this moment I only regret yourself. I have not made you happy; but I have ever felt for you all the regard and affection which you deserved. My only consolation in leaving you," he added, as he grasped her hand, and gazed fixedly upon her with his dim and failing eyes, "exists in the hope that we shall ere long meet again in eternity."

Madame de Maintenon made no rejoinder; but she soon after rose to leave the apartment, and as she crossed the threshold, exclaimed, as if unconsciously, "A pretty rendezvous he has given me! That man has never loved any one but himself." And this equally imprudent and ill-timed ejaculation was overheard by the king's apothecary, by whom it was repeated.

As she retired, the king saw in an opposite mirror the reflection of two of his valets-de-chambre, who were weeping bitterly. "Why do you shed tears?" he asked. "Did you, then, imagine that I was immortal? As for myself, I never believed that such was the case, and you should have been prepared, at my age, to lose me long ago."

After a time, the king exhibited extreme uneasiness at the absence of Madame de Maintenon, who, believing that all would shortly be over, had already departed for St. Cyr; but having been informed that her presence was required, she excused herself when she reappeared by stating that she had been uniting her prayers for his recovery with those of her pupils.

... The following day was one of agony to the expiring king. His intervals of consciousness were rare and brief. The mortification extended rapidly, and toward midday his condition became so much exasperated that it was found necessary to perform the service for the dying without delay. The mournful ceremony aroused him from his lethargy, and the surprise was general when his voice was once more heard, audibly and clearly, combined with those of the priests. At the termination of the prayers he moreover recognized the Cardinal de Rohan, and said calmly, "These are the last favors of the Church."

He then repeated several times, "*Nunc et in hora mortis*"; and finally he exclaimed, with earnest fervor, "Oh, my God, come to my aid, and hasten to help me!"

He never spoke again; for as these words escaped him he once more fell back insensible upon his pillow, and throughout the night continued unconscious of everything save bodily suffering.

At eight o'clock on the following morning, Louis XIV expired. As he exhaled his last sigh, a man was seen to approach the window of the state apartment which opened on the great balcony, and throw it suddenly back. It was the captain of the body-guard, who had no sooner attracted the attention of the populace, by whom the courtyard was thronged, in expectation of the tidings which they knew could not be long delayed, than raising his truncheon above his head, he broke it in the center, and throwing the pieces among the crowd exclaimed in a loud voice, "The king is dead!" Then seizing another staff from an attendant, without the pause of an instant, he flourished it in the air as he shouted, "Long live the king!"

And a multitudinous echo from the depths of the lately-deserted apartment answered as buoyantly, "Long live the king!"

V
ON THE EVE OF THE FRENCH
REVOLUTION

HISTORICAL NOTE

Toward the end of the eighteenth century, the masses of the French people were in misery. The nobles and the clergy together owned half of the land, but they paid hardly any taxes. The burden of taxation fell almost entirely upon the poor; and the poor had no rights which the nobles were bound to respect. Every man's life was in the hands of the king. Without trial or without even being told his offense, a person could be seized at any moment and thrown into prison for life. The court was wildly extravagant and horribly corrupt. This was the state of the kingdom when it came into the hands of Louis XVI.

The advisers of the new king had no remedy to bring forward, and at length, in 1789, the States-General, that is, representatives of the clergy, nobles, and commons, were called together. When this assembly had met before, one hundred and seventy-five years earlier, the vote had always been taken by orders, and as the clergy and nobles united, the commons had in reality no power. Now the commons declared that every man should have a vote. This would put all power into the hands of the commons, as their numbers were so much greater. For weeks there was quarreling. Then came the beginning of the Revolution, for suddenly the commons declared themselves to be the National Assembly, announced that, if the other two orders did not join them, public questions would be decided by the commons alone, and took a solemn oath not to dissolve until they had given France a Constitution. Their leader was Count Mirabeau.

In August, 1789, the assembly abolished the ancient feudal rights, and the nobility, now thoroughly alarmed, began to leave the country. Soon after, the rabble attacked Versailles and carried the royal family back to Paris, where for two years they were treated with constantly increasing audacity as the spirit of democracy spread over the land.

WHEN MARIE ANTOINETTE ENTERED PARIS

[1773]

[IN 1770, Marie Antoinette, daughter of Maria Theresa of Austria, became the wife of the dauphin who was afterwards Louis XVI. The following extract is taken from one of her letters to her mother.

The Editor.]

VERSAILLES, June 14.

MY DEAREST MOTHER,—

I absolutely blush for your kindness to me. The day before yesterday Mercy sent me your precious letter, and yesterday I received a second. That is indeed passing one's fête day happily. On Tuesday I had a fête which I shall never forget all my life. We made our entrance into Paris. As for honors, we received all that we could possibly imagine; but they, though very well in their way, were not what touched me most. What was really affecting was the tenderness and earnestness of the poor people, who, in spite of the taxes with which they are overwhelmed, were transported with joy at seeing us. When we went to walk in the Tuileries, there was so vast a crowd that we were three-quarters of an hour without being able to move either forward or backward. The dauphin and I gave repeated orders to the Guards not to beat any one, which had a very good effect. Such excellent order was kept the whole day that, in spite of the enormous crowd which followed us everywhere, not a person was hurt. When we returned from our walk we went up to an open terrace and stayed there half an hour. I cannot describe to you, my dear mamma, the transports of joy and affection which every one exhibited towards us. Before we withdrew we kissed our hands to the people, which gave them great pleasure. What a happy thing it is for persons in our rank to gain the love of a whole nation so cheaply. Yet there is nothing so precious; I felt it thoroughly, and shall never forget it.

Another circumstance, which gave great pleasure on that glorious day, was the behavior of the dauphin. He made admirable replies to every address, and remarked everything that was done in his honor, and especially the earnestness and delight of the people, to whom he showed great kindness.

HOW THE QUEEN WAS SERVED

BY MADAME CAMPAN

In order to describe the queen's private service intelligibly, it must be recollected that service of every kind was *honor*, and had not any other denomination. *To do the honors of the service*, was to present the service to an officer of superior rank, who happened to arrive at the moment it was about to be performed: thus, supposing the queen asked for a glass of water, the servant of the chamber handed to the first woman a silver gilt waiter, upon which were placed a covered goblet and a small decanter; but should the lady of honor come in, the first woman was obliged to present the waiter to her, and if Madame or the Countess d'Artois came in at the moment, the waiter went again from the lady of honor into the hands of the princess, before it reached the queen. It must be observed, however, that if a princess of the blood, instead of a princess of the family, entered, the service went directly from the first woman to the princess of the blood, the lady of honor being excused from transferring to any but princesses of the royal family. Nothing was presented directly to the queen; her handkerchief or her gloves were placed upon a long salver of gold or silver gilt, which was placed as a piece of furniture of ceremony upon a side-table, and was called *gantière*. The first woman presented to her in this manner all that she asked for, unless the tire-woman, the lady of honor, or a princess, were present, and then the gradation, pointed out in the instance of the glass of water, was always observed.

THE WARDROBE OF MARIE ANTOINETTE

BY MADAME CAMPAN

WHEN a foreign princess was married to the heir presumptive, or a son of France, it was the etiquette to go and meet her with her wedding clothes; the young princess was undressed in the pavilion usually built upon the frontiers for the occasion, and every article of her apparel, without exception, was changed; notwithstanding which, the foreign courts furnished their princesses also with rich wedding clothes, which were considered the lawful perquisites of the lady of honor and the tire-woman. It is to be observed that emoluments and profits of all kinds generally belonged to the great offices. On the death of Maria Leckzinska, the whole of her chamber furniture was given up to the Countess de Noailles, afterwards Maréchale de Mouchy, with the exception of two large rock crystal lusters, which Louis XV ordered should be preserved as appurtenances to the crown. The tire-woman was entrusted with the care of ordering materials, robes, and court dresses; and of checking and paying bills; all accounts were submitted to her, and were paid only on her signature and by her order, from shoes, up to Lyons embroidered dresses. I believe the fixed annual sum for this division of expenditure was one hundred thousand francs,[1] but there might be additional sums when the funds appropriated to this purpose were insufficient. The tire-woman sold the cast-off gowns and ornaments for her own benefit: the lace

[1] About twenty thousand dollars.

for head-dresses, ruffles, and gowns was provided by her, and kept distinct from those of which the lady of honor had the direction. There was a secretary of the wardrobe, to whom the care of keeping the books, accounts of payments, and correspondence relating to this department, was confided.

The tire-woman had, likewise, under her order a principal under-tire-woman, charged with the care and preservation of all the queen's dresses: two women to fold and press such articles as required it; two valets, and one porter of the wardrobe. The latter brought every morning into the queen's apartments, baskets covered with taffety, containing all that she was to wear during the day, and large cloths of green taffety covering the robes and the full dresses. The valet of the wardrobes on duty presented every morning a large book to the first *femme de chambre*, containing patterns of the gowns, full dresses, undresses, etc. Every pattern was marked to show to which sort it belonged. The first *femme de chambre* presented this book to the queen, on her awaking, with a pincushion; Her Majesty stuck pins in those articles which she chose for the day: one for the dress, one for the afternoon undress, and one for the full evening dress for card or supper parties, in the private apartments. The book was then taken back to the wardrobe, and all that was wanted for the day was soon after brought in, in large taffety wrappers. The wardrobe-woman who had care of the linen, in her turn, brought in a covered basket containing two or three chemises, handkerchiefs, and napkins; the morning basket was called *prêt du jour:* in the evening she brought in one containing the nightgown and nightcap, and the stockings for the next morning; this basket was called *prêt de la nuit:* they were in the department of the lady of honor, the tire-woman having nothing to do with the linen.

Nothing was put in order or taken care of by the queen's women. As soon as the toilet was over, the valets and porters belonging to the wardrobe were called in, and they carried all away in a heap, in the taffety wrappers, to the tire-woman's wardrobe, where all were folded up again, hung up, examined, and cleaned with so much regularity and care that even the cast-off clothes scarcely looked as if they had been worn. The tire-woman's wardrobe consisted of three large rooms surrounded with closets, some furnished with drawers, and others with shelves; there were also large tables in each of these rooms, on which the gowns and dresses were spread out and folded up.

For the winter, the queen had generally twelve full dresses, twelve undresses, called fancy dresses, and twelve rich hoop petticoats for the card and supper parties in the smaller apartments.

She had as many for the summer. Those for the spring served likewise for the autumn. All these dresses were discarded at the end of each season, unless indeed she retained some that she particularly liked. I am not speaking of muslin or cambric gowns, or others of the same kind; they were lately introduced; but such as these were not renewed at each returning season, they were kept several years. The chief women were charged with the keeping, care, and examination of the diamonds. This important duty was formerly confided to the tire-woman, but for many years had been included in the business of the first *femmes de chambre.*

THE FALL OF THE BASTILLE[1]

[1789]

BY ALEXANDRE DUMAS

[IN 1789, the king, alarmed by the demands for reform, dismissed Necker, the popular Minister of Finance, and called together a large body of troops in a belated attempt to stem the tide of republicanism. Instantly, Paris was in a mad excitement. The state prison, the Bastille, rose before them, grim and threatening, with its guns, so report said, trained upon the city. The Bastille stood for the despotism that was crushing them, and they sprang upon it with the fury of enraged beasts. The following extract from the "Ange Pitou" of Alexandre Dumas pictures, though with the license of the novelist, the closing scene in the capture of the Bastille by the frantic mob of Paris.

The Editor.]

AT length the fruitful imagination of the farmer gave birth to another idea. He ran toward the square. crying:

"A cart! Bring a cart here!"

Pitou considered that that which was good would be rendered excellent by being doubled. He followed Billot, vociferating, —

"Two carts! two carts!" and immediately ten carts were brought.

"Some straw and some dry hay!" cried Billot.

"Some straw and some dry hay!" reiterated Pitou, and almost instantly two hundred men came forward, each carrying a truss of straw or hay.

[1] From *Ange Pitou*. Copyright (U.S.A.), 1895, by Little, Brown, and Company.

They were obliged to call out that they had ten times more than they wanted. In an hour there was a heap of forage which would have equaled the height of the Bastille. Billot placed himself between the shafts of a cart loaded with straw, and instead of dragging it, he pushed it on before him. Pitou did the same, without knowing what it could be for, but thinking that he could not do better than to imitate the farmer. Elie and Hullin divined Billot's intention. They each seized a cart and pushed it before them into the courtyard. They had scarcely entered, when they were assailed by a discharge of grape-shot. They heard the balls strike with a whizzing sound among the straw or hay, or against the woodwork of the carts; but none of the assailants received a wound.

As soon as this discharge was over, two or three hundred men with muskets rushed on behind those who were pushing forward the carts, and, sheltered by those moving ramparts, they lodged themselves beneath the apron of the bridge itself. There Billot drew from his pocket a flint, a steel, and some tinder, formed a match by rubbing gunpowder on paper, and set fire to it. The powder ignited the paper, and the paper ignited the straw and hay. Each formed a torch for himself, and the four carts were simultaneously set fire to. The flames reached the apron, caught the timbers with their sharp teeth, and ran along the woodwork of the bridge.

A shout of joy then uttered from the courtyard was taken up by the crowd in the Square St. Antoine, and reiterated with deafening clamors. They saw the smoke rising above the walls, and they hence imagined that something fatal to the besieged was occurring. In fact, the red-hot chains detached themselves from the beams. The bridge fell, half broken and half destroyed by fire, smoking and crackling. The firemen rushed forward with their engines, and soon extinguished the flames upon the bridge. The governor ordered the Invalides to fire upon the people, but they refused. The Swiss alone obeyed; but they were not artillerymen; they were therefore obliged to abandon the guns. The French guards, on the contrary, seeing that the artillery was silenced, brought up their gun and planted it before the gate; their third shot shivered it to pieces.

The governor had gone up to the platform of the castle to see whether the promised reinforcement was approaching, when he found himself suddenly enveloped in smoke. It was then that he precipitately descended and ordered the artillerymen to fire. The refusal of the Invalides exasperated him. The breaking down of the gate made him at once comprehend that all was lost. Monsieur de Launay knew that he was hated. He felt that there was no salvation for him. During the whole time that the combat had lasted, he had matured the idea of burying himself beneath the ruins of the Bastille. At the moment he felt assured that all further defense was hopeless, he snatched a match from the hand of one of the artillerymen, and sprang towards the cellar which served as a powder-magazine.

"The powder! the powder!" cried twenty terrified voices; "the powder! the powder!"

They saw the burning match in the governor's hand. They guessed his purpose. Two soldiers rushed forward and crossed their bayonets before his breast just at the moment when he had opened the door.

THE FALL OF THE BASTILLE

"You may kill me," said De Launay, "but you cannot kill me quick enough to prevent me letting this match fall among the powder-casks; and then besieged and besiegers will all be blown to atoms."

The two soldiers stopped. Their bayonets remained crossed before De Launay's breast, but De Launay was still their commander, for all felt that he had their lives in his power. His action had nailed every one to the spot on which he stood. The assailants perceived that something extraordinary was happening. They looked anxiously into the courtyard, and saw the governor threatened and threatening in his turn.

"Hear me," cried De Launay to the besiegers; "as surely as I hold this match in my hand, with which I could exterminate you all, should any one of you make a single step to enter this courtyard, so surely will I set fire to the powder."

Those who heard these words imagined that they already felt the ground tremble beneath their feet.

"What do you wish; what do you ask?" cried several voices with an accent of terror.

"I wish a capitulation," replied De Launay, "an honorable capitulation."

The assailants pay but little attention to what the governor said; they cannot credit such an act of despair; they wish to enter the courtyard. Billot is at their head. Suddenly Billot trembles and turns pale; he just remembers Dr. Gilbert. As long as Billot had thought only of himself, it was a matter of little importance to him whether the Bastille was blown up, and he blown up with it; but Gilbert's life must be saved at any cost.

"Stop!" exclaimed Billot, throwing himself before

Elie and Hullin; "stop, in the name of the prisoners!"
And these men, who feared not to encounter death
themselves retreated, pale and trembling, in their turn.

"What do you demand?" they cried, renewing the
question they had previously put to the governor by his
own men.

"I demand that you should all withdraw," replied
De Launay fiercely. "I will not accept any proposal,
so long as there remains a single stranger in the Bastille."

"But," said Billot, "will you not take advantage of our
absence to place yourself again in a state of defense?"

"If the capitulation is refused, you shall find everything in the state it now is, — you at the gate, I where
I am now standing."

"You pledge your word for that?"

"On the honor of a gentleman."

Some of them shook their heads.

"On the honor of a gentleman," reiterated De Launay.
"Is there any one here who can still doubt, when a gentleman has pledged his honor?"

"No, no, no!" repeated five hundred voices.

"Let paper, pen, and ink be brought here to me."

The orders of the governor were instantly obeyed.

"'T is well," said De Launay. Then, turning towards
the assailants, "And now you must retire."

Billot, Hullin, and Elie set the example, and were the
first to withdraw. All the others followed them. De
Launay placed the match by his side, and began writing
the capitulation on his knee. The Invalides and the
Swiss soldiers, who felt that their existence depended
on the result, gazed at him while he was writing, with a

sort of respectful terror. De Launay looked round before allowing his pen to touch the paper. He saw that the courtyard was free of all intruders.

In an instant the people outside were informed of all that had happened within the fortress. As Monsieur de Losme had said, the population seemed to spring up from beneath the pavement. One hundred thousand men surrounded the Bastille. They were no longer merely laborers and artisans, but citizens of every class had joined them. They were not merely men in the prime of life, but children and old men had rushed forward to the fight. And all of them had arms of some description, all of them shouted vehemently. Here and there among the groups was to be seen a woman in despair, with hair dishevelled, wringing her hands, and uttering maledictions against the granite giant. She is some mother whose son the Bastille has just annihilated, some daughter whose father the Bastille has just levelled with the ground, some wife whose husband the Bastille has just exterminated. But during some moments no sounds had issued from the Bastille, no flames, no smoke. The Bastille had become as silent as the tomb. It would have been useless to endeavor to count the spots made by the balls which had marbled its surface. Every one had wished to fire a ball at the stone monster, the visible symbol of tyranny. Therefore, when it was rumored in the crowd that the Bastille was about to capitulate, that its governor had promised to surrender, they could scarcely credit the report.

Amid this general doubt, as they did not yet dare to congratulate themselves, as they were silently awaiting the result, they saw a letter pushed forth through a loophole on the point of a sword. Only between this letter and the besiegers there was the ditch of the Bastille, wide, deep, and full of water. Billot calls for a plank. Three are brought and are pushed across the ditch, but, being too short, did not reach the opposite side. Billot had them lashed together as he best could, and then ventured unhesitatingly upon the trembling bridge. The whole crowd remained breathlessly silent; all eyes were fixed upon the man who appears suspended above the ditch, whose stagnant waters resemble those of the river Cocytus. Pitou tremblingly seated himself on the edge of the slope and hid his head between his knees. His heart failed him, and he wept. When Billot had got about two thirds of the way over the plank, it twisted beneath his feet. Billot extends his arms, falls, and disappears in the ditch. Pitou utters a cry of horror and throws himself into the ditch, like a Newfoundland dog anxious to save his master. A man then approached the plank from which Billot had just before been precipitated. Without hesitation he walked across the temporary bridge. This man is Stanislaus Maillard, the usher of the Châtelet. When he had reached the spot below which Pitou and Billot were struggling in the muddy ditch, he for a moment cast a glance upon them, and seeing that there was no doubt they would regain the shore in safety, he continued to walk on. Half a minute afterwards he had reached the opposite side of the ditch, and had taken the letter which was held out to him on the point of a sword. Then, with the same tranquillity, the same firmness of step, he recrossed the ditch.

But at the moment when the crowd were pressing round him to hear the letter read, a storm of musket-balls rained down upon them from the battlements, and a frightful detonation was heard. One only cry, but one of those cries which announce the vengeance of a whole people, issues from every mouth.

"Trust, then, in tyrants!" exclaimed Gonchon.

And then, without thinking any more of the capitulation, without thinking any more of the powder-magazine, without thinking of themselves or of the prisoners, without desiring, without demanding anything but vengeance, the people rushed into the courtyard, no longer by hundreds of men, but by thousands. That which prevented the crowd from entering is no longer the musketry, but the gates, which are too narrow to admit them.

On hearing the detonation we have spoken of, the two soldiers who were still watching Monsieur de Launay threw themselves upon him: a third seized the match and extinguished it under his foot. De Launay drew the sword which was concealed in his cane, and would have turned it against his own breast, but the soldiers plucked it from him and snapped it in two. He then felt that all he could do was to abide the result; he therefore tranquilly awaited it. The people rush forward; the garrison open their arms to them, and the Bastille is taken.

THE FLIGHT OF LOUIS XVI

[1791]

BY CHARLES DUKE YONGE

[THE capture of the Bastille was followed by revolts against the nobles, which were in reality only ferocious orgies of fire and murder. Those nobles who could escape fled for their lives beyond the boundaries of France. There were rumors that the king, too, intended to flee, and a savage multitude swept out to Versailles, broke into the palace, and demanded that Louis should return to Paris. Under the charge of Lafayette, who commanded the National Guard, the king and his family were taken back to the capital. They occupied the palace of the Tuileries, but in reality they were prisoners, and a blow struck in their defense by either nobles or foreign nations would have resulted in their murder. There was only one hope, if they could make their escape to the frontier, then with foreign aid Louis and the nobles might return and overpower the revolutionists. Such an escape was carefully planned.

The Editor.]

IN such undertakings the simplest arrangements are the safest; and those devised by the queen and her advisers, the chief of whom were De Fersen and De Bouillé, were as simple as possible. The royal fugitives were to pass for a traveling party of foreigners. A transport signed by M. Montmorin, who still held the seals of the Foreign Department, was provided for Madame de Tourzel; who, assuming the name of Madame de Korff, a Russian baroness, professed to be returning to her own country with her family and her ordinary equipage. The dauphin and his sister were described as her children, the queen as their governess; while the king, himself, under the name of Durand, was to pass as their servant. Three of the old disbanded body-guard, MM. De Valory, De Malden, and De Moustier, were to attend the party, in the disguise of couriers; and, under the pretense of providing for the safe conveyance of a large sum of money which was required for the payment of the troops, De Bouillé undertook to post a detachment of soldiers at each town between Châlons and Montmédy, through which the travelers were to pass.

Some of the other arrangements were more difficult, as more likely to lead to a betrayal of the design. It was, of course, impossible to use any royal carriage, and no ordinary vehicle was large enough to hold such a party. But in the preceding year, De Fersen had had a carriage of unusual dimensions built for some friends in the south of Europe, so that he had no difficulty now in procuring another of similar pattern from the same maker; and Mr. Craufurd agreed to receive it into his stables, and at the proper hour to convey it outside the barrier.

Yet in spite of the care displayed in these arrangements, and of the absolute fidelity observed by all to whom the secret was entrusted, some of the inferior attendants about the court suspected what was in agitation. The queen, herself, with some degree of imprudence, sent away a large package to Brussels; one of her waiting-women discovered that she and Madame Campan had spent an evening in packing up jewels, and sent warning to Gouvion, an aide-de-camp of Lafayette, and to Bailly, the mayor, that the queen was at last preparing to flee. Luckily Bailly had received so many similar notices that he paid but little attention to this, or perhaps he was already beginning to feel the repentance which he afterwards exhibited at his former insolence to his sovereign, and was not unwilling to contribute to their safety by his inaction; while Gouvion was not anxious to reveal the course from which he had obtained his intelligence. Still, though nothing precise was known, the attention of more than one person was awakened to the movements of the royal family, and especially that of Lafayette, who, alarmed lest his prisoners should escape him, redoubled his vigilance, driving down to the palace every night, and often visiting them in their apartments to make himself certain of their presence. Six hundred of the National Guard were on duty at the Tuileries, and sentinels were placed at the end of every passage, and at the foot of every staircase; but fortunately a small room, with a secret door, which led into the queen's chamber, as it had been for some time unoccupied, had escaped the observation of the officers on guard, and that passage therefore offered a prospect of their being able to reach the courtyard without being perceived.

On the morning of the day appointed for the great enterprise, all in the secret were vividly excited except the queen. She alone preserved her coolness. No one could have guessed from her demeanor that she was on the point of embarking in an undertaking on which, in her belief, her own life and the lives of all those dearest to her depended. The children, who knew nothing of what was going on, went to their usual occupations: the dauphin to his garden on the terrace; Madame Royal to her lessons: and Marie Antoinette herself, after giving some orders which were to be executed in the course of the next day or two, went out riding with her sister-in-law in the Bois de Boulogne. Her conversation throughout the day was light and cheerful. She jested with the officer on guard about the reports which she understood to be in circulation about some intended flight of the king, and was relieved to find that he totally disbelieved them. She even ventured on the same jest with Lafayette himself, who replied, in his usual surly fashion, that such a project was constantly talked of; but even his rudeness could not discompose her.

As the hour drew near, she began to prepare her children. The princess was old enough to be talked to reasonably, and she contented herself therefore with warning her to show no surprise at anything that she might see or hear. The dauphin was to be disguised as a girl, and it was with great glee that he let the attendants dress him, saying that he saw that they were going to act a play. The royal supper usually took place soon after nine; at half-past ten the family separated for the night, and by eleven their attendants were all dismissed; and Marie Antoinette had fixed that hour for departing, because, even if the sentinels should get a glimpse of them, they would be apt to confound them with the crowd which usually quitted the palace at that time.

Accordingly at eleven o'clock the Count de Fersen, dressed as a coachman, drove an ordinary job-carriage into the courtyard; and Marie Antoinette, who trusted nothing to others which she could do herself, conducted Madame de Tourzel and the children downstairs, and seated them safely in the carriage. But even her nerves nearly gave way when Lafayette's coach, brilliantly lighted, drove by, passing close to her as he proceeded to the inner court to ascertain from the guard that everything was in its usual condition. In an agony of fright she sheltered herself behind some pillars, and in a few minutes the marquis drove back, and she rejoined the king, who was awaiting her summons in his own apartment, while one of the disguised body-guards went for the Princess Elizabeth. Even the children were inspired with their mother's courage. As the princess got into the carriage she trod on the dauphin, who was lying in concealment at the bottom, and the brave boy spoke not a word. While Louis himself gave a remarkable proof how, in spite of the want of moral and political resolution which had brought such miseries on himself and his country, he could yet preserve in the most critical moments his presence of mind and kind consideration for others. He was halfway downstairs when he returned to his room. M. Valory, who was escorting him, was dismayed when he saw him turn back, and ventured to remind him how precious was every instant. "I know that," replied the kind-hearted monarch; "but they will murder my servant to-morrow for having aided my escape"; and, sitting down at his table, he wrote a few lines declaring that the man had acted under his peremptory orders, and gave the note to him as a certificate to protect him from accusation. When all the rest were seated, the queen took her place. De Fersen drove them to the Porte St. Martin, where the great traveling-carriage was waiting, and, having transferred them to it, and taken a respectful leave of them, he fled at once to Brussels, which, more fortunate than those for whom he had risked his life, he reached in safety.

THE FLIGHT OF LOUIS XVI

For a hundred miles the royal fugitives proceeded rapidly and without interruption. One of the supposed couriers was on the box, another rode by the side of the carriage, and the third went on in advance to see that the relays were in readiness. Before midday they reached Châlons, the place where they were to be met by the first detachment of De Bouillé's troops, and, when the well-known uniforms met her eye, Marie Antoinette for the first time gave full expression to her feelings. "Thank God, we are saved," she exclaimed, clasping her hands; the fervor of her exclamation bearing undesigned testimony to the greatness of the fears, which, out of consideration for others, she had hitherto kept to herself; but in truth out of this employment of the troops arose all their subsequent disasters.

De Bouillé had been unwilling to send his detachments so far forward, pointing out that the notice which their arrival in the different towns was sure to attract, would do more harm than their presence as a protection could do good. But his argument had been overruled by the king himself, who apprehended the greatest danger from the chance of being overtaken, and expected it therefore to increase with every hour of the journey. De Bouillé's fears, however, were found to be the best justified by the event. In more than one town, even in the few hours that had elapsed since the arrival of the soldiers, there had been quarrels between them and the townspeople; in others, which was still worse, the populace had made friends with them and seduced them from their loyalty, so that the officers in command had found it necessary to withdraw them altogether; and anxiety at their unexpected absence had caused Louis more than once to show himself at the carriage window. More than once he was recognized by people who knew him and kept his counsel; but Drouet, the postmaster at Ste. Menehould, a town about one hundred and seventy miles from Paris, was of a less loyal disposition. He had lately been in the capital, where he had become infected with the Jacobin doctrines. He, too, saw the king's face, and on comparing his somewhat striking features with the stamp on some public documents which he chanced to have in his pocket, became convinced of his identity. He at once reported to the magistrates what he had seen, and with their sanction rode forward to the next town, Clermont, hoping to be able to collect a force sufficient to stop the royal carriage on its arrival there. But the king traveled so fast that he had quitted Clermont before Drouet reached it, and he even arrived at Varennes before his pursuer. Had he quitted that place also, he would have been in safety, for just beyond it De Bouillé had placed a strong division which would have been able to defy all resistance. But Varennes, a town on the Oise, was so small as to have no posthouse, and by some mismanagement the royal party had not been informed at which end of the town they were to find the relay. The carriage halted while M. Valory was making the necessary inquiries; and, while it was standing still, Drouet rode up, and forbade the postilions to proceed. He himself hastened on through the town, collected a few of the townspeople, and with their aid upset a cart or two on the bridge to block up the way; and, having thus made the road impassable, he roused the municipal authorities, for it was nearly midnight, and then, returning to the royal carriage, he compelled the royal family to dismount and follow him to the house of the mayor, a petty grocer, whose name was Strausse. The magistrates sounded the tocsin: the National Guard beat to arms: the king and queen were prisoners.

How they were allowed to remain so is still, after all the explanations that have been given, incomprehensible. Two officers with sixty hussars, all well disposed and loyal, were in a side street of the town waiting for their arrival, of which they were not aware. Six of the troopers actually passed the travelers in the street as they were proceeding to the mayor's house, but no one, not even the queen, appealed to them for succor; or they could have released them without an effort, for Drouet's whole party consisted of no more than eight unarmed men. And when, an hour afterwards, the officers in command learned that the king was in the town in the hands of his enemies, instead of at once delivering him, they were seized with a panic; they would not take on themselves the responsibility of acting without express orders; but galloped back to De Bouillé to report the state of affairs. In less than an hour three more detachments, amounting in all to above one hundred men, also reached the town; and their commanders did make their way to the king, and asked his orders. He could only reply that he was a prisoner, and had no orders to give; and not one of the officers had the sense to perceive that the fact of his announcing himself a prisoner was in itself an order to deliver him.

One word of command from Louis to clear the way for him at the sword's point would still have been sufficient; but he had still the same invincible repugnance as ever to allow blood to be shed in his quarrel. He preferred peaceful means, which could not but fail. With a dignity arising from his entire personal fearlessness, he announced his name and rank, his reasons for quitting Paris, and proceeding to Montmédy; declaring that he had no thought of quitting the kingdom; and demanded to be allowed to proceed on his journey; while the queen, her fears for her children overpowering all other feelings, addressed herself with the most earnest entreaties to the mayor's wife, declaring that their very lives would be in danger if they should be taken back to Paris, and imploring her to use her influence with her husband to allow them to proceed. Neither Strausse nor his wife was ill-disposed towards the king; but they had not the courage to comply with their request. And after a little time they would have found it beyond their power to let them proceed, however much they might have wished it; for the tocsin had brought up numbers of the National Guard, who were all disloyal; while some of the soldiers began to show a disinclination to act against them. And so matters stood for some hours; a crowd of townspeople, peasants, National Guards, and dragoons thronging the room; the king at times speaking quietly to his captors; the queen weeping; for the fatigue of the journey and the fearful disappointment of being thus baffled at the last moment, after she had thought that all danger was passed, had broken down even her nerves. At first, as usual, she had tried to persuade Louis to act with resolution; but when, as usual, she failed, she gave way to despair, and sat silent, with touching helpless sorrow, gazing on her children, who had fallen asleep.

At seven o'clock on the morning of the 22d, a single horseman rode into the town. He was an aide-de-camp of Lafayette. On the morning of the 21st the excitement had been great in Paris when it became known that the king had fled. The mob rose in furious tumult. They forced their way into the Tuileries, plundering the palace, and destroying the furniture. A fruit-woman took possession of the queen's bed as a stall to range her cherries on, saying that to-day it was the turn of the nation; and a picture of the king was torn down from the walls, and after being stuck up in derision outside the gates for some time, was offered for sale to the highest bidder. In the assembly the most violent language was used. An officer, whose name has been preserved through the eminence which after his death was attained by his widow and his children, General Beauharnais, was the president. And, as such, he announced that M. Bailly had reported to him that the enemies of the nation had carried off the king. The whole assembly was roused to fury at the idea of his having escaped from their power. A decree was at once drawn up in form, commanding that Louis should be seized wherever he could be found, and brought back to Paris. No one could pretend that the assembly had the slightest right to issue such an order; but Lafayette, with the alacrity which he always displayed when any insult was to be offered to the king or queen, at once sent it off by his own aide-de-camp, M. Romeuf, with instructions to see that it was carried out. The order was now delivered to Strausse; the king, with scarcely an attempt at resistance, declared his willingness to obey it; and before eight o'clock, he and his family, with their faithful bodyguard, now in undisguised captivity, were traveling back to Paris.

THE MARSEILLAISE

[1792]

BY CLAUDE JOSEPH ROUGET DE LISLE

[EARLY in 1792 it was plain that the French would be attacked by both Austria and Prussia, and the legislative assembly therefore declared war against the two countries. A few days later, De Lisle, an artillery officer, wrote the following hymn. The volunteers of Marseilles marched to Paris singing it as they went. That is why it received the name of "Marseillaise." It became the great song of the French Revolution.

The Editor.]

YE sons of freedom, wake to glory!
    Hark! hark! what myriads bid you rise!
Your children, wives, and grandsires hoary,
    Behold their tears and hear their cries!
Shall hateful tyrants, mischief breeding,
      With hireling hosts, a ruffian band,
      Affright and desolate the land,
While peace and liberty lie bleeding?
  To arms! to arms! ye brave!
    The avenging sword unsheathe;
  March on! march on! all hearts resolved
    On victory or death.

Now, now the dangerous storm is rolling,
    Which treacherous kings confederate raise;
The dogs of war, let loose, are howling,
    And lo! our walls and cities blaze;
And shall we basely view the ruin,

THE MARSEILLAISE

While lawless force, with guilty stride,
   Spreads desolation far and wide.
With crime and blood his hands imbruing.
   To arms! to arms! ye brave!
    The avenging sword unsheathe;
   March on! march on! all hearts resolved
    On victory or death.

With luxury and pride surrounded,
   The vile insatiate despots dare,
Their thirst of gold and power unbounded,
   To mete and vend the light and air!
Like beasts of burden they would lead us,
    Like gods, would bid their slaves adore;
    But man is man, and who is more?
Then shall they longer lash and goad us?
   To arms! to arms! ye brave!
    The avenging sword unsheathe;
   March on! march on! all hearts resolved
    On victory or death.

O Liberty! can man resign thee,
   Once having felt thy generous flame?
Can dungeons, bolts, or bars confine thee,
   Or whips thy noble spirit tame?
Too long the world has wept, bewailing
    That falsehood's dagger tyrants wield,
    But freedom is our sword and shield,
And all their arts are unavailing.
   To arms! to arms! ye brave!
    The avenging sword unsheathe;
   March on! march on! all hearts resolved
    On victory or death.

VI
THE REIGN OF TERROR

HISTORICAL NOTE

On September 21, 1792, a National Convention met. This consisted of two parties, the Girondists, who were moderates, and the Mountainists, or extreme radicals. Both agreed upon abolishing the monarchy, and this was done at once. The convention next proceeded to try the king for conspiring with the enemies of France and opposing the will of the people. On January 21, 1793, he was put to death.

The condition of France now seemed desperate. Austria and Prussia had declared war and their armies were advancing toward Paris. The province of Vendée was in open revolt. It was time, said Danton, the leader of the Mountainists, for audacious measures. The Girondists counseled moderation. They were overthrown and their leaders sent to the guillotine. Discontent in the provinces and in Paris was crushed down by wholesale executions. Thirteen armies were raised and equipped, the invaders were driven beyond the borders, and France was saved, though at a terrible cost of blood and treasure.

If the Revolution was merciless to its enemies, it was no less so to its friends. The heads of the Girondists had fallen at the command of the radical leaders, Marat, Danton, and Robespierre. Marat fell before the dagger of Charlotte Corday. Danton was guillotined with his followers on April 5, 1794. Herbert and the ultra-revolutionists had preceded him to the scaffold by a few days, and Robespierre was left supreme. His supremacy was of brief duration. On the 27th of August he was overthrown after a titanic struggle, and on the next day he and his followers suffered the fate they had decreed to so many others.

The downfall of Robespierre and his party ended the Reign of Terror. The Moderates once again came into power. The remaining radicals were deported, imprisoned, or executed, and the Paris mob that attempted to revive its old authority was cannonaded out of existence by Napoleon Bonaparte, a young officer who had distinguished himself at the siege of Toulon.

THE EXECUTION OF LOUIS XVI

[1793]

BY EDMOND BIRÉ

I once more take up my diary to jot down all the details I have been able to gather concerning the sacrifice of the 21st of January.

The night between the 20th and the 21st had been a cold and rainy one. At daybreak it still was raining, but the snow, which had the night before covered Paris with an immense pall, had partially disappeared. Patrols marched slowly through the streets. From all quarters came the roll of the drum and the blare of the trumpet, calling citizens to arms. House doors opened, and men, both young and old, hurried off to their various sections in obedience to the orders of the Conseil-Général of the department and the Order of the Day issued by Santerre on the 20th.

By seven o'clock more than 150,000 men were under arms at the various posts assigned them. The third legion, comprising the citizens of the Gravilliers, Arcis, and Lombard sections, is drawn up in the Place de la Révolution.

The post of honor, opposite the scaffold, at the entrance of the Champs-Élysées, is occupied by the battalions of federates from Aix and Marseilles.

At eight o'clock the rain ceases, but a thick cold mist lies upon the city. Not a single shop or warehouse is open, and all the windows are hermetically closed. In several places the following notice, written by hand, has been posted up: —

" To the People,
  " The Assembly can drag an innocent king to the scaffold, and by thus outraging the feelings of the world, bring unutterable misfortunes upon us. What has it to fear? Nothing. None but honest folk are opposed to it. Are its decrees those of a God, that they cannot be revoked? Let us save him — there is still time."

Santerre, accompanied by a formidable train of artillery, arrived at the Temple a little after eight o'clock, and went straight to the king's apartments, followed by seven or eight municipal officers and ten gendarmes. Louis received him with perfect tranquillity. "Have you come for me?" he asked. "Yes." "Very well. I want to be alone with my confessor for a few minutes, and then I will be at your disposal." Hereupon he entered an inner room, and returned almost immediately after, holding his testament in his hand. Addressing the municipal officers, he said: "Is there some member of the Commune amongst you?" The priest Jacques Roux stepped forward. "I beg you, sir, to place this document in the hands of the President of the Conseil-Général." "That's not my business," replied Jacques Roux; "I am here to take you to the scaffold." "You are right," observed the king, and thereupon handed his testament to Baudrais, a commissioner on duty in the Temple, who promised to deliver it to the Commune. After having commended Cléry, his valet, and his former servants in the Tuileries and at Versailles, to the municipal officers, he looked at Santerre, and said in a firm voice: "Let us go."

A start is made. At the top of the stairs the king's eyes fall upon Mathey, the concierge of the tower. He stops and says: "I was somewhat hasty a day or two ago; pray forgive me." They go down; the king walks across the first courtyard between a double hedge of pikes and bayonets; twice does he turn round to look at the tower in which he leaves sister, children, and wife. On reaching the second court, he finds a carriage awaiting him, with two gendarmes stationed at the door. The carriage is painted green, and is that of the Minister Clavière. Louis gets in, his confessor taking a seat beside him, whilst the front seat is occupied by a lieutenant and a quartermaster of the gendarmerie. The Abbé Edgeworth is not in clerical garb, but wears a plain black coat.

As the carriage leaves the Temple, cries of *"Mercy! Mercy!"* are uttered by some women, followed by an ominous silence.

From the Temple to the boulevard, the street was lined with more than 10,000 armed men.

Along each side of the boulevard was a line of men four deep, all carrying guns or pikes; there could not have been less than 80,000. A train of artillery headed the procession, which was composed of 12,000 to 15,000 armed men. Immediately before the king's carriage, a large number of drummers and trumpeters kept up an incessant din; behind it came more artillery.

As the carriage passed the Port Saint-Denis, four men — one of them, the eldest, flourishing a naked sword — dashed through the quadruple line of soldiers, and repeatedly shouted: "Help, Frenchmen! Help us to save the king!" To this heroic appeal there was no response, and the four royalists dashed back through the broken line and amongst the astonished crowd. The man with the sword and one of his companions succeeded in escaping, but the two others were seized just as they were entering a house in the Rue de Cléry, and were cut to pieces on the threshold. Meanwhile the procession continued to move towards the Place de la Révolution. The journey from the Temple to the end of the Rue Royale had taken more than an hour. During this time, Louis, his face half hidden by a round hat with a wide brim, was engaged in reading, from his confessor's breviary, the prayers for the dying and the Psalms of David. When the carriage at length stopped, the king, raising his head, half closed the book and said to the abbé: "Here we are, if I am not mistaken." The abbé bowed, and Louis turned once more to his breviary, and read the last verses of the psalm he had left unfinished. At that moment one of Samson's assistants opened the carriage-door and let down the step. The king calmly finished his last prayer, returned the book to the abbé, and, laying his hand on the confessor's knee, said to the lieutenant and his comrade: "Gentlemen, I recommend the abbé to your protection." Neither of the officers having replied, the king repeated in a somewhat louder tone: "I charge you to see that no harm is done him after my death." "All right — all right," replied the lieutenant; "we'll see to that." The king then got out of the carriage without any assistance; it was just twenty minutes past ten. He was wearing a brown coat and white waistcoat, gray breeches, and white stockings. His hair was neatly arranged, and his face betrayed no signs of agitation. He then advanced with a firm step to the scaffold, which had been erected between the avenue of the Champs-Élysées and the pedestal of Louis XV's statue, overturned after the 10th of August.

An immense space lined with cannons had been railed off round the scaffold. Turning to the armed masses which surround him, the king, in a tone of command, orders the drummers to be silent. They obey; but Santerre, who is on horseback a short distance off, comes hastening up, and by his orders the drummers resume their task. The headsman and his assistants now crowd round the monarch, and wish to help him to undress. He pushes them away, and, taking off his cravat with his own hands, proceeds to divest himself of his coat, under which he was wearing a white swan's-down waist-coat with sleeves. He then turns down the shirt to leave his neck free, and kneels at the feet of the Abbé Edge-worth to receive the last benediction. Rising once more, he places his foot on the first step of the ladder that leads to the scaffold; but the assistants stop him, and try to seize his hands. "What is it you want?" he asks. "To bind your hands." "Bind my hands! Never! It's not necessary; I am quite calm." The executioners raise their voices, and seem to call for assistance. "Sire," says the abbé, "in this fresh insult I see but an additional trait of resemblance between Your Majesty and the God who is about to reward you." The king submits, and, holding out his hands, says to the executioner: "Do what you will; I will drain the cup to the dregs." They then tie his hands with his handkerchief and cut off his hair.

FRANCE

All is now ready. Louis looks at the scaffold for a moment, and receives the following words from his confessor as a last encouragement: "Go, son of Saint Louis; Heaven awaits you!" Bravely he mounts the steps of the scaffold, but as they are extremely steep and his hands are tied, he leans his elbow on the abbé's arm. Whilst the priest remains kneeling on the topmost step, Louis rapidly crosses the platform, and on reaching the opposite side looks towards the Tuileries, and again imposes silence upon the drummers by an imperious gesture. In a loud voice that is heard as far as the Pont Tournant he utters these words: "Frenchmen, I die innocent of all the crimes with which I am charged." Turning to the executioners, Santerre shouts, "Don't let him speak!" A few cries of "*Mercy! Mercy!*" are heard, and the crowd shows signs of great agitation. Many of the citizens want Louis to speak, but most of them are opposed to this, and encourage the executioners to do their duty. Santerre issues an order to the drummers, and the interrupted roll of the drums is resumed with fresh vigor. The headsman's assistants now seize the king, who unresistingly allows himself to be led to the board. Whilst he is being strapped down, he utters the following words in loud, distinct tones: "I forgive all those who have sought my death; I pray to God that the blood you are about to shed may not be avenged on France. And you, unhappy people —" He says no more. It is twenty-four minutes past ten, and the knife has done its work. Whilst the men of the Republic were performing their hideous task, the man of God was on his knees on the steps of the scaffold, reciting the prayers for the dying. He did not budge till the knife had fallen; then, passing unmolested through the ranks of the soldiers, he became lost in the crowd.

The crime was perpetrated. One of the executioners —the youngest, almost a boy—took up the king's head by the hair, and showed it to the people from the four sides of the scaffold. At sight of this a few shouts of "*Vive la République!*" are raised. Soon these are multiplied, and are reëchoed back from all parts of the Place de la Révolution, and repeated along the quays—"*Vive la République!*" "*Vive la Liberté!*" "*Vive l'Égalité!*" "*May all tyrants perish so!*" Hats are stuck on the ends of guns and pikes, the citizens embrace each other in wild delight, and joining hands, they form a ring and dance round the scaffold. This example is followed in several other parts of the square, and dancing goes on as far as the Pont de la Liberté. The boys of the Collège des Quatre-Nations, who witness this horrible spectacle from their schoolroom windows, wave their caps and shout, "*Vive la République!*"

Meanwhile the National Guards, federates, and gendarmes posted round the scaffold dip their pikes, bayonets, and swords in the warm blood that is trickling down. The officers of the Marseilles battalion dip their letters in it, and as they afterwards march through the streets of the city at the head of their companies, they stick these letters on the points of their swords, and, flourishing them, shout: "This is the blood of a tyrant!"

A man climbs on to the scaffold, and plunges his naked arm into the *tyrant's* blood. He then takes a handful of it, and besprinkles the crowd that surges round the foot of the platform, eager to catch a drop or two. "Brothers," cries the man, as he performs this hideous rite —

"brothers, they have told us that the blood of Louis
Capet will be on our heads. Well, let it be. Louis Capet
has so often washed his hands in ours. Republicans, a
king's blood brings luck!"

And for this blood the crowd still hungers. People
fight to dip the tips of their fingers, a handkerchief, a pen,
or a scrap of paper, in it. A young man who looked like
an Englishman gave a boy fifteen francs to dip a very
fine linen handkerchief in the few drops of blood that
were left. One of the executioner's men, seated on the
edge of the scaffold, sells small packets of the king's hair;
the ribbon with which it was tied back fetches ten francs.
A *sans-culotte*, named Heuzé, also makes his way on
to the scaffold, and, seizing the king's coat, holds it up
at the end of a pike. The coat is immediately torn to
shreds by the crowd, and every one is anxious to secure
a piece of it. The king's hat, which was left lying on the
bottom step of the scaffold, is also torn into fragments
and distributed.

The crowd gradually disperses. The fog that has been
hanging over the city since morning has become more
dense. Every shop, workshop, and warehouse is closed;
in the afternoon a few of them are opened, as on minor
fête days. Patrols continue to parade the deserted
streets, the silence of which is only broken occasionally
by the bloodthirsty cries and savage capers of a few
abandoned wretches.

MARIE ANTOINETTE IN THE CONCIERGERIE

BY CHARLES LOUIS MÜLLER
(*French painter*, 1815–1892)

Marie Antoinette was for a time the darling of the French people. Then came criticism. She was accused of extravagance that was reckless even in a queen, of various disgraceful intrigues, and finally of being an enemy to France. Thoughtless and imprudent she certainly was, and her imperiousness and frequent haughtiness made enemies without number. At the outbreak of the French Revolution, the people of France hated her as much as they had formerly loved her. In 1793, her husband, Louis XVI, was declared guilty of tyranny, and was put to death. The Convention then ordered that she should be tried for her life. At two o'clock on the morning of October 14, 1793, she was commanded to appear before the tribunal. On the 16th, at four in the morning, the discussions came to an end, and the queen, exhausted but not terrified, was taken back to her prison.

The moment of the picture is that in which the delegates have come to announce to her the decision of the court and the order for her execution. She stands before her bed in a white dress with black at the wrists, a dress loaned her, it is said, by an actress, a fellow prisoner. The chief officer, distinguished by his sash, is reading the order aloud, and Marie Antoinette stands before him listening. Her hand rests lightly on the back of a chair. Her face is sad but resolute, and her whole bearing is marked by dignity and majesty. She is every inch a queen. The three delegates who stand just within the door are gazing upon her, one with an expression of sheer brutality, one with a look of sternness, and one, who seems unwilling to pass the threshold, with perhaps a thought of sympathy and pity. On a table at the left sits a soldier, who stares at the queen with an air of studied insolence.

A few hours later, Marie Antoinette, Queen of France, was executed.

IN THE REVOLT OF THE VENDÉE

[1793]

BY VICTOR HUGO

[THE peasants of the Vendée, a department of western
France, were devoted to the local nobles and had no sympathy with the French Revolution. They rose against the
Republican Government in 1789; and in 1793, indignant
at the conscription laws, and hoping for the aid of England,
they made angry resistance. This lasted for three years
before they were subdued.

The Editor.]

As we have just seen, the peasants, on arriving at Dol,
dispersed themselves through the town, each man following his own fancy, as happens when troops "obey
from friendship," a favorite expression with the Vendeans, — a species of obedience which makes heroes
but not troopers. They thrust the artillery out of the
way along with the baggage, under the arches of the old
market-hall. They were weary; they ate, drank, counted
their rosaries, and lay down pell-mell across the principal
street, which was encumbered rather than guarded.

As night came on, the greater portion fell asleep, with
their heads on their knapsacks, some having their wives
beside them, for the peasant women often followed their
husbands, and the robust ones acted as spies. It was a
mild July evening; the constellation glittered in the deep
purple of the sky. The entire bivouac, which resembled
rather the halt of a caravan than an army encamped,
gave itself up to repose. Suddenly, amid the dull

gleams of twilight, such as had not yet closed their eyes saw three pieces of ordnance pointed at the entrance of the street. It was Gauvain's artillery. He had surprised the main-guard. He was in the town, and his column held the top of the street.

A peasant started up, crying, "Who goes there?" and fired his musket; a cannon-shot replied. Then a furious discharge of musketry burst forth. The whole drowsy crowd sprang up with a start. A rude shock,— to fall asleep under the stars and wake under a volley of grape-shot.

The first moments were terrific. There is nothing so tragic as the aimless swarming of a thunderstricken crowd. They flung themselves on their arms; they yelled, they ran; many fell. The assaulted peasants no longer knew what they were about, and blindly shot one another. The townspeople, stunned with fright, rushed in and out of their houses, and wandered frantically amid the hubbub. Families shrieked to one another. A dismal combat ensued, in which women and children were mingled. The balls, as they whistled overhead, streaked the darkness with rays of light. A fusillade poured from every dark corner. There was nothing but smoke and tumult. The entanglement of the baggage-wagons and the cannon-carriages was added to the confusion. The horses became unmanageable; the wounded were trampled under foot. The groans of the poor wretches, helpless on the ground, filled the air. Horror here, stupefaction there. Soldiers and officers sought for one another. In the midst of all this could be seen creatures made indifferent to the awful scene by personal preoccupations. A woman sat nursing her new-born babe, seated on a bit of wall, against which her husband leaned with his leg broken; and he, while his blood was flowing, tranquilly loaded his rifle and fired at random, straight before him into the darkness. Men lying flat on the ground fired across the spokes of the wagon-wheels. At moments there rose a hideous din of clamors, then the great voices of the cannon drowned all. It was awful. It was like a felling of trees; they dropped one upon another. Gauvain poured out a deadly fire from his ambush, and suffered little loss.

Still the peasants, courageous amid their disorder, ended by putting themselves on the defensive; they retreated into the market, — a vast, obscure redoubt, a forest of stone pillars. There they again made a stand; anything which resembled a wood gave them confidence. Imânus supplied the absence of Lantenac as best he could. They had cannon, but to the great astonishment of Gauvain they did not make use of it; that was owing to the fact that the artillery officers had gone with the marquis to reconnoiter Mount Dol, and the peasants did not know how to manage the culverins and demi-culverins. But they riddled with balls the Blues who cannonaded them; they replied to the grape-shot by volleys of musketry. It was now they who were sheltered. They had heaped together the drays, the tumbrels, the casks, all the litter of the old market, and improvised a lofty barricade, with openings through which they could pass their carbines. From these holes their fusillade was murderous. The whole was quickly arranged. In a quarter of an hour the market presented an impregnable front.

This became a serious matter for Gauvain. This

market suddenly transformed into a citadel was unexpected. The peasants were inside it, massed and solid. Gauvain's surprise had succeeded, but he ran the risk of defeat. He got down from his saddle. He stood attentively studying the darkness, his arms folded, clutching his sword in one hand, erect, in the glare of a torch which lighted his battery. The gleam, falling on his tall figure, made him visible to the men behind the barricade. He became an aim for them, but he did not notice it. The shower of balls sent out from the barricade fell about him as he stood there, lost in thought. But he could oppose cannon to all these carbines, and cannon always ends by getting the advantage. Victory rests with him who has the artillery. His battery, well-manned, insured him the superiority.

Suddenly a lightning-flash burst from the shadowy market; there was a sound like a peal of thunder, and a ball broke through a house above Gauvain's head. The barricade was replying to the cannon with its own voice. What had happened? Something new had occurred. The artillery was no longer confined to one side. A second ball followed the first and buried itself in the wall close to Gauvain. A third knocked his hat off on the ground. These balls were of a heavy caliber. It was a sixteen-pounder that fired.

"They are aiming at you, Commandant," cried the artillerymen.

They extinguished the torch. Gauvain, as if in a reverie, picked up his hat. Some one had in fact aimed at Gauvain: it was Lantenac. The marquis had just arrived within the barricade from the opposite side. Imânus had hurried to meet him.

IN THE REVOLT OF THE VENDÉE

"Monseigneur, we are surprised!"

"By whom?"

"I do not know."

"Is the route to Dinan free?"

"I think so."

"We must begin a retreat."

"It has commenced. A good many have run away."

"We must not run; we must fall back. Why are you not making use of this artillery?"

"The men lost their heads; besides, the officers were not here."

"I am come."

"Monseigneur, I have sent toward Fougères all I could of the baggage, the women, everything useless. What is to be done with the three little prisoners?"

"Ah, those children!"

"Yes."

"They are our hostages. Have them taken to La Tourgue."

This said, the marquis rushed to the barricade. With the arrival of the chief the whole face of affairs changed. The barricade was ill-constructed for artillery; there was only room for two cannon; the marquis put in position a couple of sixteen-pounders, for which loopholes were made. As he leaned over one of the guns, watching the enemy's battery through the opening, he perceived Gauvain.

"It is he!" cried the marquis.

Then he took the swab and rammer himself, loaded the piece, sighted it, and fired. Thrice he aimed at Gauvain and missed. The third time he only succeeded in knocking his hat off.

"Numbskull!" muttered Lantenac; "a little lower, and I should have taken his head." Suddenly the torch went out, and he had only darkness before him. "So be it!" said he. Then turning toward the peasant gunners, he cried: "Now let them have it!"

Gauvain, on his side, was not less in earnest. The seriousness of the situation increased. A new phase of the combat developed itself. The barricade had begun to use cannon. Who could tell if it were not about to pass from the defensive to the offensive? He had before him, after deducting the killed and fugitives, at least five thousand combatants, and he had left only twelve hundred serviceable men. What would happen to the republicans if the enemy perceived their paucity of numbers? The rôles were reversed. He had been the assailant, — he would become the assailed. If the barricade were to make a sortie, everything might be lost. What was to be done? He could no longer think of attacking the barricade in front; an attempt at main force would be foolhardy: twelve hundred men cannot dislodge five thousand. To rush upon them was impossible; to wait would be fatal. He must make an end. But how?

Gauvain belonged to the neighborhood; he was acquainted with the town; he knew that the old markethouse where the Vendeans were intrenched was backed by a labyrinth of narrow and crooked streets. He turned toward his lieutenant, who was that valiant Captain Guéchamp, afterward famous for clearing out the forest of Concise, where Jean Chouan was born, and for preventing the capture of Bourgneuf by holding the dike of La Chaîne against the rebels.

"Guéchamp," said he, "I leave you in command.

Fire as fast as you can. Riddle the barricade with cannon-balls. Keep all those fellows over yonder busy."

"I understand," said Guéchamp.

"Mass the whole column with their guns loaded, and hold them ready to make an onslaught." He added a few words in Guéchamp's ear.

"I hear," said Guéchamp.

Gauvain resumed, "Are all our drummers on foot?"

"Yes."

"We have nine. Keep two, and give me seven."

The seven drummers ranged themselves in silence in front of Gauvain. Then he said: "Battalion of the Bonnet Rouge!"

Twelve men, of whom one was a sergeant, stepped out from the main body of the troop.

"I demand the whole battalion," said Gauvain.

"Here it is," replied the sergeant.

"You are twelve!"

"There are twelve of us left."

"It is well," said Gauvain.

There was a forage wagon standing near; Gauvain pointed toward it with his finger. "Sergeant, order your men to make some straw ropes and twist them about their guns, so that there will be no noise if they knock together."

A minute passed; the order was silently executed in the darkness.

"It is done," said the sergeant.

"Soldiers, take off your shoes," commanded Gauvain.

"We have none," returned the sergeant.

They numbered, counting the drummers, nineteen men; Gauvain made the twentieth. He cried: "Follow me! Single file! The drummers next to me, the battalion behind them. Sergeant, you will command the battalion."

He put himself at the head of the column, and while the firing on both sides continued, these twenty men, gliding along like shadows, plunged into the deserted lanes. The line marched thus for some time, twisting along the fronts of the houses. The whole town seemed dead; the citizens were hidden in their cellars. Every door was barred; every shutter closed; no light to be seen anywhere. Amid the silence this principal street kept up its din; the cannonading continued; the republican battery and the royalist barricade spit forth their volleys with undiminished fury.

After twenty minutes of this tortuous march, Gauvain, who kept his way unerringly through the darkness, reached the end of a lane which led into the broad street, but on the other side of the market-house. The position was turned. In this direction there was no intrenchment, according to the eternal imprudence of barricade builders; the market was open, and the entrance free among the pillars where some baggage-wagons stood ready to depart. Gauvain and his nineteen men had the five thousand Vendeans before them, but their backs instead of their faces.

Gauvain spoke in a low voice to the sergeant; the soldiers untwisted the straw from their guns; the twelve grenadiers posted themselves in line behind the angle of the lane, and the seven drummers waited with their drumsticks lifted. The artillery firing was intermittent. Suddenly, in a pause between the discharges, Gauvain waved his sword, and cried in a voice which rang like a trumpet through the silence: "Two hundred men to the right; two hundred men to the left; all the rest in the center!"

The twelve muskets fired, and the seven drums beat.

Gauvain uttered the formidable battle-cry of the Blues: "To your bayonets! Down upon them!"

The effect was prodigious. This whole peasant mass felt itself surprised in the rear, and believed that it had a fresh army at its back. At the same instant, on hearing the drums, the column which Guéchamp commanded at the head of the street began to move, sounding the charge in its turn, and flung itself at a run on the barricade. The peasants found themselves between two fires. Panic magnifies: a pistol-shot sounds like the report of a cannon; in moments of terror the imagination heightens every noise; the barking of a dog sounds like the roar of a lion. Add to this the fact that the peasant catches fright as easily as thatch catches fire; and as quickly as a blazing thatch becomes a conflagration, a panic among peasants becomes a rout. An indescribably confused flight ensued.

In a few instants the market-hall was empty; the terrified rustics broke away in all directions; the officers were powerless; Imânus uselessly killed two or three fugitives; nothing was to be heard but the cry, "Save yourselves!" The army poured through the streets of the town like water through the holes of a sieve, and dispersed into the open country with the rapidity of a cloud carried along by a whirlwind. Some fled toward Châteauneuf, some toward Plerguer, others toward Antrain.

FRANCE

The Marquis de Lantenac watched this stampede. He spiked the guns with his own hands and then retreated, — the last of all, slowly, composedly, saying to himself, "Decidedly, the peasants will not stand. We must have the English."

GIRONDISTS ON THEIR WAY TO THE GUILLOTINE

BY KARL THEODOR VON PILOTY
(*German artist*, 1826–1886)

THE Girondists wished to establish in France, in the days of the French Revolution, a republic like the United States. They were the Moderates among the Revolutionists, and they opposed the Extremists. But the Reign of Terror was at hand. Marat, Danton, and Robespierre came into power, and death was decreed to the Girondist leaders.

It is said that a friend had promised to send them a banquet on the evening of their trial, whether they were acquitted or condemned, and the promise was kept. With the most costly viands, the rarest wines, the most beautiful flowers before them, they sat in a blaze of lights for their last meal. Vergniaud presided with quiet and dignified mien. They spoke together with gravity, but without gloom, of the immortality of the soul. The still warm corpse of Valazé, one of their number who had committed suicide, had been taken back to the prison, and was ordered to be carried to the place of execution on the same cart with them. Each one kissed his dead hand. "To-morrow," they whispered, and drew his mantle gently over his face.

"The following day," Macaulay has written, "was the saddest in the sad history of the Revolution. The sufferers were so innocent, so brave, so eloquent, so accomplished, so young. Some of them were graceful and handsome youths of six or seven and twenty. Vergniaud and Gensonné were little more than thirty. In a few months the fame of their genius had filled Europe; and they were to die for no crime but this, that they had wished to combine order, justice, and mercy with freedom."

Their last moments were sublime. As they stood about the scaffold awaiting their turn to mount the stairs, they sang the Marseillaise, the chorus growing fainter and fainter as one after another laid his head upon the block until the song of the last victim was cut short by the fatal knife.

AT THE GUILLOTINE

BY CHARLES DICKENS

[THE following scene is supposed to take place in the French Revolution. In order to save the life of one of the fifty-two about to be guillotined, Sydney Carton ("Evrémonde") has exchanged clothes with him, and has taken his place among the condemned.

The Editor.]

As he stood by the wall in a dim corner, while some of the fifty-two were brought in after him, one man stopped in passing to embrace him, as having a knowledge of him. It thrilled him with a great dread of discovery; but the man went on. A very few moments after that, a young woman, with a slight girlish form, a sweet spare face in which there was no vestige of color, and large widely opened patient eyes, rose from the seat where he had observed her sitting, and came to speak to him.

"Citizen Evrémonde," she said, touching him with her cold hand. "I am a poor little seamstress, who was with you in La Force."

He murmured for answer: "True. I forget what you were accused of?"

"Plots. Though the just Heaven knows I am innocent of any. Is it likely? Who would think of plotting with a poor little weak creature like me?"

The forlorn smile with which she said it, so touched him that tears started from his eyes.

"I am not afraid to die, Citizen Evrémonde, but I

have done nothing. I am not unwilling to die, if the
Republic, which is to do so much good to us poor, will
profit by my death; but I do not know how that can be,
Citizen Evrémonde. Such a poor weak little creature!"

As the last thing on earth that his heart was to warm
and soften to, it warmed and softened to this pitiable
girl.

"I heard you were released, Citizen Evrémonde. I
hoped it was true?"

"It was. But I was again taken and condemned."

"If I may ride with you, Citizen Evrémonde, will you
let me hold your hand? I am not afraid, but I am little
and weak, and it will give me more courage."

As the patient eyes were lifted to his face, he saw
a sudden doubt in them, and then astonishment. He
pressed the work-worn, hunger-worn young fingers, and
touched his lips.

"Are you dying for him?" she whispered.

"And his wife and child. Hush! Yes."

"Oh, you will let me hold your brave hand, stranger?"

"Hush! Yes, my poor sister, to the last."

As the somber wheels of the six carts go round, they
seem to plough up a long crooked furrow among the
populace in the streets. Ridges of faces are thrown to
this side and to that, and the ploughs go steadily onward. So used are the regular inhabitants of the houses
to the spectacle, that in many windows there are no
people, and in some the occupation of the hands is not
so much as suspended, while the eyes survey the faces
in the tumbrels. Here and there, the inmate had visitors
to see the sight; then he points his finger, with some-

thing of the complacency of a curator or authorized exponent, to this cart and to this, and seems to tell who sat here yesterday, and who there the day before.

Of the riders in the tumbrels, some observe these things, and all things on their last roadside, with an impassive stare; others with a lingering interest in the ways of life and men. Some, seated with drooping heads, are sunk in silent despair; again, there are some so heedful of their looks that they cast upon the multitude such glances as they have seen in theaters, and in pictures. Several close their eyes, and think, or try to get their straying thoughts together. Only one, and he a miserable creature of a crazed aspect, is so shattered and made drunk by horror that he sings, and tries to dance. Not one of the whole number appeals, by look or gesture, to the pity of the people.

There is a guard of sundry horsemen riding abreast of the tumbrels, and faces are often turned up to some of them and they are asked some question. It would seem to be always the same question, for it is always followed by a press of people towards the third cart. The horsemen abreast of that cart frequently point out one man in it with their swords. The leading curiosity is, to know which is he; he stands at the back of the tumbrel with his head bent down, to converse with a mere girl who sits on the side of the cart, and holds his hand. He has no curiosity or care for the scene about him, and always speaks to the girl. Here and there in a long street of Saint Honoré, cries are raised against him. If they move him at all, it is only to a quiet smile, as he shakes his hair a little more loosely about his face. He cannot easily touch his face, his arms being bound.

On the steps of a church, awaiting the coming up of the tumbrels, stands the spy and prison-sheep. He looks into the first of them: not there. He looks into the second: not there. He already asks himself, "Has he sacrificed me?" when his face clears, as he looks into the third.

"Which is Evrémonde?" said a man behind him.

"That. At the back there."

"With his hand in the girl's?"

"Yes."

The man cries, "Down, Evrémonde! To the Guillotine all aristocrats! Down, Evrémonde!"

"Hush, hush!" the spy entreats him timidly.

"And why not, citizen?"

"He is going to pay the forfeit; it will be paid in five minutes more. Let him be at peace."

But the man continuing to exclaim, "Down, Evrémonde!" the face of Evrémonde is for a moment turned towards him. Evrémonde then sees the spy, and looks attentively at him, and goes his way.

The clocks are on the stroke of three, and the furrow ploughed among the populace is turning round, to come on into the place of execution, and end. The ridges thrown to this side and to that, now crumble in and close behind the last plough as it passes on, for all are following to the guillotine. In front of it, seated in chairs as in a garden of public diversion, are a number of women, busily knitting. On one of the foremost chairs, stands The Vengeance, looking about for her friend.

"Thérèse!" she cries, in her shrill tones. "Who has seen her? Thérèse Defarge!"

AT THE GUILLOTINE

"She never missed before," says a knitting-woman of the sisterhood.

"No; nor will she miss now," cries The Vengeance petulantly. "Thérèse."

"Louder," the woman recommends.

Aye! Louder, Vengeance, much louder, and still she will scarcely hear thee. Louder yet, Vengeance, with a little oath or so added, and yet it will hardly bring her. Send other women up and down to seek her, lingering somewhere; and yet, although the messengers have done dread deeds, it is questionable whether of their own wills they will go far enough to find her!

"Bad Fortune!" cries The Vengeance, stamping her foot in the chair, "and here are the tumbrels! And Evrémonde will be dispatched in a wink, and she not here. See her knitting in my hand, and her empty chair ready for her. I cry with vexation and disappointment!"

As The Vengeance descends from her elevation to do it, the tumbrels begin to discharge their loads. The ministers of Sainte Guillotine are robed and ready. Crash! — A head is held up, and the knitting-women, who scarcely lifted their eyes to look at it a moment ago when it could think and speak, count One.

The second tumbrel empties and moves on! the third comes up. Crash! — And the knitting-women, never faltering or pausing in their work, count Two.

The supposed Evrémonde descends, and the seamstress is lifted out next after him. He has not relinquished her patient hand in getting out, but still holds it as he promised. He gently places her with her back to the crashing engine that constantly whirrs up and falls, and she looks into his face and thanks him.

"But for you, dear stranger, I should not be so composed, for I am naturally a poor little thing, faint of heart; nor should I have been able to raise my thoughts to Him who was put to death, that we might have hope and comfort here to-day. I think you were sent to me by Heaven."

"Or you to me," says Sydney Carton. "Keep your eyes upon me, dear child, and mind no other object."

"I mind nothing while I hold your hand. I shall mind nothing when I let it go, if they are rapid."

"They will be rapid. Fear not!"

The two stand in the fast-thinning throng of victims, but they speak as if they were alone. Eye to eye, voice to voice, hand to hand, heart to heart, these two children of the Universal Mother, else so wide apart and differing, have come together on the dark highway, to repair home together and to rest in her bosom.

"Brave and generous friend, will you let me ask you one last question? I am very ignorant, and it troubles me — just a little."

"Tell me what it is."

"I have a cousin, an only relative and an orphan, like myself, whom I love very dearly. She is five years younger than I, and she lives in a farmer's house in the south country. Poverty parted us, and she knows nothing of my fate — for I cannot write — and if I could, how should I tell her! It is better as it is."

"Yes, yes: better as it is."

"What I have been thinking as we came along, and what I am still thinking now, as I look into your kind, strong face which gives me so much support, is this: If the Republic really does good to the poor, and they come

334

to be less hungry, and in all ways to suffer less, she may live a long time; she may even live to be old."

"What then, my gentle sister?"

"Do you think" — the uncomplaining eyes, in which there is so much endurance, fill with tears, and the lips part a little more and tremble — " that it will seem long to me, while I wait for her in the better land where I trust both you and I will be mercifully sheltered?"

"It cannot be, my child; there is no Time there, and no trouble there."

"You comfort me so much! I am so ignorant. Am I to kiss you now? Is the moment come?"

"Yes."

She kisses his lips; he kisses hers; they solemnly bless each other. The spare hand does not tremble as he releases it; nothing worse than a sweet, bright constancy is in the patient face. She goes next before him — is gone; the knitting-women count Twenty-two.

"I am the Resurrection and the Life, saith the Lord: he that believeth in me, though he were dead, yet shall he live: and whosoever liveth and believeth in me, shall never die."

The murmuring of many voices, the upturning of many faces, the pressing on of many footsteps in the outskirts of the crowd, so that it swells forward in a mass, like one great heave of water, all flashes away. Twenty-three.

THE FALL OF ROBESPIERRE

[1794]

BY THOMAS CARLYLE

[THE supremacy of Robespierre marked the climax of the Reign of Terror. Up to this time the executions in Paris had averaged about sixty a week. Now they rose to nearly two hundred and fifty. This could not continue. Fear drove other members of the Committee of Public Safety to unite against Robespierre. Hitherto the Convention had been controlled by him, but for some time he had held aloof from its meetings and there was a chance that his power might at last be overthrown. With each side it was a question of life or death, for the members of the party that was outvoted in the Convention could expect nothing but the guillotine. On the 27th of July, or the ninth Thermidor by the Revolutionary calendar, the decisive struggle took place.

The leaders of the Mountainists were Maximilien Robespierre, Saint-Just, and Couthon. Their opponents, the Men of the Plain, were led by Barras and Tallien. Henriot was commander of the Paris militia and a follower of Robespierre. Tinville was public prosecutor. The Jacobins were a powerful society of revolutionists.

The Editor.]

TALLIEN'S eyes gleamed bright, on the morrow, Ninth of Thermidor, "about nine o'clock," to see that the Convention had actually met. Paris is in rumor: but at least, we are met, in Legal Convention here; we have not been snatched seriatim; treated with a *Pride's Purge* at the door. "*Allons*, brave men of the Plain, late Frogs of the Marsh!" cried Tallien, with a squeeze of the hand, as he passed in; Saint-Just's sonorous voice being now audible from the Tribune, and the game of games begun.

Saint-Just is verily reading that report of his; green Vengeance, in the shape of Robespierre, watching nigh. Behold, however, Saint-Just has read but few sentences, when interruption rises, rapid *crescendo;* when Tallien starts to his feet, and Billaud and this man starts, and that, — and Tallien, a second time, with his: "Citoyens, at the Jacobins last night, I trembled for the Republic. I said to myself, if the Convention dare not strike the Tyrant, then I myself dare; and with this will I do it if need be," said he, whisking out a clear-gleaming Dagger, and brandishing it there: the Steel of Brutus, as we call it. — Whereat we all bellow, and brandish, impetuous acclaim. "Tyranny! Dictatorship! Triumvirate!" And the *Salut* Committee-men accuse, and all men accuse, and uproar, and impetuously acclaim. And Saint-Just is standing motionless, pale of face; Couthon ejaculating, "Triumvir?" with a look at his paralytic legs. And Robespierre is struggling to speak, but President Thuriot is jingling the bell against him, but the Hall is sounding against him like an Æolus-Hall: and Robespierre is mounting the Tribune-steps and descending again; going and coming, like to choke with rage, terror, desperation: — and mutiny is the order of the day!

O President Thuriot, thou that wert Elector Thuriot, and from the Bastille battlements sawest Saint-Antoine rising like the Ocean-tide, and hast seen much since, sawest thou ever the like of this? Jingle of bell, which thou jinglest against Robespierre, is hardly audible amid the Bedlam-storm; and men rage for life. "President of

Assassins," shrieks Robespierre, "I demand speech of you for the last time!" It cannot be had. "To you, O virtuous men of the Plain," cries he, finding audience one moment, "I appeal to you!" The virtuous men of the Plain sit silent as stones. And Thuriot's bell jingles, and the Hall sounds like Æolus's Hall. Robespierre's frothing lips are grown "blue"; his tongue dry, cleaving to the roof of his mouth. "The blood of Danton chokes him!" cry they. "Accusation! Decree of Accusation!" Thuriot swiftly puts that question. Accusation passes; the incorruptible Maximilien is decreed Accused.

"I demand to share my Brother's fate, as I have striven to share his virtues," cries Augustin, the younger Robespierre; Augustin also is decreed; and Couthon, and Saint-Just, and Lebas, they are all decreed; and packed forth, — not without difficulty, the Ushers almost trembling to obey. Triumvirate and Company are packed forth in *Salut* Committee-room; their tongue cleaving to the roof of their mouth. You have but to summon the Municipality; to cashier Commandant Henriot, and launch Arrest at him; to regulate formalities; hand Tinville his victims; It is noon: the Æolus-Hall has delivered itself; blows now victorious, harmonious, as one irresistible wind.

And so the work is finished? One thinks so: and yet it is not so. Alas, there is yet but the first-act finished; three or four other acts still to come, and an uncertain catastrophe! A huge city holds in it so many confusions; seven hundred thousand human heads; not one of which knows what its neighbor is doing, nay, not what itself is doing. — See, accordingly, about three in the afternoon, Commandant Henriot, how instead of sitting cashiered, arrested, he gallops along the Quais, followed by Municipal Gendarmes, "trampling down several persons!" For the Townhall sits deliberating, openly insurgent: Barriers to be shut; no Gaoler to admit any Prisoner this day; — and Henriot is galloping towards the Tuileries, to deliver Robespierre. On the Quai de la Ferraillerie, a young Citoyen, walking with his wife, says aloud: "Gendarmes, that man is not your Commandant; he is under arrest." The Gendarmes strike down the young Citoyen with the flat of their swords.

Representatives themselves (as Merlin the Thionviller), who accost him, this puissant Henriot flings into guardhouses. He bursts towards the Tuileries Committee-room, "to speak with Robespierre"; with difficulty, the Ushers and Tuileries Gendarmes, earnestly pleading and drawing saber, seize this Henriot; get the Henriot Gendarmes persuaded not to fight; get Robespierre and Company packed into hackney-coaches, sent off under escort to the Luxembourg and other Prisons. This then *is* the end. May not an exhausted Convention adjourn now, for a little repose and sustenance, "at five o'clock"?

An exhausted Convention did it; and repented it. The end was not come; only the end of the *second-act*. Hark, while exhausted Representatives sit at victuals, — tocsin bursting from all steeples, drums rolling in the summer evening; Judge Coffinhal is galloping with new gendarmes, to deliver Henriot from Tuileries Committee-room, and does deliver him! Puissant Henriot vaults on horseback; sets to haranguing the Tuileries Gendarmes; corrupts the Tuileries Gendarmes, too; trots off with them to Townhall. Alas, and Robespierre is not in Prison: the Gaoler showed his Municipal order,

durst not, on pain of his life, admit any Prisoners; the
Robespierre Hackney-coaches, in this confused jangle
and whirl of uncertain Gendarmes, have floated safe
— into the Townhall! There sit Robespierre and Company, embraced by Municipals and Jacobins, in sacred
right of Insurrection; redacting Proclamations; sounding tocsins; corresponding with sections and Mother
Society. Is not here a pretty enough third-act of a
natural Greek Drama; the catastrophe more uncertain
than ever?

The hasty Convention rushes together again, in the
ominous nightfall: President Collot, for the chair is his,
enters with long strides, paleness on his face; claps-on
his hat; says with solemn tone: "Citoyens, armed Villains have beset the Committee-rooms, and got possession of them. The hour is come, to die at our post!"
"*Oui*," answer one and all: "We swear it!" It is no
rhodomontade this time, but a sad fact and necessity;
unless we *do* at our posts, we must verily die. Swift,
therefore, Robespierre, Henriot, the Municipality, are
declared Rebels, put *Hors la Loi*, Out of Law. Better
still, we appoint Barras Commandant of what Armed-
force is to be had; send Missionary Representatives to
all Sections and quarters, to preach, and raise force; will
die at least with harness on our back.

What a distracted City; men riding and running,
reporting and hearsaying; the Hour clearly in travail,—
child not to be *named* till born! The poor prisoners in
the Luxembourg hear the rumor; tremble for a new September. They see men making signals to them, on sky-
lights and roofs, apparently signals of hope; cannot in
the least make out what it is. We observe, however, in

the eventide, as usual, the Death-tumbrels faring South-eastward, through Saint-Antoine, towards their Barrier du Trone. Saint-Antoine's tough bowels melt; Saint-Antoine surrounds the Tumbrels; says, It shall not be. O Heavens, why should it! Henriot and Gendarmes, scouring the streets that way, bellow, with waved sabers, that it must "Quit hope, ye poor Doomed!" The Tumbrels move on.

But in this set of Tumbrels there are two other things notable: one notable person; and one want of a notable person. The notable person is Lieutenant-General Loiserolles, a nobleman by birth, and by nature; laying down his life here for his son. In the Prison of Saint-Lazare, the night before last, hurrying to the Grate to hear the Death-list read, he caught the name of his son. The son was asleep at the moment. "I am Loiserolles," cried the old man at Tinville's bar, an error in the Christian name is little; small objection was made. — The want of the notable person, again, is that of Deputy Paine![1] Paine has sat in the Luxembourg since January; and seemed forgotten; but Fouquier had pricked him at last. The Turnkey, List in hand, is marking with chalk the outer doors of to-morrow's *Fournée*. Paine's outer door happened to be open, turned back on the wall; the Turnkey marked it on the side next him, and hurried on: another Turnkey came, and shut it; no chalk-mark now visible, the *Fournée* went without Paine. Paine's life lay not there. —

Our fifth-act, of this natural Greek Drama, with its natural unities, can only be painted in gross; somewhat

[1] Tom Paine, the American pamphleteer and author of *The Age of Reason.*

as that antique Painter, driven desperate, did the *foam*.
For through this blessed July night, there is clangor,
confusion very great, of marching troops; of Sections
going this way, Sections going that; of Missionary
Representatives reading Proclamations by torchlight;
Missionary Legendre, who has raised force somewhere,
emptying out the Jacobins, and flinging their key on the
Convention table: "I have locked their door; it shall be
Virtue that re-opens it." Paris, we say, is set against
itself, rushing confused, as Ocean-currents do; a huge
Mählstrom, sounding there, under cloud of night. Convention sits permanent on this hand; Municipality most
permanent on that. The poor prisoners hear tocsin and
rumor; strive to bethink them of the signals apparently
of hope. Meek continual Twilight streaming up, which
will be Dawn and a To-morrow, silvers the Northern
hem of Night; it wends and wends there, that meek
brightness like a silent prophecy, along the great ring-
dial of the Heaven. So still, eternal! and on Earth, all is
confused shadow and conflict; dissidence, tumultuous
gloom and glare; and "Destiny as yet sits wavering,
and shakes her doubtful urn."

About three in the morning, the dissident Armed-
Forces have *met*. Henriot's Armed Force stood ranked
in the Place de Grève; and now Barras's, which he has
recruited, arrives there, and they front each other, cannon bristling against cannon. Citoyens! cries the voice
of Discretion loudly enough, Before coming to blood-
shed, to endless civil-war, hear the Convention Decree
read: "Robespierre and all rebels Out of Law!" — Out
of Law? There is terror in the sound. Unarmed Citoyens disperse rapidly home. Municipal Cannoneers, in

sudden whirl, anxiously unanimous, range themselves on the Convention side, with shouting. At which shout, Henriot descends from his upper room, far gone in drink as some say; finds his Place de Grève empty; the cannon's mouth turned *towards* him; and on the whole, — that it is now the catastrophe!

Stumbling in again, the wretched drunk-sobered Henriot announces: "All is lost!" "*Misérable*, it is thou that hast lost it!" cry they; and fling him, or else he flings himself out of window: far enough down; into masonwork and horror of cesspool; not into death, but worse. Augustin Robespierre follows him; with the like fate. Saint-Just, they say, called on Lebas to kill him; who would not. Couthon crept under a table; attempting to kill himself; not doing it. — On entering that Sanhedrim of Insurrection, we find all as good as extinct; undone, ready for seizure. Robespierre was sitting on a chair, with pistol-shot blown through, not his head, but his under jaw; the suicidal hand had failed. With prompt zeal, not without trouble, we gather these wrecked Conspirators; fish up even Henriot and Augustin, bleeding and foul; pack them all, rudely enough, into carts; and shall, before sunrise, have them safe under lock and key. Amid shoutings and embracings.

Robespierre lay in an anteroom of the Convention Hall, while his Prison-escort was getting ready; the mangled jaw bound up on a table, a deal-box his pillow; the sheath of the pistol is still clenched convulsively in his hand. Men bully him, insult him: his eyes still indicate intelligence; he speaks no word. "He had on the sky-blue coat he had got made for the Feast of the Être Suprême" — O reader, can thy hard heart hold out against that? His trousers were nankeen; the stockings had fallen down over the ankles. He spake no word more in this world.

And so, at six in the morning, a victorious Convention adjourns. Report flies over Paris as on golden wings; penetrates the Prisons; irradiates the faces of those that were ready to perish: turnkeys and *moutons*, fallen from their high estate, look mute and blue. It is the 28th day of July, called 10th of Thermidor, year 1794. Fouquier had but to identify; his prisoners being already Out of Law. At four in the afternoon, never before were the streets of Paris seen so crowded. From the Palais de Justice to the Place de la Révolution, for *thither* again go the Tumbrels this time, it is one dense stirring mass; all windows crammed; the very roofs and ridge-tiles budding forth human Curiosity, in strange gladness. The Death-tumbrels, with their motley Batch of Outlaws, some Twenty-three or so, from Maximilien to Mayor Fleuriot and Simon the Cordwainer, roll on. All eyes are on Robespierre's Tumbrel, where he, his jaw bound in dirty linen, with his half-dead Brother, and half-dead Henriot, lie shattered; their "seventeen hours" of agony about to end. The Gendarmes point their swords at him, to show the people which is he. A woman springs on the Tumbrel; clutching the side of it with one hand; waving the other Sibyl-like; and exclaims: "The death of thee gladdens my very heart, *m'énivre de joie*"; Robespierre opened his eyes: "*Scélérat* [scoundrel], go down to Hell, with the curses of all wives and mothers": — At the foot of the Scaffold, they stretched him on the ground till his turn came. Lifted aloft, his eyes again opened; caught the bloody axe. Samson wrenched the coat off him; wrenched the dirty linen from his jaw: the jaw fell powerless, there burst from him a cry; — hideous to hear and see. Samson, thou canst not be too quick!

Samson's work done, there bursts forth shout on shout of applause. Shout, which prolongs itself not only over Paris, but over France, but over Europe, and down to this generation. Deservedly, and also undeservedly. O unhappiest advocate of Arras, wert thou worse than other Advocates? Stricter man, according to his Formula, to his Credo and his Cant, of probities, benevolences, pleasures-of-virtue, and such like, lived not in that age. A man fitted, in some luckier settled age, to have become one of those incorruptible barren Pattern-Figures, and have had marble-tablets and funeral-sermons. His poor landlord, the Cabinet-maker in the Rue Saint-Honoré, loved him; his Brother died for him. May God be merciful to him, and to us!

VII
NAPOLEON BONAPARTE

HISTORICAL NOTE

ACCORDING to the new constitution framed by the Convention, the executive power was put into the hands of five "Directors." As England and Austria persisted in their opposition, the young commander, Napoleon Bonaparte, was sent by this Directory to strike a blow at Austria in Italy, then at England in Egypt; but a new coalition was formed against France by the leading States of Europe. The French arms met with disaster, and the French people declared that the Directors in their jealousy of Napoleon's evident ability had sent away the only commander who could bring them success. Napoleon had kept close watch of affairs at home, and now he promptly set sail for France, drove the Council of Five Hundred, one of the two legislative bodies, from their chamber, and became at a blow the ruler of France.

He made himself first consul, then Emperor. He conquered one ruler after another, placing his generals or members of his family upon the vacant thrones. Fortune was with him until he set out on a Russian campaign, in which his losses were terrible. Russia, Prussia, Sweden, and England now united against him. Paris was taken by the allies, and Napoleon was sent to Elba. Louis XVIII became king; but Napoleon suddenly returned, and for one hundred days he was again Emperor. Then came the famous battle of Waterloo. Napoleon was defeated and sent to St. Helena, where he died.

THE EIGHTEENTH BRUMAIRE

BY FRANÇOIS BOUCHOT

(*French artist*, 1800–1842)

As soon as Napoleon had returned from Egypt, he began plotting the overthrow of the Directorate. On November 9, 1799, the eighteenth Brumaire, in the Revolutionary calendar, he dispersed the Council of Five Hundred, the legislative branch of the Government, after scenes of wild disorder. The event was thus described by Napoleon in a proclamation that he immediately issued: —.

"I entered the Council of Five Hundred, alone, unarmed, my head uncovered. Daggers are at once raised against me; twenty assassins fly at me and strike at my breast. The grenadiers of the legislative body, whom I had left at the door, rush in to interpose between the assassins and me. They drag me out. At the same moment cries of *Outlaw* are raised against the protector of the law. They crowd around the president (Lucien Bonaparte) with threats in their mouths, and arms in their hands; they call on him for a declaration of outlawry; word is sent out to me; I give orders to have him saved from their rage, and six grenadiers bring him out. Immediately after this the grenadiers of the legislative body charge into the hall and clear it. Alarmed, the factions disperse and go away.

"People of France, you will doubtless recognize in my conduct the zeal of a soldier of liberty, of a citizen devoted to the Republic."

The same day the president of the council, Lucien Bonaparte, Napoleon's brother, called together the members who were in sympathy with this act, declared the Directorate abolished, and prepared a new constitution. This placed all power in the hands of a First Consul — who was, of course, Napoleon himself. Two other consuls were to be appointed by him, but their office was merely advisory.

THE BATTLE OF EYLAU

[1807]

BY ISAÁC McLELLAN

[At Eylau, on the 8th of February, 1807, Napoleon attacked
the combined armies of Russia and Prussia, but failed to
obtain a decisive victory. The battle was fought in a blinding
snowstorm and was one of the bloodiest of modern times.

The Editor.]

FAST and furious falls the snow;
Shrilly the bleak tempests blow,
With a sound of wailing woe,
    O'er the soil;
Where the watch-fires blaze around,
Thick the warriors strew the ground,
Each in weary slumber bound,
    Worn with toil.

Harken to the cannon-blast!
Drums are beating fierce and fast:
Fierce and fast the trumpets cast
    Warning call.
Form the battle's stern parade,
Charge the musket, draw the blade;
Square and column stand arrayed,
    One and all.

On they rush in stern career,
Dragoon and swart cuirassier;

FRANCE

Hussar-lance and Cossack-spear
    Clanging meet!
Now the grenadier of France
Sinks beneath the Imperial lance;
Now the Prussian horse advance,
    Now retreat.

Davoust, with his line of steel,
Storms their squadrons till they reel,
While his ceaseless cannon-peal
    Rends the sky.
'Gainst that crush of iron hail
Naught may Russia's ranks avail;
Like the torn leaves in the gale,
    See, they fly!

Through the battle's smoky gloom
Shineth Murat's snowy plume;
Fast his cohorts to their doom
    Spur the way.
Platoff, with his desert horde,
Is upon them with the sword;
Deep his Tartar-spears have gored
    Their array.

With his thousands, Augereau
Paints with blood the virgin snow;
Low in war's red overthrow
    Sleep they on!
Helm and breastplate they have lost,
Spoils that long shall be the boast

THE ·BATTLE OF EYLAU

Of the savage-bearded host
    Of the Don.

Charge, Napoleon! Where be those
At Marengo quelled thy foes;
Crowning thee at Jena's close
    Conqueror?
At this hour of deadly need
Faintly thy old guardsmen bleed;
Vain dies cuirassier and steed,
    Drenched with gore.

Sad the frosty moonbeam shone
O'er the snows with corses strewn,
Where the frightful shriek and groan
    Rose amain:
Loud the night-wind rang their knell;
Fast the flaky horrors fell,
Hiding in their snowy cell
    Heaps of slain!

Many a year hath passed and fled
O'er that harvest of the dead;
On thy rock the Chief hath sped,
    St. Helene!
Still the Polish peasant shows
The round hillocks of the foes,
Where the long grass rankly grows,
    Darkly green.

THE RETREAT FROM MOSCOW

[1812]

BY VICTOR HUGO

It snowed. A defeat was our conquest red!
For once the Eagle was hanging its head.
Sad days! the Emperor turned slowly his back
On smoking Moscow, blent orange and black.
The winter burst, avalanche-like, to reign
Over the endless blanched sheet of the plain.
Nor chief, nor banner in order could keep,
The wolves of warfare were 'wildered like sheep.
The wings from center could hardly be known
Through snow o'er horses and carts o'erthrown,
Where froze the wounded. In the bivouacs forlorn
Strange sights and gruesome met the breaking morn:
Mute were the bugles, while the men bestrode
Steeds turned to marble, unheeding the goad.
The shells and bullets came down with the snow
As though the heavens hated these poor troops below.
Surprised at trembling, though it was with cold,
Who ne'er had trembled out of fear, the veterans bold
Marched stern; to grizzled mustache hoar-frost clung
'Neath banners that in leaden masses hung.
It snowed, went snowing still. And chill the breeze
Whistled upon the glassy, endless seas,
Where naked feet on, on forever went,
With naught to eat, and not a sheltering tent.
They were not living troops as seen in war,

THE RETREAT FROM MOSCOW

But merely phantoms of a dream, afar
In darkness wandering, amid the vapor dim, —
A mystery; of shadows a procession grim,
Nearing a blackening sky, into its rim.
Frightful, since boundless, solitude behold
Where only Nemesis wove, mute and cold,
A net all snowy with its soft meshes dense,
A shroud of magnitude for host immense;
Till every one felt as if left alone
In a wide wilderness where no light shone,
To die, with pity none, and none to see
That from this mournful realm none should get free.
Their foes the frozen North and Czar — That, worse.
Cannons were broken up in haste accurst
To burn the frames and make the pale fire high,
Where those lay down who never woke, or woke to die.
Sad and commingled, groups that blindly fled
Were swallowed smoothly by the desert dread.
'Neath folds of blankness, monuments were raised
O'er regiments. And History, amazed,
Could not record the ruin of this retreat,
Unlike a downfall known before the defeat
Of Hannibal — reversed and wrapped in gloom!
Of Attila, when nations met their doom!
Perished an army — fled French glory then.
Though there the Emperor! he stood and gazed
At the wild havoc, like a monarch dazed
In woodland hoar, who felt the shrieking saw —
He, living oak, beheld his branches fall, with awe.
Chiefs, soldiers, comrades died. But still warm love
Kept those that rose all dastard fear above,
As on his tent they saw his shadow pass —

FRANCE

Backwards and forwards, for they credited, alas!
His fortune's star! it could not, could not be
That he had not his work to do — a destiny?
To hurl him headlong from his high estate,
Would be high treason in his bondman, Fate,
But all the while he felt himself alone,
Stunned with disasters few have ever known.
Sudden, a fear came o'er his troubled soul,
What more was written on the Future's scroll?
Was this an expiation? It must be, yea:
He turned to God for one enlightening ray.
"Is this the vengeance, Lord of Hosts?" he sighed,
But the first murmur on his parched lips died.
"Is this the vengeance? Must my glory set?"
A pause: his name was called; of flame a jet
Sprang in the darkness — a Voice answered: "No! Not
        yet."
Outside still fell the smothering snow.
Was it a voice indeed? or but a dream!
It was the vulture's, but how like the sea-bird's scream.

THE RETREAT FROM MOSCOW

BY ADOLPHE YVON

(French painter, 1817–1893)

In 1811 Napoleon was at the height of his power; in 1812 he had taken a long step toward his fall. This was his invasion of Russia, undertaken because of the union of the Czar with the enemies of the emperor. At the head of 500,000 men, Napoleon crossed the Russian boundaries. On the banks of the Niemen he repulsed 300,000 Russians and marched onward through storm and tempest and amid the sufferings of famine. Both French and Russians were driving on toward Moscow. They met at the Borodino, and in the awful conflict that followed more than 80,000 men were slain. Soon after the Russian army evacuated Moscow, taking with it most of the inhabitants. In this city Napoleon had expected to find food in plenty for his starving troops. The condition of the place has been described as follows: —

"When Napoleon rode into the ancient capital, it was as silent as the desert, and he took up his residence in the Kremlin as if he were about to sleep in a tomb. But suddenly, at midnight, a hundred glares of light showed that the people had not yet all deserted. The vast city was in flames in every direction, and the baffled French, enveloped in fire, were compelled to seek refuge in the desolate surrounding country. Napoleon lingered over the splendid ruins until Oct. 19, when all his proposals for a peaceful settlement of difficulties being rejected, he was reluctantly compelled to order a retreat. At first the weather was fine and only moderately cold; but soon the snow, the rain, fatigue, and swarms of harassing Cossacks threw the dispirited Frenchmen into disorder. Then commenced that terrible retreat of 120,000 men, which for suffering and horror has no parallel in the annals of our race. The loss of the French and their auxiliaries, in this campaign, was 125,000 slain, 132,000 dead of fatigue, hunger, disease, and cold, and 193,000 made prisoners. Yet the author of this fearful waste of human life had scarcely reached Paris when he issued orders for new conscriptions, and still thought of prosecuting the war!"

THE COMING OF LOUIS XVIII

[1814]

BY LOUISA MÜHLBACH

[AFTER the execution of Louis XVI, his little son was recognized by England and Russia as Louis XVII. He is believed to have died from the neglect and cruelty of his jailers. In 1814, Paris was overwhelmed by the forces of the leading States of Europe. Napoleon was exiled to the little island of Elba, and Louis XVIII, brother of Louis XVI, was set upon the throne of France.

The Editor.]

THE restoration was complete. The allied powers had left France at last, and Louis XVIII was now absolute master of France. In him, in the returned members of his family, and the exiles streaming homeward from all directions, old France was represented — the France of unrestricted royal power, brilliant manners, intrigues, luxury, aristocracy, and frivolity. In opposition to them stood young France, the generation trained by Napoleon and the Revolution — the new aristocracy which possessed no other ancestors than its great achievements and its fame.

These two parties stood face to face, old and young France, struggling at the court of Louis XVIII, carrying on an hourly, untiring warfare, except that young France, which had always been accustomed to come off victorious, now suffered daily new defeats and humiliations. For it was now old France that carried the day. And it conquered, not by virtue of its courage, its achievements — it conquered by virtue of its past, which was now to be connected directly with the present, regardless of the chasm that yawned between.

King Louis had of course promised all his subjects, in the compact of April 11, that their titles and dignities should remain intact; and the new dukes, princes and marshals, counts and barons, might appear at court. But they played there only a sorry, humiliating part, and were made to feel keenly that they were only tolerated, not welcome.

The gentlemen who had been entitled before the Revolution to enter the king's equipage, retained the right now, and the doors thereof never once opened to the gentlemen of the new Napoleonic nobility.

The Duchess of Angoulême was the shining example of the ladies of Saint-Germain in their intolerance and high-handed scorn of the now obsolete Empire. She was the most unrelenting of all in her attitude toward the new era and its representatives, and she, the daughter of the guillotined royal pair, had herself suffered long in the Temple, and had made the acquaintance of the horrors of revolution in their direst forms. She meant now to try to forget the time which she could not avenge, and to appear as if it had never been.

At one of the first dinners which the king gave to the allied powers, the Duchess of Angoulême sat beside the King of Bavaria, and, pointing to the Grand Duke of Baden, she asked: "Is not that the prince who married a princess of Napoleon's creation? What weakness, to ally himself thus with that general."

The duchess forgot, or did not wish to remember, that

the King of Bavaria and the Emperor of Austria, who sat at the duchess's other side and could not fail to hear everything that she said, had allied themselves to the "general."

When she had resumed possession of her former dwelling in the Tuileries, the Duchess of Angoulême asked old Dubois, her former piano-tuner, who had held the same office under the Empire and was showing the duchess the fine new instrument purchased by Josephine, where her own, the duchess's piano, was.

This piano had been a wretched old spinet, and the duchess was surprised not to find it, ignoring the thirty years that had passed since she last saw it, and acting as though August 10, 1792, the day when the people destroyed the Tuileries, had never been.

It had become a matter of principle to ignore the time from 1795 to 1814, and the Bourbons seemed really to have forgotten wholly that, between the last levée of Louis XVI, and to-day's receptions of Louis XVIII, there lay more than a passing night. The duchess seemed amazed that people whom she had known as small children had grown up in her absence, and she tried to greet every one as she had done in 1789.

After Josephine's death the Count of Artois visited Malmaison, which had scarcely existed before the Revolution, and was wholly due to Josephine's sense of art and her love of the beautiful.

At Malmaison the empress, who had a great love of botany, had built superb greenhouses in which the plants of the whole world were represented; for all the princes of Europe, knowing the empress' taste, had rivaled one another in the days of her greatness in their eagerness to send her rare and precious plants and flowers. The Prince Regent of England had even found means, during the war with France, to send some rare slips to the empress, and the greenhouses of Malmaison finally became the most complete of all Europe, and a real storehouse of treasures for botanists.

The Count of Artois went to inspect the famous dwelling of the Empress Josephine, and when the greenhouses, with their rarities, were shown him, he exclaimed, as if recognizing the plants of 1789: —

"Ah! there are our old plants from the Trianon!"

And as the Bourbons, their lords and masters, so did the exiles return with the same ideas which they had taken with them. They proposed to renew all the habits, customs, and pretensions of 1789. They were so occupied with the contemplation of their own deserts that they had eyes or ears for nothing else, yet the only service which they had rendered was their emigration. And now they proposed to be rewarded for that.

Every one of the exiles demanded some recompense, either in the form of a position or a pension, and found it incomprehensible if the same were not instantly withdrawn from their present possessors.

There was one continuous intrigue and cabal until, at last, old France did actually succeed in supplanting new France in place, power, and pension, as it had already done in the honors of the courts. All the higher positions of the army were filled with the marquises, dukes, and counts of ancient France, who had been embroidering tapestries or tying silk threads in Coblentz while new France was upon the field of battle. And now these valiant exiles proposed to teach the soldiers of the empire the old routine of 1780.

Meanwhile the cleverest and most wide-awake of all these gentlemen was their lord and master, Louis XVIII. He recognized the faults and errors of all those who surrounded him, and had very little confidence in the people of the court. But he could not emancipate himself from their influence; and after he had, in the face of the will and opinion of his whole family, his court and ministers, given a charter to his people, and placated them in spite of the resistance of Monsieur and the Prince of Condé, who habitually called the charter *Mademoiselle la Constitution de 1791*, Louis retired into the interior of the Tuileries, and left it to Blacas to manage the details of Government. The king thought the more important affairs alone worthy of his attention.

THE RETURN OF NAPOLEON FROM ELBA

[1815]

ANONYMOUS

[THE determination of Louis XVIII and the Royalists to put everything back where it was before the Revolution aroused great dissatisfaction. Many began to long for the return of Napoleon. In March, 1815, their wish came to pass, for Napoleon landed on the shores of France. He had only a few followers, but as he pushed on to Paris, his old soldiers hurried forward to join him. His whole journey was one glowing welcome.

The following account was written by an English lady, a partisan of the Bourbons, who was in Paris at the time of Napoleon's arrival.

The Editor.]

WE were enjoying the breezes of a fine March morning when suddenly an officer issued from the palace and whispered to us that *Bonaparte had landed!* Had a thunderbolt fallen at our feet its effects could not have produced a more terrible sensation than did this unexpected intelligence on our hearts. We instantly returned home, and that night it was no longer a secret in Paris. Some could not conceal the terror the name of Napoleon always inspires; others, judging from their own loyal sentiments, exclaimed, "The hand of God is to be seen in this!" Another party, appreciating present circumstances, rejoiced in the idea that he would be taken and secured forever; as if Napoleon, in risking the chance of success, had not secured the means of insuring it! The king issued an *ordonnance* declaring him a traitor. The Chamber of Deputies was convened, an express sent for Marshal Ney. The king, preserving admirable calmness and confidence in his subjects, received the ambassadors, saying, "Write, gentlemen, to your respective courts that I am in good health, and that the mad enterprise of this man will no longer trouble the repose of Europe nor my own." The Prince de Condé, notwithstanding his advanced age, offered his services.

His Majesty passed in review the troops, addressed the most flattering compliments to their generals, who surrounded him, and said to General Rapp, "Notwithstanding that this is not the siege of Dantzic, I count always upon your courage and fidelity!" Rapp, affected, turned away and exclaimed, "One must be a villain to betray such a king." He rendered himself justice, and unconsciously pronounced his own panegyric in advance. When the Duc de Berri appeared he was received with enthusiasm. *La Maison du Roi* solicited to march with him against their common enemy, but elsewhere all remained in a state of apathy. An extensive confederacy on one side, want of means on the other, an inefficient organization in every department — our great confidence was in Ney; Ney departed with promises to bring back Napoleon dead or alive. He kissed the king's hand, and, shedding tears, renewed his oaths of fidelity for himself and his army.

The Duc de Feltre (Clarke) was named minister of war. Our fluctuating hopes rose and fell like the mercury in a weather-glass, but this nomination revived them. Clarke had been called "*the calculating Irishman*," but the loyal party now extol him, and say that he forgot himself at the epoch that others forgot only what they owed to their king. "What will Talleyrand do? Will he, amidst the congregated ministers of the Allies, remain steady to his last oaths to Louis?" was constantly echoing through our salons during the first days of consternation.

The streets were quieter than usual; every person seemed to have a more serious mien, and to be preoccupied. Of the *beau-monde* some had fled, others kept within their hotels. No carriages of the opulent contested the passage with the cabriolets or with the vehicles of commerce, no belles skipped lightly along. In the shops few purchasers, and those few looking gloomy and silent; suspicion and fear seemed to predominate. Entering two or three shops where I had been in the habit of purchasing, they exclaimed, "Softly! softly! mademoiselle; speak low, we are surrounded with spies." At the open stalls, and in the shops on the bridges and on the quays, the proprietors were busily occupied in removing the engravings, and other emblems of the Bourbons, and replacing those of the usurper and his military partisans. Ladders were placed at the corners of the streets and against the shops, while workmen were effacing the names and brevets of the Bourbon dynasty, to be replaced by those of the Corsican family, or in haste substituting a design analogous to the merchandise within. We entered for a moment the Chamber of Deputies. The flags taken in the different campaigns were brought from their concealed dépôts. The President's chair, embroidered with fleur-de-lis, was being removed. "Where will you find another?" I hastily demanded. "The old chair is in the garret," was the quick reply.

THE RETURN OF NAPOLEON FROM ELBA

In a few moments it was brought down; the portraits of the king and of the princes were already removed from their frames, and those of Napoleon and Maria Louisa had replaced them.

[On the 19th of March cries were heard of "*Vive le Roi !*" in the square of Louis XV. On the morning of the 20th they were supplanted by shouts of "*Vive l'Empereur !*"]

The next morning I determined to see Napoleon, but when our carriage arrived at the Pont Royal thousands were collected there. Our servant advised us to descend and proceed on foot. The crowd civilly made way: they were waiting to see the review. An unusual silence prevailed, interrupted only by the cries of the children, whom the parents were thumping with energy for crying "*Vive le Roi !*" instead of "*Vive l'Empereur !*" which some months before they had been thumped for daring to vociferate! A friend recommended us to proceed to the review, to see which he had the good-nature to procure me admittance to a small apartment in the Tuileries, and from the window I saw and heard for the first time the scourge of the Continent — his martial, active figure, mounted on his famed white horse. He harangued with energetic tone (and in those bombastic expressions we have always remarked in all his manifestoes, and which are so well adapted to the French) the troops of the divisions of Lefol and Defour. There was much embracing of the "Ancient Eagles " of the Old Guard, much mention of "great days and souvenirs dear to his heart," of the "scars of his brave soldiers," which, to serve his views, we will reopen without remorse. The populace were tranquil, as I had remarked them on the bridge. Inspirited by my still unsatisfied curiosity I rejoined my escort and proceeded to the gardens, where not more than thirty persons were collected under the windows. There was no enthusiastic cry, at least none seemed sufficient to induce him to show himself. In despair at not being able to contemplate his physiognomy at greater advantage, I made my cavalier request some persons in the throng to cry, "*Vive l'Empereur!*" Some laughed and replied, "Wait a moment," while others advised us to desire some of the children to do so. A few francs thrown to the latter soon stimulated their voices into cries of the loyalty of the day, and Napoleon presented himself at the window, but he retired often and reappeared. A few persons arrived from the country and held up petitions, which he sent an aide-de-camp to receive. His square face and figure struck me with involuntary emotion. I was dazzled, as if beholding a supernatural being. There was a sternness spread over his expansive brow, a gloom on the lids of his darkened eye, which rendered futile his attempts to smile. Something Satanic sported round his mouth, indicating the ambitious spirit of the soul within!

Much agitation seemed to reign in the salon. The ministers and generals paced up and down with their master in reciprocal agitation and debate. The palace has now the appearance of a fortress, the retreat of a despot, not the abode of a sovereign confiding in the loyalty of his people, and recalled by their unanimous voice, but feeling that he is only welcomed back by military power, whose path was smoothed by the peasantry of Dauphiny. A range of artillery is now placed before it; soldiers stretched on straw repose under the finely-arched corridors, and military casqued heads even appear from the uppermost windows. Napoleon had the gallant consideration the day after his return to renew the guard of honor at the hôtel of the Dowager Duchess of Orléans, to whom he has always accorded the respect due to royalty.

WHEN NAPOLEON RETURNED FROM ELBA

[1815]

BY NAPOLEON BONAPARTE

[EVEN at the distance of a century, there is in Napoleon's shortest proclamations something that thrills the reader. In his warm appreciation of the past deeds of his troops, his conviction of their ability to surpass even these, and especially in his undoubting confidence in their eagerness to do his will, there is less of the stern commander than of the devoted brother. It is no wonder that his soldiers loved him, and counted their lives as nothing if only they might obey the orders of such a leader.

The Editor.]

SOLDIERS! we were not defeated!

Soldiers! In my exile I have heard your voice. I have come to you through every obstacle, every danger. Your general, called to the throne by the voice of the people and raised on your bucklers, is back among you; come to him! Pluck off the colors that the nation has proscribed, and that, for twenty-five years, were the rallying point of all the enemies of France. Put on the tricolor cockade; you wore it in our great days. Here are the eagles you had at Ulm, at Austerlitz, at Jena, at Eylau, at Friedland, at Tudela, at Eckmühl, at Essling, at Wagram, at Smolensk, at the Moskowa, at Lützen, at Wurschen, at Montmirail! Do you believe that the little handful of Frenchmen who are so arrogant to-day can support their sight? They will return whence they came; there let them reign as they pretend they did reign these last nineteen years.

Soldiers, rally around the standard of your chief! Victory will advance at the double! The Eagle, with the national colors, will fly from steeple to steeple to the towers of Notre Dame. Then will you be able to display your honorable scars. Then will you be able to claim the credit of your deeds, as the liberators of your country. In your old age, surrounded and honored by your fellow-citizens, all will respectfully listen while you narrate your great deeds; you will be able to say with pride: "And I also was one of that Grand Army that twice entered the walls of Vienna, of Rome, of Berlin, of Madrid, of Moscow, and that cleansed Paris from the stain left on it by treason and the presence of the enemy!"

WATERLOO

[1815]

BY VICTOR HUGO

THE EMPEROR PUTS A QUESTION TO THE GUIDE LACOSTE

At the moment when Wellington drew back, Napoleon started up. He saw the plateau of Mont St.-Jean suddenly laid bare and the front of the English army disappear. It rallied, but kept concealed. The Emperor half rose in his stirrups. The flash of a victory passed into his eyes.

Wellington hurled back on the Forest of Soignes and destroyed; that was the final overthrow of England by France; it was Cressy, Poitiers, Malplaquet, and Ramillies avenged. The man of Marengo was wiping out Agincourt.

The Emperor, then, contemplating this terrible turn of fortune, swept his glass for the last time over every point of the battle-field. His Guard, standing behind, with grounded arms, looked up to him with a sort of religion. He was reflecting; he was examining the slopes, noting the ascents, scrutinizing the tufts of the trees, the square rye field, the footpath; he seemed to count every bush. He looked for some time at the English barricades on the two roads, two large abattis of trees, that on the Genappe road above La Haye Sainte, armed with two cannon, which alone, of all the English artillery, bore upon the bottom of the field of battle, and that of the Nivelles road, where glistened the Dutch bayonets of Chassé's brigade. He noticed near that barricade the old chapel of St. Nicholas, painted white, which is at the corner of the cross-road toward Braine l'Alleud. He bent over and spoke in an undertone to the guide Lacoste. The guide made a negative sign of the head, probably treacherous.

The Emperor rose up and reflected. Wellington had fallen back. It remained only to complete this repulse by a crushing charge.

Napoleon, turning abruptly, sent off a courier at full speed to Paris to announce that the battle was won.

Napoleon was one of those geniuses who rule the thunder.

He had found his thunderbolt.

He ordered Milhaud's cuirassiers to carry the plateau of Mont St.-Jean.

THE UNLOOKED-FOR

They were 3500. They formed a line of half a mile. They were gigantic men on colossal horses. There were twenty-six squadrons, and they had behind them, as a support, the division of Lefebvre-Desnouettes, the 106 gensdarmes d'élite, the chasseurs of the guard, 1197 men, and the lancers of the guard, 880 lances. They wore casques without plumes, and cuirasses of wrought iron, with horse pistols in their holsters and long saber-swords. In the morning they had been the admiration of the whole army, when, at 9 o'clock, with trumpets sounding, and all the bands playing "Veillons au salut de l'empire," they came, in heavy columns, one of their batteries on their flank, the other at their center, and deployed in two ranks between the Genappe road and Frischemont, and took their position of battle in this powerful second line, so wisely made up by Napoleon, which, having at its extreme left the cuirassiers of Kellermann and at its extreme right the cuirassiers of Milhaud, had, so to speak, two wings of iron.

Aide-de-camp Bernard brought them the Emperor's order. Ney drew his sword and placed himself at their head. The enormous squadrons began to move.

Then was seen a fearful sight.

All this cavalry, with sabers drawn, banners waving, and trumpets sounding, formed in column by divisions, descended with an even movement and as one man — with the precision of a bronze battering-ram opening a breach — the hill of La Belle-Alliance, sank into the formidable depths where so many men had already fallen, disappeared in the smoke, then rising from this valley of shadow reappeared on the other side, still compact and serried, mounting at full trot, through a cloud of grape emptying itself upon them, the frightful acclivity of mud of the plateau of Mont St.-Jean. They rose, serious and menacing, imperturbable; in the intervals of the musketry and artillery could be heard the sound of this colossal tramp. Being in two divisions, they formed two columns; Wathier's division had the right, Delord's the left. From a distance they would be taken for two immense serpents of steel stretching themselves toward the crest of the plateau. That ran through the battle like a prodigy.

Nothing like it had been seen since the taking of the grand redoubt at La Moscowa, by the heavy cavalry; Murat was not there, but Ney was there. It seemed as if this mass had become a monster, and had but a single mind. Each squadron undulated and swelled like the ring of a polyp. They could be seen through the thick smoke as it was broken here and there. It was one pell-mell of casques, cries, sabers, a furious bounding of horses among the cannon, and the flourish of trumpets, a terrible and disciplined tumult; over all the cuirasses, like the scales of a hydra.

These recitals appear to belong to another age. Something like this vision appeared, doubtless, in the old Orphic epics which tell of centaurs, antique happan-thropes, those titans with human faces, and chests like horses, whose gallop scaled Olympus, horrible, invulner-able, sublime; at once gods and beasts.

An odd numerical coincidence, twenty-six battalions, were to receive these twenty-six squadrons. Behind the crest of the plateau, under cover of the masked battery, the English infantry formed in thirteen squares, two battalions to the square and upon two lines — seven on the first and six on the second — with musket to the shoulder, and eye upon their sights, waiting calm, silent, and immovable. They could not see the cuirassiers, and the cuirassiers could not see them. They listened to the rising of this tide of men. They heard the increasing sound of three thousand horses, the alternate and meas-ured striking of their hoofs at full trot, the rattling of the cuirasses, the clicking of sabers, and a sort of fierce roar of the coming host. There was a moment of fearful si-lence; then, suddenly a long line of raised arms bran-dishing sabers appeared above the crest, with casques, trumpets, and standards, and three thousand faces with gray mustaches, crying, *"Vive l'Empereur!"* All this cavalry debouched on the plateau, and it was like the beginning of an earthquake.

All at once, tragic to relate, at the left of the English, and on our right, the head of the column of cuirassiers reared with a frightful clamor. Arrived at the culminating point of the crest, unmanageable, full of fury, and bent upon the extermination of the squares and cannons, the cuirassiers saw between themselves and the English a ditch, a grave. It was the sunken road of Ohain.

It was a frightful moment. There was the ravine, unlooked for, yawning at the very feet of the horses, two fathoms deep between its double slope. The second rank pushed in the first, the third pushed in the second, the horses reared, threw themselves over, fell upon their backs and struggled with their feet in the air, piling up and overturning their riders, no power to retreat; the whole column was nothing but a projectile. The force acquired to crush the English crushed the French. The inexorable ravine could not yield until it was filled; riders and horses rolled in together pell-mell, grinding each other, making common flesh in this dreadful gulf, and when this grave was full of living men the rest marched over them and passed on. Almost a third of the Dubois' brigade sank into this abyss.

Here the loss of the battle began.

A local tradition, which evidently exaggerates, says that two thousand horses and fifteen hundred men were buried in the sunken road of Ohain. This undoubtedly comprises all the other bodies thrown into this ravine on the morrow after the battle.

Napoleon, before ordering this charge of Milhaud's

cuirassiers, had examined the ground, but could not see this hollow road, which did not make even a wrinkle on the surface of the plateau. Warned, however, and put on his guard by the little white chapel which marks its junction with the Nivelles road, he had, probably, on the contingency of an obstacle, put a question to the guide, Lacoste. The guide had answered no. It may almost be said that from this shake of a peasant's head came the catastrophe of Napoleon.

Still other fatalities must arise.

Was it possible that Napoleon should win this battle? We answer — no! Why? Because of Wellington? Because of Blücher? No! Because of God.

For Bonaparte to be conqueror at Waterloo was not in the law of the nineteenth century. Another series of facts were preparing in which Napoleon had no place. The ill will of events had long been announced.

It was time that this vast man should fall.

The excessive weight of this man in human destiny disturbed the equilibrium. This individual counted of himself more than the universe besides. These plethoras of all human vitality concentrated in a single head, the world mounting to the brain of one man, would be fatal to civilization if they should endure. The moment had come for incorruptible supreme equity to look to it. Probably the principles and elements upon which regular gravitations in the moral order as well as in the material depend, began to murmur. Reeking blood, overcrowded cemeteries, weeping mothers, — these are formidable pleaders. When the earth is suffering from a surcharge, there are mysterious moanings from the deeps which the heavens hear.

377

FRANCE

Napoleon had been impeached before the infinite and his fall was decreed.

He vexed God.

Waterloo is not a battle; it is the change of front of the universe.

THE PLATEAU OF MONT ST.-JEAN

At the same time with the ravine, the artillery was unmasked.

Sixty cannon and thirteen squares thundered and flashed into the cuirassiers. The brave General Delord gave the military salute to the English battery.

All the English flying artillery took position in the squares at a gallop. The cuirassiers had not even time to breathe. The disaster of the sunken road had decimated but not discouraged them. They were men who, diminished in number, grew greater in heart.

Wathier's column alone had suffered from the disaster; Delord's which Ney had sent obliquely to the left, as if he had a presentiment of the snare, arrived entire.

The cuirassiers hurled themselves upon the English squares.

At full gallop, with free rein, their sabers in their teeth, and their pistols in their hands, the attack began.

There are moments in battle when the soul hardens a man even to changing the soldier into a statue, and all this flesh becomes granite. The English battalions, desperately assailed, did not yield an inch.

Then it was frightful.

All sides of the English squares were attacked at once. A whirlwind of frenzy enveloped them. This frigid in-

378

fantry remained impassible. The first rank, with knee on the ground, received the cuirassiers on their bayonets, the second shot them down; behind the second rank, the cannoneers loaded their guns, the front of the square opened, made way for an eruption of grape, and closed again. The cuirassiers answered by rushing upon them with crushing force. Their great horses reared, trampled upon the ranks, leaped over the bayonets and fell, gigantic in the midst of these four living walls. The balls made gaps in the ranks of the cuirassiers, the cuirassiers made breaches in the squares. Files of men disappeared, ground down beneath the horses' feet. Bayonets were buried in the bellies of these centaurs. Hence a monstrosity of wounds never, perhaps, seen elsewhere. The squares, consumed by this furious cavalry, closed up, without wavering. Inexhaustible in grape, they kept up an explosion in the midst of their assailants. It was a monstrous sight. These squares were battalions no longer, they were craters; these cuirassiers were cavalry no longer, they were a tempest. Each square was a volcano attacked by a thunder-cloud; the lava fought with the lightning.

The square, on the extreme right, the most exposed of all, being in the open field, was almost annihilated at the first shock. It was formed of the 75th Regiment of Highlanders. The piper in the center, while the work of extermination was going on, profoundly oblivious of all about him, casting down his melancholy eye full of the shadows of forests and lakes, seated upon a drum, his bagpipe under his arm, was playing his mountain airs. These Scotchmen died thinking of Ben Lothian, as the Greeks died remembering Argo. The saber of a cuirassier, striking down the pibroch and the arm which bore it, caused the strain to cease by killing the player.

The cuirassiers, relatively few in number, lessened by the catastrophe of the ravine, had to contend with almost the whole of the English army; but they multiplied themselves; each man became equal to ten. Nevertheless, some Hanoverian battalions fell back. Wellington saw it and remembered his cavalry. Had Napoleon, at that very moment, remembered his infantry, he would have won the battle. This forgetfulness was his great, fatal blunder.

Suddenly the assailing cuirassiers perceived that they were assailed. The English cavalry was upon their back. Before them, the squares, behind them Somerset; Somerset with the fourteen hundred dragoon guards. Somerset had on his right Dornberg, with his German light horse, and on his left Trip, with the Belgian carbineers. The cuirassiers, attacked front, flank, and rear, by infantry and cavalry, were compelled to face in all directions. What was that to them? They were a whirlwind. Their valor became unspeakable.

Besides, they had behind them the ever-thundering artillery. All that was necessary in order to wound such men in the back. One of their cuirasses, with a hole in the left shoulder blade, made by a musket ball, is in the collection of the Waterloo Museum.

With such Frenchmen only such Englishmen could cope.

It was no longer a conflict; it was a darkness, a fury, a giddy vortex of souls and courage, a hurricane of sword flashes. In an instant the fourteen hundred horse guards were but eight hundred. Fuller, their lieutenant-colonel, fell dead. Ney rushed up with the lancers and chasseurs of Lefebvre-Desnouettes. The plateau of Mont St.-Jean was taken, retaken, and taken again. The cuirassiers left the cavalry to return to the infantry, or, more correctly, all this terrible multitude wrestled with each other without letting go their hold. The squares still held. There were twelve assaults. Ney had four horses killed under him. Half of the cuirassiers lay on the plateau. This struggle lasted two hours.

The English army was terribly shaken. There is no doubt, if they had not been crippled in their first shock by the disaster of the sunken road, the cuirassiers would have overwhelmed the center and decided the victory. This wonderful cavalry astounded Clinton, who had seen Talavera and Badajos. Wellington, though three fourths conquered, was struck with heroic admiration. He said, in a low voice, "Splendid!"

The cuirassiers annihilated seven squares out of thirteen, took or spiked sixty pieces of cannon, and took from the English regiments six colors, which three cuirassiers and three chasseurs of the guard carried to the Emperor before the farm of La Belle-Alliance.

The situation of Wellington was growing worse. This strange battle was like a duel between two wounded infuriates, who, while yet fighting and resisting, lose all their blood. Which of the two shall fall first?

The struggle of the plateau continued.

How far did the cuirassiers penetrate? None can tell. One thing is certain: the day after the battle a cuirassier and his horse were found dead under the frame of the hay-scales at Mont St.-Jean, at the point where the four roads from Nivelles, Genappe, La Hulpe, and Brussels meet. This horseman had pierced the English lines. One of the men who took away the body still lives at Mont St.-Jean. His name is Dehaze; he was then eighteen years old.

Wellington felt he was giving away. The crisis was upon him. The cuirassiers had not succeeded, in this sense, that the center was not broken. All holding the plateau, nobody held it; and, in fact, it remained for the most part with the English. Wellington held the village and the crowning plain. Ney held only the crest and the slope. On both sides they seemed rooted in this funeral soil.

But the enfeeblement of the English appeared irremediable. The hemorrhage of this army was horrible. Kempt, on the left wing, called for reinforcements. "Impossible," answered Wellington, "we must die on the spot we now occupy." Almost at the same moment — singular coincidence, which depicts the exhaustion of both armies — Ney sent to Napoleon for infantry, and Napoleon exclaimed: "Infantry! where does he expect me to take them? Does he expect me to make them?"

However, the English army was farthest gone. The furious onslaughts of these great squadrons, with iron cuirasses and steel breastplates had ground up the infantry. A few men about a flag marked the place of a regiment; battalions were now commanded by captains or lieutenants. Alten's division, already so cut up at La Haye Sainte, was almost destroyed; the intrepid Belgians of Van Kluze's brigade strewed the rye field along the Nivelles road; there were hardly any left of those Dutch grenadiers who, in 1811, joined to our ranks in Spain, fought against Wellington, and who, in 1815,

rallied on the English side, fought against Napoleon.
The loss of officers was heavy. Lord Uxbridge, who
buried his leg next day, had a knee fractured. If, on
the side of the French, in this struggle of the cuirassiers,
Delord, l'Hériter, Colbert, Dnop, Travers, and Blan-
card were *hors de combat*, on the side of the English
Alten was wounded, Barne was wounded, Delancey was
killed, Van Meeren was killed. Ompteda was killed, the
entire staff of Wellington was decimated, and England had the worst share in this balance of blood. The
2d Regiment of foot guards had lost five lieutenant-
colonels, four captains and three ensigns; the first battalion of the 30th Infantry had lost twenty-four officers
and one hundred and twelve soldiers; the 79th Highlanders had twenty-four officers wounded, eighteen
officers killed, and four hundred and fifty soldiers slain.
Cumberland's Hanoverian hussars, an entire regiment,
having at its head Colonel Hacke, who was afterward
court-martialed and broken, had drawn rein before the
fight, and were in flight in the Forest of Soignes, spreading the panic as far as Brussels. Carts, ammunition-
wagons, baggage-wagons, ambulances full of wounded,
seeing the French gain ground and approach the forest,
fled precipitately; the Dutch, sabered by the French
cavalry cried "Murder!" From Vert Coucou to Groe-
nendael, for a distance of nearly six miles in the direction
toward Brussels, the roads, according to the testimony
of witnesses still alive, were choked with fugitives. This
panic was such that it reached the Prince of Condé at
Malines, and Louis XVIII at Ghent. With the exception of the small reserve drawn up in echelon behind
the hospital established at the farm of Mont St.-Jean,

and the brigades of Vivian and Vandeleur on the flank of the left wing, Wellington's cavalry was exhausted. A number of batteries lay dismounted. These facts are confessed by Siborne; and Pringle, exaggerating the disaster, says even that the Anglo-Dutch army was reduced to 34,000 men. The Iron Duke remained calm, but his lips were pale. The Austrian commissary, Vincent, the Spanish commissary, Olava, present at the battle of the English staff, thought the Duke was beyond hope. At 5 o'clock Wellington drew out his watch, and was heard to murmur these somber words: "Blücher or night."

It was about this time that a distant line of bayonets glistened on the heights beyond Frischemont.

Here is the turning-point in this colossal drama.

BAD GUIDE FOR NAPOLEON: GOOD GUIDE FOR BÜLOW

We understand the bitter mistake of Napoleon; Grouchy hoped for, Blücher arriving; death instead of life.

Destiny has such turnings. Awaiting the world's throne, St. Helena became visible.

If the little cowboy, who acted as guide to Bülow, Blücher's lieutenant, had advised him to debouch from the forest about Frischemont rather than below Planchenoit, the shaping of the nineteenth century would perhaps have been different. Napoleon would have won the battle of Waterloo. By any other road than below Planchenoit, the Prussian army would have brought up at a ravine impassable for artillery, and Bülow would not have arrived.

Now, an hour of delay, as the Prussian general,

Müffling, declares, and Blücher would not have found Wellington in position; "the battle was lost."

It was time, we have seen, that Bülow should arrive. He had bivouacked at Dion le Mont, and started on at dawn. But the roads were impracticable, and his division stuck in the mire. The cannon sank to the hubs in the ruts. Furthermore, he had to cross the Dyle on the narrow bridge of Wavre; the street leading to the bridge had been fired by the French; the caissons and artillery wagons, being unable to pass between two rows of burning houses, had to wait till the fire was extinguished. It was noon before Bülow could reach Chapelle St.-Lambert.

Had the action commenced two hours earlier it would have been finished at four o'clock, and Blücher would have fallen upon a field already won by Napoleon. Such are these immense chances, proportioned to an infinity, which we cannot grasp.

As early as midday the Emperor, first of all, with his field-glass, perceived in the extreme horizon something which fixed his attention. He said: "I see yonder a cloud which appears to me to be troops." Then he asked the Duke of Dalmatia: "Soult, what do you see toward Chapelle St.-Lambert?" The marshal, turning his glass that way, answered, "Four or five thousand men, sire. Grouchy, of course." Meanwhile, it remained motionless in the haze. The glasses of the whole staff studied "the cloud" pointed out by the Emperor. Some said: "They are columns halting." The most said: "It is trees." The fact is that the cloud did not stir. The Emperor detached Domon's division of light cavalry to reconnoiter this obscure point.

Bülow, in fact, had not moved. His vanguard was very weak and could do nothing. He had to wait for the bulk of his *corps d'armée*, and he was ordered to concentrate his force before entering into line; but at five o'clock, seeing Wellington's peril, Blücher ordered Bülow to attack, and uttered these remarkable words: "We must give the English army a breathing spell."

Soon after, the divisions of Losthin, Hiller, Hacke, and Ryssel deployed in front of Lobau's corps, the cavalry of Prince William of Prussia debouched from the wood of Paris, Planchenoit was in flames, and the Prussian balls began to rain down even in the ranks of the Guard in reserve behind Napoleon.

THE GUARD

The rest is known; the irruption of a third army, the battle thrown out of joint, eighty-six pieces of artillery suddenly thundering forth, Pirch the First coming up with Bülow, Ziethen's cavalry led by Blücher in person, the French crowded back, Marcognet swept from the plateau of Ohain, Durutte dislodged from Papelotte, Donzelot and Quiot recoiling, Lobau taken *en écharpe*, a new battle falling at nightfall upon our dismantled regiments, the whole English line assuming the offensive and pushed forward, the gigantic gap made in the French army, the English grape and the Prussian grape lending mutual aid, extermination, disaster in front, disaster in flank, the Guard entering into line amid this terrible crumbling.

Feeling that they were going to their death they cried out: "*Vive l'Empereur!*" There is nothing more touching in history than this death agony bursting forth in acclamations.

The sky has been overcast all day. All at once, at this very moment—it was eight o'clock at night—the clouds in the horizon broke, and through the elms on the Nivelles road streamed the sinister red light of the setting sun. The rising sun shone upon Austerlitz.

Each battalion of the Guard, for this final effort, was commanded by a general. Friant, Michel, Roguet, Harlet, Mallet, Poret de Morvan, were there. When the tall caps of the grenadiers of the Guard, with their large eagle plates, appeared, symmetrical, drawn up in line, calm, in the smoke of that conflict, the enemy felt respect for France; they thought they saw twenty victories entering upon the field of battle with wings extended, and those who were conquerors, thinking themselves conquered, recoiled; but Wellington cried "Up, Guards, and at them!" The red regiment of English Guards lying behind the hedges, rose up, a shower of grape riddled the tricolored flag fluttering about our eagles, all hurled themselves forward, and the final carnage began. The Imperial Guard felt the army slipping away around them in the gloom, and the vast overthrow of the rout; they heard the "*Sauve qui peut!*"[1] which had replaced the "*Vive l'Empereur!*" and, with flight behind them, they held on their course, battered more and more and dying faster and faster at every step. There were no weak souls or cowards there. The privates of that band were as heroic as their general. Not a man flinched from the suicide.

Ney, desperate, great in all the grandeur of accepted

[1] Save yourselves.

387

death, bared himself to every blow in this tempest. He had his horse killed under him. Reeking with sweat, fire in his eyes, froth upon his lips, his uniform unbuttoned, one of his epaulets half cut away by the saber stroke of a horse guard, his badge of the Grand Eagle pierced by a ball, bloody, covered with mud, magnificent, a broken sword in his hand, he said: "Come! and see how a marshal of France dies upon the field of battle!" But in vain; he did not die. He was haggard and exasperated. He flung this question at Drouet d'Erlon: "What! are you not going to die?" He cried out·in the midst of all this artillery which was mowing down a handful of men: "Is there nothing, then, for me? Oh! I would that all these English balls were buried in my body!" Unhappy man! thou wast reserved for French bullets!

THE CATASTROPHE

The rout behind the Guard was dismal.

The army fell back rapidly from all sides at once, from Hougomont, from La Haye Sainte, from Papelotte, from Planchenoit. The cry: "Treachery!" was followed by the cry: "*Sauve qui peut!*" A disbanding army is a thaw. The whole bends, cracks, snaps, floats, rolls, falls, crushes, hurries, plunges. Mysterious disintegration. Ney borrows a horse, leaps upon him, and without hat, cravat, or sword, plants himself in the Brussels road, arresting at once the English and the French. He endeavors to hold the army, to call them back, he reproaches them, he grapples with the rout. He is swept away. The soldiers flee from him, crying: "*Vive le Marshal Ney!*" Durutte's two regiments come and go, frightened and tossed between the sabers of the Uhlans and the fire of the brigades of Kempt, Best, Pack, and Rylandt; rout is the worst of all conflicts; friends slay each other in their flight; squadrons and battalions are crushed and dispersed against each other, enormous foam of the battle. Lobau at one extremity, like Reille at the other, is rolled away in the flood. In vain does Napoleon make walls with the remains of the Guard; in vain does he expend his reserve squadrons in a last effort. Quiot gives way before Vivian, Kellermann before Vandeleur, Lobau before Bülow, Moraud before Pirch, Doman and Lubervic before Prince William of Prussia. Guyot, who had led the Emperor's squadrons to the charge, falls under the feet of the English Horse. Napoleon gallops along the fugitives, harangues them, urges, threatens, entreats. The mouths, which in the morning were crying "*Vive l'Empereur*," are now agape; he is hardly recognized. The Prussian cavalry, just come up, spring forward, fling themselves upon the enemy, saber, cut, hack, kill, exterminate. Teams rush off, the guns are left to the care of themselves; the soldiers of the train unhitch the caissons and take the horses to escape; wagons upset, with their four wheels in the air, block up the road, and are accessories of massacre. They crush and they crowd; they trample upon the living and the dead. Arms are broken. A multitude fills roads, paths, bridges, plains, hills, valleys, woods, choked up by this flight of forty thousand men. Cries, despair; knapsacks and muskets cast into the rye; passages forced at the point of the sword; no more comrades, no more officers, no more generals; inexpressible dismay. Ziethen sabering France at his ease. Lions become kids. Such was this flight.

FRANCE

At Genappe there was an effort to turn back, to form a line, to make a stand. Lobau rallied three hundred men. The entrance to the village was barricaded, but at the first volley of Prussian grape all took to flight again and Lobau was captured. The marks of that volley of grape are still to be seen upon the old gable of a brick ruin at the right of the road, a short distance before entering Genappe. The Prussians rushed into Genappe, furious, doubtless, at having conquered so little. The pursuit was monstrous. Blücher gave orders to kill all. Roguet had set this sad example by threatening with death every French grenadier who should bring him a Prussian prisoner. Blücher surpassed Roguet. The general of the Young Guard, Duhesme, caught at the door of a tavern in Genappe, gave up his sword to a hussar of death, who took the sword and killed the prisoner. The victory was completed by the assassination of the vanquished. Let us punish, since we are history; old Blücher disgraced himself. This ferocity filled the disaster to the brim. The desperate rout passed through Genappe, passed through Quatre Bras, passed through Sombreffe, passed through Frasness, passed through Thuin, passed through Charleroi, and stopped only at the frontier. Alas! who now was flying in such wise? The grand army.

This madness, this terror, this falling to ruins of the highest bravery which ever astonished history, can that be without cause? No. The shadow of an enormous right hand rests on Waterloo. It is the day of destiny. A power above man controlled that day. Hence, the loss of mind in dismay; hence, all these great souls yielding up their swords. Those who had conquered Europe fell to the ground, having nothing more to say or to do, feeling a terrible presence in the darkness. *Hoc erat in fatis.*[1] That day the perspective of the human race changed. Waterloo is the hinge of the nineteenth century. The disappearance of the great man was necessary for the advent of the great century. One, to whom there is no reply, took it in charge. The panic of heroes is explained. In the battle of Waterloo there is more than a cloud, there is a meteor. God passed over it.

In the gathering night, on a field near Genappe, Bernard and Bertrand seized by a flap of his coat and stopped a haggard, thoughtful, gloomy man, who, dragged thus far by the current of the rout, had dismounted, passed the bridle of his horse under his arm, and, with bewildering eye, was returning alone toward Waterloo. It was Napoleon endeavoring to advance again, mighty somnambulist of a vanished dream.

[1] So fate decreed.

EVENING OF THE BATTLE OF WATERLOO

BY ERNEST CROFTS

(*English painter*, 1847)

On the evening of the Battle of Waterloo, Napoleon's one hope lay in the charge of the Imperial Guard. Of this charge John S. C. Abbott says: —

"The fate of the world trembled in the balance. Not a drum beat the charge. Not a bugle uttered its inspiriting tones. Not a cheer escaped the lips of those proud, indomitable men. Silently, sternly, unflinchingly, they strode on till they arrived within a few yards of the batteries and bayonets which the genius of Wellington had arrayed to meet them.... Napoleon gazed with intense anxiety upon the progress of this heroic band, till, enveloped in clouds of smoke, it was lost to sight.

"At the same moment the Prussians came rushing upon the field, with infantry, cavalry, and artillery, entirely overpowering the feeble and exhausted squadrons left to oppose them. A gust of wind swept away the smoke, and as the anxious eye of Napoleon pierced the tumult of the battle to find his Guard, it had disappeared. Almost to a man they were weltering in blood. A mortal paleness overspread the cheek of the Emperor. The French army also saw that the Guard was annihilated. An instantaneous panic struck every heart. With exultant shouts the army of Blücher and of Wellington rushed upon the plain, and a scene of horror ensued at which humanity shudders."

With a cry of "Save yourselves," the French troops broke and fled in confusion. Napoleon, protected by a few of the Guard, was swept along with the rout. At Genappe a last desperate effort was made to check the fugitives, and a handful of men rallied for a moment to hold back the Prussian cavalry that were thundering at their heels. Taking advantage of their heroic stand, Napoleon hastily left his coach, and, mounting a horse, set out at full gallop for Paris.

THE DEATH OF NAPOLEON

BY ISAAC McLELLAN

[On the night of Napoleon's death, St. Helena was swept by a terrible storm. All night the dying Emperor fought over his battles in delirium, but as the storm ceased he grew calmer, and just at sunrise he died.

The Editor.]

Wild was the night, yet a wilder night
  Hung round the soldier's pillow;
In his bosom there waged a fiercer fight
  Than the fight on the wrathful billow.

A few fond mourners were kneeling by,
  The few that his stern heart cherished;
They knew by his glazed and unearthly eye
  That life had nearly perished.

They knew by his awful and kingly look,
  By the order hastily spoken,
That he dreamed of days when the nations shook,
  And the nations' hosts were broken.

He dreamed that the Frenchman's sword still slew,
  And triumphed the Frenchman's "Eagle";
And the struggling Austrian fled anew,
  Like the hare before the beagle.

THE DEATH OF NAPOLEON

The bearded Russian he scourged again,
  The Prussian's camp was routed,
And again on the hills of haughty Spain
  His mighty armies shouted.

Over Egypt's sands, over Alpine snows,
  At the Pyramids, at the mountain,
Where the wave of the lordly Danube flows,
  And by the Italian fountain;

On the snowy cliffs, where mountain streams
  Dash by the Switzer's dwelling,
He led again, in his dying dreams,
  His hosts, the broad earth quelling.

Again Marengo's field was won,
  And Jena's bloody battle;
Again the world was overrun,
  Made pale at his cannon's rattle.

He died at the close of that darksome day,
  A day that shall live in story;
In the rocky land they placed his clay,
  " And left him alone with his glory."

VIII
THE FRANCO-PRUSSIAN WAR

HISTORICAL NOTE

AFTER the battle of Waterloo, Napoleon was forced to abdicate, and was banished to the island of St. Helena, where he died in 1821. Louis XVIII was again set upon the throne. His brother, Charles X, who succeeded him, manifested all the Bourbon stubbornness, and in 1830 he was driven into exile. Louis Philippe, a descendant of Louis XIII, was made sovereign.

There was still a party determined upon a republican form of government. Its strength increased, and in 1848, Louis Philippe was obliged to flee. The republic was established, and Louis Napoleon Bonaparte, nephew of Napoleon I, was chosen president. In 1852, he succeeded in making himself emperor. This Napoleon III was eager to emulate the military glory of the great Napoleon, less from motives of personal ambition than to win popularity for his Government. A pretext was found for declaring war with Prussia. France was beaten and had to accept severe terms of peace. The emperor with his wife, the Empress Eugénie, and son fled to England. For the third time, the government of France became a republic, and such it remains.

THE WHITE FLAG OF SEDAN

[1870]

BY ÉMILE ZOLA

[THIERS and the Liberals opposed the war with Prussia, but the Bonapartists were wildly enthusiastic about it and the glory it would surely bring to their country. They made small preparation for war, but declared themselves "ready to the last gaiter-button." As a matter of fact, France was as unprepared for war as a country could be. The emperor was no commander, and was only in the way. The French invaded Germany, but were driven back by the Germans and pursued into France. After the disastrous battle of Gravelotte, the French were forced to retreat to Metz. While the siege of this place was going on, the other French forces were brought together at Sedan. Here the French fought brilliantly, but the army was surrounded, and Napoleon III was obliged to deliver up his sword to William I.

The news of this catastrophe made its way to Paris, and a republic was instantly proclaimed. Half of the French army was destroyed, and the other half was shut up in Metz. The war resolved itself into a struggle for Paris, and after a brave defense an armistice was announced. Four months later, terms of peace were agreed to.

"Delaherche" was a prosperous manufacturer of Sedan.

The Editor.]

DELAHERCHE then went off, explaining that he should speedily return with positive information. As soon as he was in the Rue Maqua he was surprised at the number of soldiers who were already returning from the field without their weapons, and with their uniforms in shreds, soiled with dust. He could not, however, obtain any precise details from those whom he endeavored to question. Some, who were quite stupefied, replied that they did n't know; whilst others had such a deal to relate, and gesticulated so furiously, and talked so extravagantly, that they resembled madmen. He therefore directed his steps once more towards the Sub-Prefecture, thinking to himself that all the news must flow thither. As he was crossing the Place du Collège, a couple of guns, doubtless the only remaining pieces of some battery, came up at a gallop, and stranded beside the footway. On reaching the High Street he had to acknowledge that the town was becoming quite crowded with fugitives. Three dismounted hussars were sitting in a doorway, dividing a loaf of bread; two others were slowly leading their horses by the bridle, at a loss for a stable where they might tether them; officers, too, were running wildly hither and thither, looking as if they did not know where they were going. On the Place Turenne a sub-lieutenant advised Delaherche not to linger there, for the shells were falling very frequently, a splinter of one of them having just broken the railing around the statue of the great captain, the victor of the Palatinate. And, as Delaherche was swiftly gliding along the Rue de la Sous-Prefecture, he saw a couple of projectiles explode, with a frightful crash, on the bridge spanning the Meuse.

Reaching the Sub-Prefecture, he was standing in front of the porter's lodge, seeking a pretext to ask for one of the aides-de-camp and question him, when a youthful voice called him by name: "Monsieur Delaherche! come in quick; it's anything but pleasant outside."

The speaker was Rose, his work-girl, whom he had

not thought of. Thanks to her, however, every door would be opened to him. He entered the lodge and accepted a seat.

"Just fancy," began Rose, "all this business has made mother quite ill; she's in bed, and can't get up. So there's only me, you see, for father is at the citadel, being a National Guard. A little while ago the emperor again wanted to show his bravery, for he went out again and was able to get to the end of the street, as far as the bridge. But then a shell fell in front of him, and the horse of one of his equerries was killed. And so he came back again — not surprising, is it? What would you have him do?"

"Then you know how we are situated — what do the officers say?"

She gave him a little look of astonishment. Amid all these abominations, but little of which she understood, she bustled about assiduously, retaining her gay freshness, with her fine hair and her clear eyes, the eyes of the child she was. "No, I know nothing," she said; "at twelve o'clock I took up a letter for Marshal MacMahon. The emperor was with him. They remained shut up together for nearly an hour, the marshal in bed, and the emperor on a chair close to the mattress. I know that, because I saw them when the door was opened."

"What were they saying?"

She again looked at him, and could not help laughing.

"Why, I don't know," she answered. "How could I know? Nobody in the world knows what they said to one another."

That was true, and Delaherche made a gesture as though to apologize for his foolish question. Still the

FRANCE

idea of that supreme conversation worried him; how interesting it must have been! What decision could they have come to?

"And now," added Rose, "the emperor has gone back into his private room, where he's conferring with two generals who arrived just now from the battle-field." She paused and glanced towards the house-steps: "Look! here comes one of the generals — and look! here's the other."

Delaherche hastily stepped out of the lodge and recognized Generals Douay and Ducrot, whose horses were waiting. He watched them get into the saddle again and gallop off. After the abandonment of the plateau of Illy, each, on his own side, had hastened into the town to warn the emperor that the battle was lost. They furnished him with precise details of the situation; the army and Sedan were now completely enveloped, and the disaster would prove frightful.

For a few minutes the emperor walked up and down his room in silence, with the wavering step of a sick man. The only person there besides himself was an aide-de-camp, standing erect and silent near a door. And, with a disfigured face which was now twitching with a nervous tic, Napoleon kept pacing to and fro between the chimney-piece and the window. His back appeared to have become more bent, as though a world had fallen upon it; and his dim eyes, veiled by their heavy lids, bespoke the resignation of the fatalist who has played and lost his final game with Destiny. Each time, however, that he reached the window, set ajar, he gave a start which, for a second, made him pause; and during one of those brief halts, he raised a trembling hand and muttered:

"Oh! those guns, those guns! one has heard them ever since the morning."

From that spot, indeed, the roaring of the batteries of the Marfée and Frénois hills reached the ear with extraordinary violence — it was a rolling thunder, which not merely rattled the window panes, but shook the very walls, a stubborn, incessant, exasperating uproar. And the emperor must have reflected that the struggle was henceforth a hopeless one, that all resistance was becoming a crime. What could it avail, why should more blood be spilt, more limbs be shattered, more heads be carried off, more and more dead be ever and ever added to those already scattered across the country-side? Since they, the French, were vanquished, since it was all over, why continue the massacre any longer? Sufficient abomination and suffering already cried out aloud under the sun.

Once more did the emperor reach the window, and again he began to tremble, with his hands raised. "Oh! those guns, those guns! Will they never stop?"

Perhaps the terrible thought of his responsibility was arising within him, with a vision of the thousands of bleeding corpses stretched upon the ground over yonder, through his fault. Perhaps, though, it was but the melting of his heart — the pitiful heart of a dreamer, of a man in reality good-natured and haunted by humanitarian notions. And albeit Fate had dealt him this frightful blow — which was crushing and sweeping away his fortune as though it were but a bit of straw — he yet found tears for others, was distracted that this useless butchery should still continue, and lacked the strength to endure it any longer. That villainous cannonade was now rending his breast, at each moment increasing his agony.

"Oh! those guns, those guns! Make them stop firing at once — at once."

And then this emperor, who, having confided his powers to the empress-regent, no longer had any throne; this generalissimo, who, since he had surrendered the supreme command to Marshal Bazaine, no longer commanded, awoke once more to the exercise of his power — to the irresistible needment of being the master for the last time. Since his stay at Châlons he had kept in the background, had not given an order; content, in his resignation, to become nothing more than a nameless and cumbersome inutility, a troublesome parcel carried along among the baggage-train of the troops. And it was only in the hour of defeat that the emperor again awoke within him; the first, the only order that he was yet to give, in the scared compassion of his heart, was to hoist the white flag upon the citadel to beg a truce.

"Oh! those guns, those guns! Take a sheet, a table-cloth, no matter what! Run quickly, tell them to stop those guns!"

The aide-de-camp hastily left the room, and the emperor continued his wavering march from the chimney-piece to the window, whilst the batteries kept on thundering, shaking the house from top to bottom.

Delaherche was still talking with Rose when a sergeant, on duty at the Sub-Prefecture, ran into the lodge: "Mademoiselle," said he, "we can't find anything. I can't see a servant anywhere. Do you happen to have any linen—a piece of white linen?' '

"Will a napkin do?"

"No, no; that would n't be large enough. Half a sheet would do."

Rose, ever obliging, had already darted to the wardrobe. "I have n't any half-sheets," said she. "A large piece of white linen — no, I don't see anything that would suit you — Oh! would you like a tablecloth?"

"A tablecloth? Nothing could be better; that's exactly what we want." And as he turned to go he added: "We are going to make a white flag of it, and hoist it on the citadel, to ask for peace. Much obliged, mademoiselle."

Delaherche gave a start of involuntary delight. At last, then, they were going to have quietness. It occurred to him, however, that his joy was unpatriotic, and he restrained it. Nevertheless his lightened heart beat quickly, and he eagerly watched a colonel and a captain, who, followed by the sergeant, were now coming out of the Sub-Prefecture with hasty steps. The colonel was carrying the tablecloth, rolled up, under his arm. It occurred to Delaherche to follow them, and he took leave of Rose, who was quite proud of having provided that cloth. Just then it struck two o'clock.

The cannonade seemed to have become still more violent whilst the captain was dying; a second shell had fallen in the garden, cutting down one of the centenarian trees. Moreover, a conflagration of considerable magnitude had broken out in the Faubourg of La Cassine, and some terror-stricken people cried out that all Sedan was burning. It would be the end of everything if this bombardment were to continue for any length of time with such fearful violence.

405

"It's incomprehensible. I'm going back!" exclaimed Delaherche, at last, quite beside himself.

"Where to?" asked Bouroche.

"Why, to the Sub-Prefecture, to ascertain whether the emperor's playing the fool with us when he talks of hoisting the white flag."

For a few seconds the major remained dumbfounded by this idea of the white flag, defeat, and capitulation, which broke upon him amid his powerlessness to save the poor mangled fellows who were being brought to him in such numbers. He made a gesture of furious despair. "Well, go to the devil!" he shouted; "we are none the less done for."

Once outside, Delaherche experienced far greater difficulty than before in making his way through the groups of people, which were now much larger. The streets were every minute filling with the stream of disbanded soldiers. He questioned several of the officers he met, but none of them had seen the white flag upon the citadel. At last, however, a colonel declared that he had espied it there for an instant; it had been taken down almost as soon as hoisted. That seemed to explain everything; either the Germans had not perceived it, or else, seeing it appear and disappear, they had realized that the last agony was at hand, and had thereupon redoubled their fire. Indeed, a story was already circulating of a general who, at sight of the flag, had flown into a mad rage, had rushed upon it, and torn it down with his own hands, breaking the staff, and trampling the linen under foot. And thus the Prussian batteries were still firing; the projectiles rained upon the roofs and the streets, houses were burning, and a woman had just had her head smashed, at the corner of the Place Turenne.

On reaching the Sub-Prefecture, Delaherche did not find Rose in the lodge. Every door of the house was now open; the rout was beginning. He entered and went upstairs, meeting only a few scared people, none of whom inquired his business. Whilst he was hesitating on the first-floor landing, he came upon the young girl.

"Oh, Monsieur Delaherche, matters are getting much worse," said she. "There, make haste and look if you want to see the emperor."

A door at the left hand stood ajar, and, through the opening, one could perceive Napoleon III, who had resumed his wavering march from the chimney-piece to the window. He tramped up and down without a pause, despite his intolerable sufferings.

An aide-de-camp had just entered the room — it was he who had carelessly left the door ajar — and the emperor was heard asking in a voice enervated by wretchedness: "But why are they still firing, monsieur, when I have had the white flag hoisted?"

Still did he experience the same unbearable torment at sound of that cannonade which never ceased, but on the contrary increased in violence every minute. It struck him in the heart each time that he drew near to the window. Still more blood, still more human lives destroyed through his fault! Each minute added more corpses to the pile, to no purpose whatever. And, commiserative dreamer that he was, his whole being revolted at the thought of this slaughter; and a dozen times already he had put the same despairing question to those who entered the room: "But why are they still firing when I have had the white flag hoisted?"

Delaherche did not manage to catch the muttered answer of the aide-de-camp. Besides, the emperor had not paused in his walk. Faint though he felt each time that he reached the window, he yielded to the needment of returning thither. His pallor had increased, his long-drawn mournful face, but imperfectly cleansed of the paint with which it had been brightened that morning, plainly told his agony.

At that moment a vivacious little man, in a dusty uniform, whom Delaherche recognized as General Lebrun, crossed the landing and pushed the door open, without waiting to be announced. And the emperor's anxious voice could immediately be distinguished, once more asking: "But why, General, why are they still firing when I have had the white flag hoisted?"

The aide-de-camp came out of the room and shut the door behind him, so that Delaherche could not even hear the general's reply. All was blank again.

"Ah!" repeated Rose, "things are getting bad, I can tell it by the gentlemen's faces. It's like my tablecloth, which I shall never see again; some say it has been torn up. After all, it's the emperor whom I pity the most, for he's in a worse state even than the marshal. He would be far better in his bed than in that room, where he's wearing himself out with walking."

She was quite affected, and her pretty, fair face expressed sincere compassion; for which reason Delaherche, whose Bonapartist fervor had been sensibly cooling the last two days, considered her rather foolish. He lingered with her downstairs, however, whilst watching for General Lebrun's departure. And when the general came down he followed him.

General Lebrun had explained to the emperor that if he desired to ask for an armistice, a letter signed by the commander-in-chief of the French forces must be transmitted to the commander-in-chief of the German armies. He had then offered to write the letter in question and to start in search of General de Wimpffen, by whom it should be signed. And now he was carrying this letter away, and his only fear was that he might be unable to find Wimpffen, for he did not know on what part of the field he was. The crush by this time had become so great that he was compelled to walk his horse through Sedan, thus enabling Delaherche to follow him as far as the Ménil gate.

Once on the highway, however, General Lebrun put his horse at a gallop, and as he was approaching Balan, he was lucky enough to perceive General Wimpffen. A few minutes previously the latter had written to the emperor: "Sire, come and place yourself at the head of your troops; they will esteem it an honor to open you a passage through the enemy's lines." Accordingly, at the first word of a truce he flew into a furious passion. No, no! he would sign nothing; he meant to fight. It was then half-past three o'clock, and shortly afterwards came the last onslaught, that heroic, despairing attempt to pierce through the Bavarians by marching yet once more upon Bazeilles. To restore the spirits of the soldiers, lies were circulated along the streets of Sedan and across the surrounding fields. "Bazaine is coming up! Bazaine is coming up!" was the cry. It was a dream that many had indulged in since the morning, thinking, each time that the Germans unmasked a fresh battery, that the guns they heard were those of the army of Metz.

Some twelve hundred men were got together, disbanded soldiers of all arms, from every corps; and along the road, swept by the enemy's projectiles, the little column dashed with glorious gallantry, at the double-quick. It was superb at first; the men who fell did not arrest the dash of the others, and some five hundred yards were covered with a perfect fury of courage. But the ranks were speedily thinned, and the bravest at last fell back. What could be done, indeed, against such overwhelming numbers? This effort was but the mad temerity of a commander who refused to be beaten. And at last General de Wimpffen found himself alone with General Lebrun, on that road to Balan and Bazeilles, which they finally had to abandon. No course now remained but to retreat under the walls of Sedan.

And now the formidable drama was drawing to a close. From that wooded height of La Marfée, King William had just beheld the junction of his troops. It was accomplished; the Third Army, under the orders of the Crown Prince, his son, which had proceeded by way of St. Menges and Fleigneux, was taking possession of the plateau of Illy, whilst the Fourth Army, commanded by the Crown Prince of Saxony, reached the meeting place by way of Daigny and Givonne, after turning the wood of La Garenne. Thus the Eleventh and Fifth German Corps joined hands with the Twelfth Corps and the Prussian Guard. And the supreme effort made to break the circle at the very moment when it was closing up, that useless but glorious charge of General Margueritte's division, had wrung an admiring exclamation from the king: "Ah! the brave fellows!" Now the mathematical, inexorable encompassment was completed, the vise-chops had met; and at a glance the king could survey the immense wall of men and guns enveloping the vanquished army. On the north the grasp pressed closer and closer home, throwing the fugitives back into Sedan under the redoubling fire of the batteries which fringed the horizon all around in an unbroken line. On the south Bazeilles, conquered, empty, and mournful, was burning away, throwing up whirling clouds of spark-laden smoke; whilst the Bavarians, now masters of Balan, were leveling their guns at three hundred yards from the gates of Sedan itself. And the other batteries, those on the left bank at Pont-Maugis, Noyers, Frénois, and Wadelincourt, which for nearly twelve hours had been firing without a pause, were now thundering even yet more loudly, completing the impassable belt of flames, even under the king's feet.

Somewhat tired, however, King William laid his fieldglass aside for a moment, and continued examining the scene without its help. The sun was descending obliquely towards the woods, sinking to rest in a sky of unspotted purity; it gilded the whole vast stretch of country, bathed it in so limpid a light that the smallest objects acquired remarkable distinctness. The king could distinguish the houses of Sedan, with their little black window bars, the ramparts and the fortress, all the complicated defensive works, clearly and sharply outlined. Then all around, scattered amid the fields, were the villages, fresh-colored and shiny as with varnish, like the farmhouses one finds in boxes of toys. On

the left was Donchéry, at the edge of the level plain; on
the right were Douzy and Carignan in the meadows. It
seemed as though one could count the trees of the Forest
of the Ardennes, whose sea of verdure stretched away to
the frontier. In the crisp light, the lazily winding Meuse
looked like a river of pure gold, and the fearful blood-
smeared battle, seen from this height, under the sun's
farewell rays, became as it were a delicate piece of painting. Some corpses of cavalry soldiers, and dead horses
with their bellies ripped open, scattered bright touches
over the plateau of Floing. Towards the right, in the
direction of Givonne, the eye was amused by the scram-
bles of the retreat, the vortex of running, falling black
specks; whilst on the peninsula of Iges, on the left, a
Bavarian battery, whose guns looked no bigger than
lucifer matches, was served with such clock-work regularity, that it seemed like some piece of mechanism,
carefully put together. And all this was victory — victory
surpassing hope, overwhelming; and the king felt no remorse whatever as he looked down upon all those tiny
corpses, those thousands of men occupying less space
than the dust of the roads, that immense valley where
neither the conflagrations of Bazeilles, the massacres of
Illy nor the anguish of Sedan could prevent impassive
nature from remaining beauteous in this the serene close
of a lovely day.

All at once, however, Delaherche perceived a French
general, clad in a blue tunic and mounted on a black
horse, who was ascending the slopes of La Marfée, preceded by a hussar carrying a flag of truce. It was General Reille, charged by the emperor to deliver this letter
to the King of Prussia: —

THE WHITE FLAG OF SEDAN

SIR, MY BROTHER, — Not having been able to die in the midst of my troops, it only remains for me to place my sword in Your Majesty's hands. — I am Your Majesty's good Brother,

NAPOLEON.

In his eagerness to stop the slaughter, since he was no longer the master, the emperor delivered himself up, hoping that he might thereby soften the victor. And Delaherche saw General Reille, who was unarmed and carried merely a riding-whip, rein in his horse at ten paces from the king, alight, and then step forward and deliver the letter. The sun was sinking in a far-spreading, roseate glow; the king seated himself on a chair, rested his arm on the back of another one held by a secretary, and replied that he accepted the sword, pending the dispatch of an officer empowered to treat for the capitulation.

THE DEFENSE OF CHAMPIGNY

BY JEAN BAPTISTE ÉDOUARD DETAILLE

(Born in Paris, 1848)

THIS picture shows an incident in the siege of Paris by the German Army during the Franco-Prussian War. The French, having taken Champigny, fortified themselves in the village, and defended, foot by foot, the house and inclosures against the attack of the Germans.

In the center of the picture is General Faron, commander of this division. The sappers are making embrasures in the wall to allow the sharpshooters to fire under protection, and are barricading the openings with all kinds of material. In the background by the wall may be seen the artillerists placing the battery guns in position.

Special interest attaches to this painting from the fact that Detaille was soldier as well as artist, having himself been a member of the "Garde Mobile," during the siege of Paris.

ONE DAY UNDER THE COMMUNE

[1871]

BY JOHN LEIGHTON

[ACCORDING to the terms of the treaty of Versailles, which ended the Franco-Prussian War, France ceded to Germany some 4700 square miles of territory, and agreed to pay within three years five billion francs for indemnification. The Red Republicans, or Communists, rebelled against these humiliating terms, and the capital now fell into the hands of the "Commune of Paris." By order of the National Government the regular army was brought up, and a second siege of Paris took place, infinitely more full of horrors than the previous one by the Germans. The Government at length got control, and the Third Republic was fully organized, under the presidency of Thiers.

The author of the following extract was in Paris at the time of the Commune.

The Editor.]

THE roaring of cannon close at hand, the whizzing of shells, volleys of musketry. I hear this in my sleep, and awake with a start. I dress and go out. I am told the troops have come in. "How? Where? When?" I ask of the National Guards who come rushing down the street, crying out, "We are betrayed!" They, however, know but very little. They have come from the Trocadéro, and have seen the red trousers of the soldiers in the distance. Fighting is going on near the viaduct of Auteuil, at the Champ de Mars. Did the assault take place last night or this morning? It is quite impossible

416

to obtain any reliable information. Some talk of a civil engineer having made signals to the Versaillais; others say a captain in the navy was the first to enter Paris. Suddenly about thirty men rush into the streets, crying, "We must make a barricade." I turn back, fearing to be pressed into the service. The cannonading appears dreadfully near. A shell whistles over my head. I hear some one say, "The batteries of Montmartre are bombarding the Arc de Triomphe"; and strangely enough, in this moment of horror and uncertainty, the thought crosses my mind that now the side of the arch on which is the bas-relief of Rude will be exposed to the shells. On the Boulevard there is only here and there a passenger hurrying along. The shops are closed; even the cafés are shut up; the harsh screech of the mitrailleuse grows louder and nearer. The battle seems to be close at hand, all round me. A thousand contradictory suppositions rush through my brain and hurry me along, and here on the Boulevard there is no one that can tell me anything. I walk in the direction of the Madeleine, drawn there by a violent desire to know what is going on, which silences the voice of prudence. As I approach the Chaussée d'Antin, I perceive a multitude of men, women. and children running backwards and forwards, carrying paving-stones. A barricade is being thrown up; it is already more than three feet high. Suddenly I hear the rolling of heavy wheels; I turn, and a strange sight is before me — a mass of women in rags, livid, horrible, and yet grand, with the Phrygian cap on their heads, and the skirts of their robes tied around their waists, were harnessed to a mitrailleuse, which they dragged along at full speed; other women pushing vigorously behind. The whole procession, in its somber colors, with dashes of red here and there, thunders past me; I follow it as fast as I can. The mitrailleuse draws up a little in front of the barricade, and is hailed with wild clamors by the insurgents. The Amazons are being unharnessed as I come up. "Now," said a young gamin, such as one used to see in the gallery of the Théâtre Porte St.-Martin, "don't you be acting the spy here, or I will break your head open as if you were a Versaillais."—"Don't waste ammunition," cried an old man with a long white beard — a patriarch of civil war — "don't waste ammunition; and as for the spy, let him help to carry paving-stones. Monsieur," said he, turning to me with much politeness, "will you be so kind as to go and fetch those stones from the corner there?"

I did as I was bid, although I thought, with anything but pleasure, that if at that moment the barricade were attacked and taken, I might be shot before I had the time to say, "Allow me to explain." But the scene which surrounds me interests me in spite of myself. Those grim hags, with their red head-dresses, passing the stones I give them rapidly from hand to hand, the men who are building them up only leaving off for a moment now and then to swallow a cup of coffee, which a young girl prepares over a small tin stove; the rifles symmetrically piled; the barricade, which rises higher and higher; the solitude in which we are working — only here and there a head appears at a window, and is quickly withdrawn; the ever-increasing noise of the battle; and, over all, the brightness of a dazzling morning sun—all this has something sinister, and yet horribly fascinating about it. While we are at work they talk; I listen. The Versaillais have been coming in all night. The Porte de la Muette and the Porte Dauphine have been surrendered by the 13th and the 113th battalions of the first arrondissement. "Those two numbers 13 will bring them ill luck," says a woman. Vinoy is established at the Trocadéro, and Douai at the Point du Jour: they continue to advance. The Champ de Mars has been taken from the Federals after two hours' fighting. A battery is erected at the Arc de Triomphe, which sweeps the Champs Élysées and bombards the Tuileries. A shell has fallen in the Rue du Marché Saint-Honoré. In the Cours-la-Reine the 138th battalion stood bravely. The Tuileries is armed with guns, and shells the Arc de Triomphe. In the Avenue de Marigny the gendarmes have shot twelve Federals who had surrendered; their bodies are still lying on the pavement in front of the tobacconist's. Rue de Sèvres, the *Vengeurs de Flourens* have put to flight a whole regiment of the line: the *Vengeurs* have sworn to resist to a man. They are fighting in the Champs Élysées, around the Ministère de la Guerre, and on the Boulevard Haussmann. Dombrowski has been killed at the Château de la Muette. The Versaillais have attacked the Western Saint-Lazare Station, and are marching towards the Pépinière barracks. "We have been sold, betrayed, and surprised; but what does it matter, we will triumph. We want no more chiefs or generals; behind the barricades every man is a marshal!"

Close to Saint-Germain l'Auxerrois women are busy pulling down the wooden seats; children are rolling empty wine-barrels and carrying sacks of earth. As one nears the Hôtel de Ville the barricades are higher, better armed, and better manned. All the Nationals here look ardent, resolved, and fierce. They say little, and do not shout at all. Two guards, seated on the pavement, are playing at picquet. I push on, and am allowed to pass. The barricades are terminated here, and I have nothing to fear from paving-stones. Looking up, I see that all the windows are closed, with the exception of one, where two old women are busy putting a mattress between the window and the shutter. A sentinel, mounting guard in front of the Café de la Compagnie du Gaz, cries out to me, "You can't pass here!" I therefore seat myself at a table in front of the café, which has doubtless been left open by order, and where several officers are talking in a most animated manner. One of them rises and advances towards me. He asks me rudely what I am doing there. I will not allow myself to be abashed by his tone, but draw out my pass from my pocket and show it to him, without saying a word. "All right," says he; and then seats himself by my side, and tells me, "I know it already, that a part of the left bank of the river is occupied by the troops of the Assembly, that fighting is going on everywhere, and that the army on this side is gradually retreating.—Street fighting is our affair, you see," he continues. "In such battles as that, the merest gamin from Belleville knows more about it than MacMahon. . . . It will be terrible. The enemy shoots the prisoners." (For the last two months the Commune had been saying the same thing.) "We shall give no quarter."—I ask him, "Is it Delescluze who is determined to resist?"—"Yes," he answers. "Lean forward a little. Look at those three windows to the left of the trophy. That is the Salle de l'État-Major. Delescluze is there giving orders, signing commissions. He has not slept for three days. Just now I scarcely knew him, he was so worn out with fatigue. The Committee of Public Safety sits permanently in a room adjoining, making out proclamations and decrees." — "Ha, ha!" said I, "decrees!" — "Yes, citizen, he has just decreed heroism!" The officer gives me several other bits of information: tells me that "Lullier this very morning has had thirty *réfractaires* shot, and that Rigault has gone to Mazas to look after the hostages." While he is talking, I try to see what is going on in the Place de l'Hôtel de Ville. Two or three thousand Federals are there, some seated, some lying on the ground. A lively discussion is going on. Several little barrels are standing about on chairs; the men are continually getting up and crowding round the barrels, some have no glasses, but drink in the palms of their hands. Women walk up and down in bands, gesticulating wildly. The men shout, the women shriek. Mounted expresses gallop out of the Hôtel, some in the direction of the Bastille, some towards the Place de la Concorde. The latter fly past us crying out, "All's well!" A man comes out on the balcony of the Hôtel de Ville and addresses the crowd. All the Federals start to their feet enthusiastically. — "That's Valles," says my neighbor to me. I had already recognized him. I frequently saw him in the students' quarter in a little *crémerie* in the Rue Serpente. He was given to making verses, rather bad ones by the bye; I remember one in particular, a panegyric on a green coat. They used to say he had a situation as a professional mourner. His face even then wore a bitter and violent expression. He left poetry for journalism, and then journalism for politics. To-day he is spouting forth at a window of the Hôtel de Ville. I cannot catch a word of what he says; but as he retires he is wildly applauded. Such applause pains me sadly. I feel that these men and these women are mad for blood, and will know how to die. Alas! how many dead and dying already! Neither the cannonading nor the musketry has ceased an instant.

I now see a number of women walk out of the Hôtel, the crowd makes room for them to pass. They come our way. They are dressed in black, and have black crape tied round their arms and a red cockade in their bonnets. My friend the officer tells me that they are the governesses who have taken the places of the nuns. Then he walks up to them and says, "Have you succeeded?" — "Yes," answers one of them, "here is our commission. The school-children are to be employed in making sacks and filling them with earth, the eldest ones are to load the rifles behind the barricades. They will receive rations like National Guards, and a pension will be given to the mothers of those who die for the republic. They are mad to fight, I assure you. We have made them work hard during the last month; this will be their holiday!" The woman who says this is young and pretty, and speaks with a sweet smile on her lips. I shudder. Suddenly two staff officers appear and ride furiously up to the Hôtel de Ville; they have come from the Place Vendôme. An instant later and the trumpets sound. The companies form in the Place, and great agitation reigns in the Hôtel. Men rush in and out. The officers who are in the café where I am get up instantly, and go to take their places at the head of their men. A rumor spreads that the Versaillais have taken the barricades on the Place de la Concorde. — "By Jove! I think you had better go home," says my neighbor to me, as he clasps his sword-belt; "we shall have hot work here, and that shortly." I think it prudent to follow this advice. One glance at the Place before I go. The companies of Federals have just started off by the Rue de Rivoli and the quays at a quick march, crying, "*Vive la Commune!*" a ferocious joy beaming in their faces. A young man, almost a lad, lags a little behind; a woman rushes up to him, and lays hold of his collar, screaming, "Well, and you! are you not going to get yourself killed with the others?"

I reach the Rue Vieille-du-Temple, where another barricade is being built up. I place a paving-stone upon it and pass on. Soon I see open shops and passengers in the streets. This tradesmen's quarter seems to have outlived the riot of Paris. Here one might almost forget the frightful civil war which wages so near, if the conversation of those around did not betray the anguish of the speakers, and if you did not hear the cannon roaring out unceasingly, "People of Paris, listen to me! I am ruining your houses. Listen to me! I am killing your children."

On the Boulevards more barricades; some nearly finished, others scarcely commenced. One constructed near the Porte Saint-Martin looks formidable. That spot seems destined to be the theater of bloody scenes, of riot and revolution. In 1852, corpses lay piled up behind the railing, and all the pavement was tinged with blood. I return home profoundly sad; I can scarcely think — I feel in a dream, and am tired to death; my eyelids droop of themselves; I am like one of those houses there with closed shutters.

Near the Gymnase I meet a friend who I thought was at Versailles. We shake hands sadly. "When did you come back?" I ask. — "To-day; I followed the troops." — Then turning back with me he tells me what he has seen. He had a pass, and walked into Paris behind the artillery and the line, as far as the Trocadéro, where the soldiers halted to take up their line of battle. Not a single man was visible along the whole length of the quays. At the Champ de Mars he did not see any insurgents. The musketry seemed very violent near Vaugirard on the Pont Royal and around the Palais de l'Industrie. Shells from Montmartre repeatedly fell on the quays. He could not see much, however, only the smoke in the distance. Not a soul did he meet. Such frightful noise in such solitude was fearful. He continued his way under the shelter of the parapet. On one place he saw some gamins cutting huge pieces of flesh off the dead body of a horse that was lying in the path. There must have been fighting there. Down by the water a man fishing while two shells fell in the river, a little higher up, a yard or two from the shore. Then he thought it prudent to get nearer to the Palais de l'Industrie. The fighting was nearly over then, but not quite. The Champs Élysées was melancholy in the extreme; not a soul was there. This was only too literally true, for several corpses lay on the ground. He saw a soldier of the line lying beneath a tree, his forehead covered with blood. The man opened his mouth as if to speak as he heard the sound of footsteps, the eyelids quivered and then there was a shiver, and all was over.

ONE DAY UNDER THE COMMUNE

My friend walked slowly away. He saw trees thrown down and bronze lamp-posts broken; glass crackled under his feet as he passed near the ruined kiosques. Every now and then turning his head he saw shells from Montmartre fall on the Arc de Triomphe and break off large fragments of stone. Near the Tuileries was a confused mass of soldiery against a background of smoke. Suddenly he heard the whizzing of a ball and saw the branch of a tree fall. From one end of the avenue to the other, no one; the road glistened white in the sun. Many dead were to be seen lying about as he crossed the Champs Élysées. All the streets to the left were full of soldiery; there had been fighting there, but it was over now. The insurgents had retreated in the direction of the Madeleine. In many places tricolor flags were hanging from the windows, and women were smiling and waving their handkerchiefs to the troops. The presence of the soldiery seemed to reassure everybody. The concierges were seated before their doors with pipes in their mouths, recounting to attentive listeners the perils from which they had escaped; how balls pierced the mattresses put up at the windows, and how the Federals had got into the houses to hide. One said, "I found three of them in my court; I told a lieutenant they were there, and he had them shot. But I wish they would take them away; I cannot keep dead bodies in my house." Another was talking with some soldiers, and pointing out a house to them. Four men and a corporal went into the place indicated, and an instant afterwards my friend heard the cracking of rifles. The concierge rubbed his hands and winked at the bystanders, while another was saying, "They respect nothing, those Federals; during the battle they came in to steal. They wanted to take away my clothes, my linen, everything I have; but I told them to leave that, that it was not good enough for them, that they ought to go up to the first floor, where they would find clocks and plate, and I gave them the key. Well, messieurs, you would never believe what they have done, the rascals! They took the key and went and pillaged everything on the first floor!" My friend had heard enough, and passed on. The agitation everywhere was very great. The soldiers went hither and thither, rang the bells, went into the houses and brought out with them pale-faced prisoners. The inhabitants continued to smile politely but grimly. Here and there dead bodies were lying in the road. A man who was pushing a truck allowed one of the wheels to pass over a corpse that was lying with its head on the curbstone. "Bah!" said he, "it won't do him any harm." The dead and wounded were, however, being carried away as quickly as possible.

The cannon had now ceased roaring, and the fight was still going on close at hand — at the Tuileries doubtless. The townspeople were tranquil and the soldiery disdainful. A strange contrast; all these good citizens smiling and chatting, and the soldiers, who had come to save them at the peril of their lives, looking down upon them with the most careless indifference. My friend reached the Boulevard Haussmann; there the corpses were in large numbers. He counted thirty in less than a hundred yards. Some were lying under the doorways; a dead woman was seated on the bottom stair of one of the houses. Near the church of "La Trinité" were two guns, the reports from which were deafening; several of the shells fell in a bathing establishment in the Rue Taitbout opposite the Boulevard. On the Boulevard itself, not a person was to be seen. Here and there dark masses, corpses doubtless. However, the moment the noise of the report of a gun had died away, and while the gunners were reloading, heads were thrust out from doors to see what damage had been done — to count the number of trees broken, benches torn up, and kiosques overturned. From some of the windows rifles were fired. My friend then reached the street he lived in and went home. He was told during the morning they had violently bombarded the Collège Chaptal, where the Zouaves of the Commune had fortified themselves; but the engagement was not a long one, they made several prisoners and shot the rest.

My friend shut himself up at home, determined not to go out. But his impatience to see and hear what was going on forced him into the streets again. The Pépinière barracks were occupied by troops of the line; he was able to get to the New Opera without trouble, leaving the Madeleine, where dreadful fighting was going on, to the right. On the way were to be seen piled muskets, soldiers sitting and lying about, and corpses everywhere. He then managed, without incurring too much danger, to reach the Boulevards, where the insurgents, who were then very numerous, had not yet been attacked. He worked for some little time at the barricade, and then was allowed to pass on. It was thus that we had met. Just as we were about to turn up the Faubourg Montmartre a man rushed up saying that three hundred Federals had taken refuge in the church of the Madeleine, followed by gensdarmes, and had gone on fighting for more than an hour. "Now," he finished up by saying, "if the curé were to return, he would find plenty of people to bury!"

I am now at home. Evening has come at last; I am jotting down these notes just as they come into my head. I am too much fatigued both in mind and body to attempt to put my thoughts into order. The cannonading is incessant, and the fusillade also. I pity those that died, and those that kill! Oh! poor Paris, when will experience make you wiser?

THE SOLDIERS' DREAM

BY JEAN BAPTISTE ÉDOUARD DETAILLE
(*French artist*, 1848)

IN the "Soldiers' Dream," a bivouac of weary troops is
pictured. They have made a long day's march with knapsacks on their backs. Their caps have not shielded them
from the sun, nor have their cloaks from the rain. At the
place of bivouac they have dried themselves as best they
were able at the smoky fires of green wood, and now, half
dead with sleep, they have flung themselves down upon the
ground. They are wrapped in their cloaks, their heads rest
upon their knapsacks, their feet are toward the fire. Stacks
of arms stretch far away toward the horizon; and on two of
these in the foreground lies the flag of the division, new and
fresh, not yet torn by ball and shell, the flag of victories to
come.

The chill night of September is drawing to a close, and far
in the east the first rays of the dawn may be seen. The young
soldiers are dreaming of battle and victory. High up on the
clouds above them are pictured the battles of the past. Here
are the flags of Lodi, Arcole, Marengo, Hohenlinden, Austerlitz, Jena, Eylau, Wagram, and Borodino, together with
those of Trocadero and of Algiers, of Isly, and of Inkerman,
Solferino, and Puebla. Here are the cuirassiers and the
charging squadrons; here are the white, the tricolor, pikes,
eagles, and victorious banners, torn by grapeshot and ball.
On the ground below these lie the men. To-morrow they may
awake to wounds and death, but to-night they dream of
glory.

Made in the USA
Columbia, SC
07 April 2022